TWENTY-FIVE YEARS ON
The two Germanies 1970

by

Stanley Radcliffe, M.A., Ph.D.
Senior Lecturer in German, University of Bristol

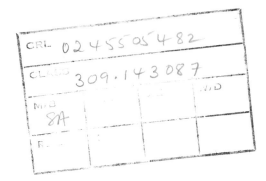

HARRAP   LONDON

First published in Great Britain 1972
by GEORGE G. HARRAP & CO. LTD
182–4 High Holborn, London WC1V 7AX

© *Stanley Radcliffe* 1972

ISBN 0 245 50548 2

Printed in Great Britain by
WILLMER BROTHERS LIMITED, BIRKENHEAD

Table of Contents

List of Maps

Acknowledgements

I should like briefly to express my gratitude to all those who have helped me in their various ways with the production of this book. My debt is particularly great to the services of the German Federal Embassy, above all to Herr Sulzbach, and to the staff of Inter Nationes. Likewise I have to thank the staff of the Deutsch-Britische Gesellschaft of East Berlin, for the supply of much valuable material on East Germany. The London office of the BDI has very kindly sent me their report for 1969-70, and my colleagues Brian Keith-Smith and Horst Claus have supplied information on West German company law and housing costs. The final word of thanks must be to Mrs M. Taylor and Mrs E. Laidlaw for their ready assistance in the typing of this work, and to Robin Sawers for his advice and guidance at all stages of the production of the book.

Bristol 1972   S.R.

Introduction

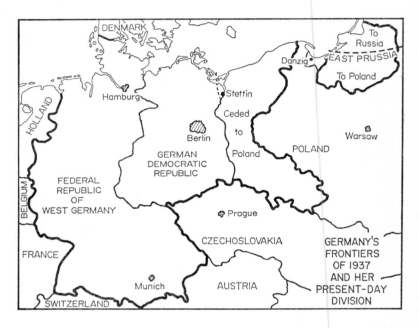

The year 1970 found post-war Germany twenty-five years old. A quarter of a century had passed since the final destruction of Nazi tyranny in Europe, and throughout these twenty-five years Germany had—whether she wished it or not—featured as a prominent figure in the turbulent arena of European politics. Within this same period Germany herself underwent a singular transformation. We may, indeed, no longer speak of one Germany; for today we are confronted with a Germany divided into two, or even three, parts. The largest of these parts comprises the *Bundesrepublik Deutschland*, the Federal Republic of Germany, with sixty million inhabitants. To the east of West Germany, and divided from her by a continuous belt of scorched no man's land, lies the *Deutsche Demokratische Republik*, with seventeen million inhabitants. Further still to the east and beyond the much-invoked Oder-Neisse Line, lie the 'lost territories', those parts of a former Germany which are now incorporated into Poland or even Russia herself, and whose territorial area is actually greater than that of the East German Republic. An asset and a bargaining counter which the West Germans have not found easy to renounce. Thus did the legacy of Yalta, Potsdam and the Cold War confront the world of 1970, its problems still basically unresolved. And, tangible symbol of this convoluted problem, the city of Berlin stands, part under four-power military jurisdiction, part capital of the East German state; isolated outpost of Bonn's Western-style democracy, show window for the West (and soon, now, for the East), and potential flashpoint for a world-wide holocaust.

The year 1970 had further interesting connotations, for it marked the coming of age of the German republics of both East and West. The Federal Republic of Germany became twenty-one years old in September, and the German Democratic Republic in the October of that year. During these twenty-one years the two states had been growing progressively away from each other, developing institutions and acquiring a character specifically their own. Each has succeeded, in its own separate way, in achieving a recovery from the destruction and disintegration of 1945 that is little short of the miraculous—the so-called *Wirtschaftswunder*. Much has been heard in the West (and rightly so) of the triumphs and achievements of the Federal Republic; little has been heard of those of the DDR. It is proposed, in the pages that follow, to attempt a survey of the principal achievements of both states since 1945, and to assess the nature of the present-day reality. This will include a study of the political institutions, the administrative systems, the achievements of industry and commerce, the roles of management and labour, the concept of the Welfare State, social life, educational theory and practice, and the position of culture and the arts. We shall at times discover patterns of development so divergent that all talk of a reunification of Germany flies in the face of reality. Even the West German Chancellor, Herr Willy Brandt, acknowledged the reality of two separate German entities on his historic goodwill mission to Erfurt in March of the year 1970.

The question of reunification is not one that can be—nor indeed will be—left for the Germans themselves to settle. It can only be dealt within the much wider context of the European and even global confrontation of East and West. Eastern Germany is tied into the pattern of the Soviet bloc economy and the Warsaw Pact defence system just as effectively as West Germany is an integral part of EEC and NATO. The full acceptance of East Germany into the community of the Eastern European bloc can be dated from the year 1957, when Russia and Poland made their final peace with her, and took active steps to promote her recovery. Today she is a vital factor in the trading life of the Comecon states, an advanced Communist position facing the Western world. Some details of these commitments and relationships will be examined in the pages that follow.

A Germany divided no longer rouses fears in the Russians of a resurgent *Drang nach Osten*, with all its terrible memories of suffering and destruction. (Another significant anniversary, occurring in January 1971, was the centenary of the creation of the modern German Reich, under the dominance of Bismarck's Prussia, calling into being the most feared power in Europe.) The West German state securely built by Konrad Adenauer into the NATO system is thereby rendered incapable of a private imperialism; it is, however, also secure against the dangers of a Communist take-over by the East.

Against this background we have the new phenomenon of the search for a détente between East and West in Europe, paralleled— as indeed it must be—by negotiations between the two Germanies. The implications of this development and the prospects for its success are the subject of the final section of this study. Should reunification become generally acknowledged as an impossible goal, the problem will still remain of the future relationship of the two states, and particularly of the status of Berlin. The foundering of the attempt initiated in 1968 would signal the failure not just of a German, but of a European effort at reconciliation, and would leave a mood of bitterness, recrimination and despair in its trail.

We believe that from this varied analysis the reader will derive a sense of the quality of present-day life of both the Federal Republic of the West and the Democratic Republic of the East, together with some hard statistical facts on which to base his own continuing study of the German situation.

Section I

Constitution and Political Structure

A. WEST GERMANY

1. *Constitution*

The West Germans will explain that their system of laws and procedures does not represent a final constitution for Germany, since it was drawn up and approved only by the western half of the country, and still awaits examination and approval by the eastern half. They desired, in other words, an all-German constitution, whose political basis would obviously be some form of union between the separate parts of Germany. The West Germans therefore drew up a Basic Law (*Grundgesetz*) to regulate their political affairs in the meantime. They nevertheless frequently claimed to speak on behalf of the East Germans, regarding them as mute prisoners of an absolutist régime. This attitude has clearly needed modification in the interests of the attempted rapprochement between the two German states.

The failure of the occupying powers to agree on a common policy for Germany in December 1947 led to the decision by the Western allies to establish a West German state, whose government should be based on a provisional democratic constitution drawn up by the citizens themselves (London Agreements, June 1948). Accordingly the legislatures of the existing eleven states[1] in the Western occupation zones—themselves only recently elected, and half-regretful at the implicit widening of the division of Germany, chose 65 delegates to a 'Parliamentary Council', whose task it was to draft the Basic Law. These proposals, formulated in May 1949, and approved by the regional parliaments with the exception of Bavaria, were accepted with some reservations by the three Military Governors, and formed the basis on which in August 1949 the first free, direct, secret and general elections took place for a federal West German parliament. With the establishment of a Federal Government, in September 1949, the three Military Governments were replaced by High Commissions (an Occupation Statute, itself finally to be annulled in May 1955, defined the powers still to be retained by them) and the Basic Law became effective.

The Basic Law defines and guarantees the democratic rights of the

[1] This includes West Berlin. Baden and Württemberg were separate states until 1952, and the Saar was only incorporated after a plebiscite in January 1957.

11

individual, in particular the freedom of conscience and belief, of the press and public opinion, of peaceful assembly and the sanctity of private property and inheritance, pronouncing them to be inalienable and unassailable. The fundamental principles of the state structure, including its federal basis, are also declared to be unalterable. The traditional democratic separation of the powers of the legislative, executive and judicial organs of state is observed, while further safeguards against absolutist tendencies exist in the federal composition of the republic and the supervisory control exercised by a supreme constitutional court (*Bundesverfassungsgericht*). Article One of the Basic Law states: "The Federal Republic of Germany is a democratic and social federated state. All political power of the state rests with the people. It is exercised by the people, in elections and plebiscites and by special organs of the legislative, the executive power and the judiciary. The dignity of the individual in inviolable. It is the duty of all organs of the government to respect and protect it." The freedom of the individual is therefore placed superior to the power of the state, and he is guaranteed legal redress against any infringement of his personal rights. At the same time, the freedom-based structure of the state is guaranteed against anti-democratic forces, and opponents of the system expose themselves to the loss of their civil rights.

The preamble of the Basic Law also refers to the seeking for integration into a greater European whole, a supra-national community of peoples which will help secure the peace and stability of Europe and indeed of the world—a clear rejection of absolutist or nationalistic intentions. Limitations on her own sovereignty are thereby rendered constitutionally possible.

The constitution lays down the federal nature of the West German republic (*Bundesrepublik*), which comprises ten provincial states or *Länder*, plus the specially-related *Land* of West Berlin. The *Länder*, whose individual integrity and authority are guaranteed as of right (Article 28) are, in order of size: Bavaria (27,200 sq. miles), Lower Saxony (18,200 sq. miles), Baden-Württemberg (13,800 sq. miles), North Rhine-Westphalia (13,100 sq. miles), Hesse (8,100 sq. miles), Rhineland-Palatinate (7,600 sq. miles), Schleswig-Holstein (6,000 sq. miles), the Saar (990 sq. miles), Hamburg (228 sq. miles) and Bremen (156 sq. miles).[2] Each *Land* has its own provincial parliament (*Landtag*), with guaranteed rights of its own, as well as being represented in the Federal Parliament at Bonn. A *Land* is further subdivided into districts (*Kreise*), while the smallest unit of administration is the commune, or *Gemeinde*. Each of these units again has its powers and responsibilities defined by the Basic Law. The main power in

---

[2] They vary considerably in density of population.

the country is vested in the Federal Parliament, which has its permanent seat in the Federal capital, Bonn.

Three categories of legislation are recognized by the Basic Law, which defines the powers of the various levels of government to enact them (Section VII). **Exclusive legislation** (*ausschließliche Gesetzgebung*) reserves to the Federal Parliament alone such national or 'security' matters as foreign affairs, defence, state finance, justice, post and telegraph services, customs and excise, commercial and trade treaties. **Concurrent legislation** (*konkurrierende Gesetzgebung*) on the other hand is permitted to the *Land* parliaments in all matters where the Federal authority does not seek to use its own power to legislate (Article 74 of the Basic Law). All economic matters are covered under this head, though the State does reserve to itself the prerogative of legislating for those taxes, levies and dues whose product is required mainly by the Federal authority. The *Länder* in their turn enjoy certain 'exclusive' powers, being granted the sole right to legislate in the fields of culture and the arts, most aspects of education (see page 186), religious affairs, police, local government, radio and television and the like. The third category is that of **framework legislation** (*Rahmengesetzgebung*), in which the Federal authority lays down the bounds within which the regions may legislate separately: it covers such matters as the public services, and film and press laws.

2. *Parliamentary System*

It is convenient to begin our survey with the Federal Parliament, and here we find two representative bodies, the Lower House (*Bundestag*) and the Upper House (*Bundesrat*), both of which are involved in the enactment of legislation, as in our own country at Westminster. The *Bundestag* is elected directly, on a national basis, for a period of four years. The deputies are full-time members and receive a salary (plus expenses), of roughly £3,200 per annum[3], their attendance at parliament being compulsory with a fine levied for non-attendance. The Federal Chancellor has a salary of about £9,000 a year, plus allowances of £3,000. Ministers receive £7,000 a year.

The leader of the government is the Federal Chancellor (*Bundeskanzler*), who is appointed to his office by the head of state, the Federal President, as the man commanding a parliamentary majority and the support of his own party. The chancellor can only be dismissed if the *Bundestag* can produce a majority vote in support of

---

3 This sum was increased to about £8,750 in 1971, and is tax-free; increases of like proportion were made to ministerial salaries.

his proposed successor—technically known as the constructive vote of no confidence. In this way much of the danger of parliamentary instability is removed, for no chancellor can be dismissed before his successor in office has been determined. The chancellor, once appointed, proceeds to the choosing of his ministers, who must again be appointed by the president. The *Bundestag* then proceeds to the election of its officers (Speaker, deputy speakers and clerks). The dates for the opening and closing of sessions of the *Bundestag* are fixed by the deputies themselves, but the president also has the power to recall parliament in an emergency. An early recall of parliament can likewise be effected at the instance of the chancellor or by a petition of one third of the deputies. Secret sessions of the house are determined by a two thirds vote of those present. *Bundestag* deputies enjoy the protection of parliamentary privilege and also receive free railway travel and an expenses allowance.

The composition of the *Bundesrat*, the upper house, is very different. Its membership is smaller than that of the *Bundestag* and is a fixed number; whereas that of the *Bundestag* is subject to minor fluctuations (see p. 21). There is no direct election to the *Bundesrat*, its 45 members being appointed by the provincial assemblies, the *Landtage*, to whom they remain responsible. These representatives are mandated to vote as directed by their respective *Land* governments and do not enjoy the freedom of conscience permitted to the deputies of the *Bundestag*: they therefore vote en bloc, and one delegate can cast the collective vote for his *Land*. *Bundesrat* members can also be replaced at the discretion of their *Landtag* superiors. Each *Land* is allocated seats in the *Bundesrat* in accordance with its population, ranging from the maximum of 5 seats for the large *Länder* to 3 seats for the small city states, as follows:

Land	Population (1968)	Seats
North-Rhine-Westphalia	16,800,000	5
Bavaria	10,300,000	5
Baden-Württemberg	8,800,000	5
Lower Saxony	6,900,000	5
Hesse	5,400,000	4
Rhineland-Palatinate	4,600,000	4
Schleswig-Holstein	2,500,000	4
West Berlin	2,200,000	4
Hamburg	1,860,000	3
Saarland	1,130,000	3
Bremen	751,000	3

Since West Berlin is not a fully integrated part of the West German state, being still subject to Big Four control, its delegates—like those in the *Bundestag* also—may not vote in plenary sessions, though they are free to do so in committee.

The presidency of the *Bundesrat* is held on a rotating principle, for a year at a time, by the chief minister of one of the *Länder*. This is an important post, for in the prolonged absence of the Federal President, the president of the *Bundesrat* assumes his responsibilities.

The *Bundesrat* constitutes a secure safeguard of the federal principle in West Germany. Its prime function could well be defined as that of defending the interests of the individual *Länder*. Certain legislation can only become effective with the approval of the upper house, in particular laws concerning the administration of the *Länder* and important financial legislation—so-called 'consent laws' (*Zustimmungsgesetze*).

The *Bundesrat*, not being an elective body, is in permanent existence, though its party political balance will obviously be subject to periodic change in consequence of *Land* elections and the resulting shifts in political power at *Landtag* level (see below). Plenary sessions of the *Bundesrat*, however, only occur every second week and are of very brief duration, most of the work being done in the committees.

As a general principle, sessions of both the *Bundesrat* and *Bundestag* are public.

3. Legislation

Parliamentary bills can be initiated from any of three different sources. They can be introduced by the government, by private members, or by the *Bundesrat*. The great majority are initiated by the government itself. For a private member's bill to succeed, the support of his party is generally necessary, and fifteen sponsors are required for its introduction into the *Bundestag*.

On its first presentation to the *Bundestag*, a bill usually receives a formal first reading and then passes to the appropriate standing committee of the house for detailed examination. These parliamentary committees, twenty-three in number, are made up of between fifteen and twenty-seven deputies, appointed according to the relative party strengths in the *Bundestag*. The draft bill produced by this committee then returns to the house for a second reading. The vital work on the bill will have been done by the committee, which has the right to call in representatives of the government and even outside experts to give evidence, in its detailed examination of the proposed bill, which will now incorporate amendments arising from members' criticisms and the views of those consulted. The emerging draft is likely to meet most of the requirements of all parties, and after a debate on the second reading a vote is taken. If no further amendments have been proposed, the third reading follows immediately, the entire bill being debated and voted upon. Amendments at this stage must be supported by at least fifteen members. If the second reading has produced amendments, the third reading can be delayed for forty-eight hours at the insistence of ten or more deputies, to enable printed copies of the proposed amendments to be distributed.

If the bill is approved by the *Bundestag* it passes to the *Bundesrat*, which will already have had three weeks' notice in which to comment on proposed government legislation before its actual tabling in the *Bundestag*. The bill is then examined by the appropriate standing committee of the *Bundesrat*—there are fourteen of these—which gathers the views of the various *Länder* and reports back to the *Bundesrat*. Many bills—just over half of those so far submitted—are known as 'simple', that is to say, they do not require the approval of the *Bundesrat*, which can however request the *Bundestag* to re-examine details of its proposals (the so-called *Einspruchsrecht*). The remaining bills come under the definition of 'consent laws' (*Zustimmungsgesetze*) and require the approval of the *Bundesrat* before they can become law. They concern matters which affect the prerogatives or interests of the *Länder*. A negative vote of the *Bundesrat* can be reversed by the *Bundestag* in the case of 'simple' bills, although a two-thirds negative majority in the *Bundesrat* can only be reversed by a two-thirds vote in the *Bundestag*. On its final approval, a bill goes to the Federal President for signature and enters into force after an interval of fourteen days.

Few government-proposed bills have failed to gain the final approval of the *Bundesrat*. Between 1949 and 1961 only fourteen out of 826 bills requiring *Bundesrat* approval were rejected; such bills must then fail. Much of the ironing-out of differences is carried out by the body known as the Mediation Committee (*Vermittlungsausschuß*), which contains members from both houses, eleven from the *Bundestag*, according to party strength and eleven from the *Bundesrat*, one chosen from each *Land*. These committee members are not bound by directions from either party or *Land*. The chairmanship is held for three months alternately by *Bundesrat* and *Bundestag* members. The task of this Mediation Committee is to produce amendments to the disputed bill which are designed to overcome the opposition. This is normally achieved, the interests of the *Länder* usually prevailing. Of 183 bills submitted to the Mediation Commitee up to 1962, only seventeen finally miscarried.

Bills promoted by the *Bundesrat* pass first to the *Bundestag*, where they follow the same course as other proposed legislation. Only fifty-one such measures were in fact proposed between 1949

16

and 1961, compared with a total of 3,065 bills and ordinances submitted by the government. Basically the function of the *Bundesrat* is to ensure the co-operation of the *Länder* in the legislative and administrative work of the state and to protect their interests. Legislation which affects them financially or administratively *must* be approved by the *Bundesrat*, in particular the Federal laws on taxes, whose yields are shared by the *Länder* and their sub-divisions. The portion taken from the income and corporation taxes by the *Länder* is also a fixed sum and can only be altered by agreement of the *Bundesrat*.

Liaison between *Bund* and *Länder* is also furthered by the special government Ministry for *Bundesrat* and *Land* Affairs. Its duties are to act as an information channel between Bonn and the provincial assemblies, and particularly to keep the *Bundesrat* informed on government policy.

Parliamentary voting is usually carried out by the raising of hands for or against a motion, no exact count being taken. In cases of doubt, however, members go out into the lobbies and are counted as they return through doors marked *Ja, Nein* or *Enthaltung* ('abstention'). A personal vote, in which members record their name and vote on an individual card, may be taken if requested by fifty or more members. More than half of the deputies must be present to constitute a quorum of the *Bundestag*.

A two-thirds vote of *both* houses is necessary to impeach the Federal President. Both houses must also produce a two-thirds majority to effect any amendment to the Basic Law. There is only very limited scope for amendment here, however, since such basic principles as those of federalism, the separation of powers and the pre-eminence of individual rights are declared by the Basic Law to be permanent and unalterable features of the West German state.

Members of the *Bundestag* are able to question ministers in a number of ways. On matters of importance a question bearing the signature of thirty deputies is answered orally and a debate follows. Less important matters, needing the signature of only fifteen members, are answered in writing. The institution known as question time has more recently been introduced into the *Bundestag*, the first hour of a plenary session being devoted to it. This enables members to question the government on a wide range of matters, and if not satisfied with the answer they receive, they may ask up to two supplementary questions.

The Federal President is elected by a meeting of the whole *Bundestag* and an equivalent number of deputies from the *Land* parliaments, made up according to party strengths. He is appointed for a period of five years, which may be renewed for one further five year term. An absolute majority is required for his election, but

17

B

if, after the second ballot, no candidate has qualified, a simple majority in the third ballot is allowed to settle the issue. The president is head of state, but his powers are not very extensive. His duties are mainly of a representative nature. He receives the accredited diplomatic missions of foreign countries in West Germany, accredits her own envoys and represents his country on official visits abroad. He has certain powers of free pardon and his approval is required in the appointment of judges, officers and civil servants, though he has no say in their selection. Together with the Supreme Constitutional Court, he checks the admissibility of parliamentary bills passed to him for signature. He can also dissolve the *Bundestag* within 21 days of its having refused a government vote of confidence without electing a new chancellor. In a state of emergency, the president does possess greater powers to intervene in the machinery of government, being empowered to approve legislation which the *Bundestag* has rejected but which the government of the day regards as urgent and to which the *Bundesrat* has given approval. Such suspension of normal constitutional practice may only, however, be applied for a period of six months, and only once during his term of office.

4. *The Electoral System*

The right to vote is extended by the Basic Law to all persons who have reached the age of 18, irrespective of sex, religion, social status or political beliefs. *Bundestag* legislation was approved in June 1970 which reduced the age of franchise to 18.[4] Exceptions to this rule exist only in the case of the mentally defective and those under arrest or serving prison sentences. Members of the armed forces are, for the first time in German history, also allowed to vote. The register of electors, compiled from the official police record of residents, must be placed on public display some time before elections, and those who find their name missing can apply to have it included. (N.B. registration is not the responsibility of the citizen, but of the local authority). Voting facilities outside one's residential district are available to all those who will be prevented from voting at their local polling station; they are more readily granted and more widely used than in Britain. In the Federal elections of 1965, 8% of the vote in the Rhineland-Palatinate and 8·6% in North Rhine-Westphalia and more than one million votes altogether were recorded in this way: many people voted while on holiday.

[4] It was already in force for the Hamburg elections of March 1970 and in certain other *Länder*.

A person wishing to stand as a candidate for election had previously to be at least 25 years of age, but since June 1970 this agebar has been lowered to 21. Candidates nominated by their party for a constituency must be chosen by secret ballot at a meeting of the district members—a democratic improvement on previous German practice. In large cities with several constituencies, candidates can be nominated for all electoral districts by the same assembly. The results of these ballots must be published, and a transcript of the proceedings must be handed in at the same time as the nomination papers, including details of the announcement of the meeting and the number of those present at the ballot. To qualify for official recognition a new party must first submit to the Federal authorities details of its constitution, the names of its principal officers, its party programme and the chief sources of its funds. The Federal Constitutional Court can rule against the legality of any party whose procedures or aims are not in accord with democratic principles. At least 500 voters from the appropriate constituency must also provide their signatures in support of a new party's candidate. Independent candidates may also stand, provided they are likewise supported by the signatures of 500 electors.

Elections to the *Bundestag* normally take place every four years, the first being held in 1949. In these Federal elections the elector has two votes, one which he casts for a candidate standing in his local constituency, and a second one which he may cast for any party which is campaigning in his *Land*. West Germany thus has a two-fold voting system. The Federal territory is divided up into 247 constituencies, from which roughly half of the *Bundestag* members are elected on a simple majority vote. The remaining seats in the *Bundestag* (just over half of the total) are allocated on the basis of the total number of votes polled in the *Länder* by each of the contending parties.[5]

The voting paper received by the voter is therefore rather more complex than that encountered in Britain. It is divided into two halves, to represent each of his two votes. On the left hand side appear, arranged in order of political strengths in the outgoing *Bundestag*, the names of all the candidates standing in his constituency, together with their address, profession and party affiliation. The names of candidates from parties not represented in the outgoing *Bundestag* are listed in the sequence in which their nominations were handed in. They appear at the bottom of the list. The voter makes his cross in a small circle against the **candidate** of his

[5] Prior to 1953, 60% of the seats were allocated to constituency votes, 40% to P.R. This was changed to a 50:50 basis in 1953, in answer to the complaint by the smaller parties that the older system penalised them.

choice. The right hand side of the voting slip offers him a choice from all the political parties campaigning, again arranged in the order of their numerical representation in the old *Bundestag*, and with the names of the area candidates on each party list added in small print. In similar fashion he makes his mark against the name of the **party** of his choice. It is thus possible with one's first option to vote for a candidate of outstanding personal merit who does not belong to one's favoured party, and still to record a vote for that party with one's second option.

It has been argued that the party-list system is undemocratic, in that it allows a party to place on its *Land* list persons who would never stand a chance in a constituency contest, but to whom it owes some kind of party obligation. Against this it is pointed out that many able brains, who would be hopeless fighting a constituency campaign but have much to offer the *Bundestag* in terms of expert knowledge or wide experience of affairs, can be brought into Parliament through this means. It has also been objected that the arranging of names on the ballot paper in the order of their previous parliamentary strengths places at a disadvantage those at the bottom of the list, suggesting that they are 'also-rans', and demands have been made for an alphabetical arrangement instead. It is possible also for a candidate to 're-ensure' his chances of election, by having his name entered for a constituency contest at the same time as being included on his *Land* list; many candidates are known to do this.

To avoid the situation of a *Bundestag* full of small splinter parties (one of the complications of government-forming in the Weimar republic of 1919–1933) two qualifying hurdles are imposed on parties wishing to be represented at either *Bundestag* or *Landtag* level. No party is granted representation which has not obtained either 5% of the national vote, or won at least three constituency seats. Numerous small parties have been excluded from the *Bundestag* on this score.

The composition of the *Bundestag* in terms of party strength remains fixed for a further four years once an election is complete. There are no by-elections in West Germany; in the event of the death or retirement of a member, his seat simply passes to the next name on the party list.

The distribution of seats from the party list vote is a somewhat complex business, and is carried out according to the Maximum Ratio Method (*Höchstzahlverfahren*) evolved by the Belgian d'Hondt. In this system, the total vote cast for each party is divided progressively by 1, 2, 3 etc. and the seats are then allocated to the highest remaining totals until all seats have been distributed. Thus, supposing the three parties A, B and C to have polled 3 million,

2 million and $\frac{1}{2}$ million votes respectively, and there being 12 seats to allocate, the calculation would proceed as follows:

Party A Total poll: 3 million	*Party B* Total poll: 2 million	*Party C* Total poll: $\frac{1}{2}$ million
$\div$ by 1 = 3,000,000 = 1st seat	$\div$ by 1 = 2,000,000 = 2nd seat	$\div$ by 1 = 500,000 = 9th seat
$\div$ by 2 = 1,500,000 = 3rd seat	$\div$ by 2 = 1,000,000 = 4th seat	$\div$ by 2 = 250,000
$\div$ by 3 = 1,000,000 = 4th seat	$\div$ by 3 = 666,606 = 7th seat	$\div$ by 3 = 166,666
$\div$ by 4 = 750,000 = 6th seat	$\div$ by 4 = 500,000 = 9th seat	$\div$ by 4 = 125,000
$\div$ by 5 = 600,000 = 8th seat	$\div$ by 5 = 400,000	$\div$ by 5 = 100,000
$\div$ by 6 = 500,000 = 9th seat	$\div$ by 6 = 333,333	$\div$ by 6 = 83,333
$\div$ by 7 = 428,571 = 12th seat	$\div$ by 7 = 285,714	$\div$ by 7 = 71,428

Party A thus receives 7 seats, Party B 4 seats and Party C 1 seat. The allocation of seats for each *Land* is based almost entirely on the proportional distribution of the second votes and not on the constituency contests which have been settled by the casting of first votes. All seats are initially distributed according to the party list vote, and then the number of constituencies won by the separate parties is deducted from the number they have been allotted on this party list basis. The seats which then remain available to each party are now awarded to those candidates whose names stand on the *Land* lists, in the sequence in which they were arranged for the election. It occasionally happens that a party has done so well in the constituencies that few seats remain vacant for distribution to its party list candidates, and leading party members have occasionally failed to be returned as a result. Sometimes a party will win more constituency seats than it is entitled to *proportionately* on the basis of the *Land*-list vote. When this happens, the candidates who have won in the constituencies retain their seats, and the number of members in the *Bundestag* is increased correspondingly. This can obviously cause slight variations in the size of the *Bundestag*.

Campaigning methods have undergone a dramatic change since the days of the first post-war Federal election of 1949. In the early days of the republic, election campaigns were conducted in a somewhat heavy, intellectual manner, the appeal being mainly to the party-faithful. Admission to election rallies would most likely be by ticket only. Heckling and hostile questions were regarded as bad taste, and interrupters were ejected. The former Federal Chancellor, Dr Adenauer, has been known to open his meeting with the performance of an entire Mozart symphony. However, styles rapidly changed, and especially under the impact of American campaigning methods the parties' projection of themselves has taken matters almost to the opposite extreme. Give-away presents, pop music and 'go-go' girls have been part of the more recent presentation. The party leaders themselves have undertaken whistle-stop or airborne speaking-tours of the entire country, and far more meetings are held at local level. Vast sums of money have been expended on advertising campaigns. It is estimated that four to five times as much money is expended by the parties in their campaigns as by their counterparts in Great Britain. The 1957 Federal elections are said to have cost the main parties nearly 55 million DM, and the cost for the subsequent elections of 1961 and 1965 to have increased by 33% and 45% respectively.[6] Chief spender has been the right-centre CDU party, which has received considerable financial assistance from big business. All parties are concerned to imprint on the elector's brain the initial letters of the party's name, and the magic abbreviations CDU, FDP, SPD and so forth confront the citizen at every turn, on huge street hoardings, in whole-page newspaper advertisements, on television and cinema screens, and on a myriad little posters that appear overnight like mushrooms on lamp-posts, post-boxes, and any other prominent anchorage. Plentiful printed literature is distributed—often at a sponsor's expense—and fleets of cinema vans also tour the country showing films in support of a particular party. It was reported in 1957 that the ruling CDU party had 400 such vans at its disposal, while the opposition SPD had ten. The CDU in this campaign even organized a railway train, complete with cinema, loudspeakers, posters and propaganda displays which toured every town in the country on its behalf.

In addition to the parties' own financing of their campaigns they also qualify for certain assistance from public funds. Legislation of 1969 allows 2·50 DM to be allocated for every registered elector, to cover spending by the parties on any matter directly connected with a Federal election. With an electorate of over 38 million voters, this produced a sum of 96·8 million DM in 1969. To be entitled to claim from this fund a party must poll at least $2\frac{1}{2}\%$ of the second vote (*i.e.* that for the party lists), and the money is distributed in proportion to the number of votes received. Parties are also allowed tax deductions on donations and contributions not exceeding 600 DM, but must publicly account for the sources of all their funds (Article 21 of the Basic Law). Some of the *Land* administrations have instituted a similar levy, at the rate of 1·50 DM per elector, but the indications are that rising election costs will induce them to increase this to 2·50 DM in the near future.

Public opinion polls, once ignored by the political parties, now play an increasingly dominant role at election times, and campaign tactics are often adjusted in accordance with the findings of the various survey organizations.

Polling day itself is either a Sunday or a public holiday and the polling booths are open from 8 a.m. until 6 p.m. (In special cases the time may be extended to 9 p.m.) The voter on entering the polling booth receives his voting paper and an envelope. After re-

[6] *Der Spiegel* (22.9.1965) put the estimated cost of the 1965 campaigning at 85 million DM—about £8 million at that time.

cording his two votes in private, he places the paper in its envelope and delivers it to the official in charge for whom he must establish his identity. The envelope is then placed in a locked box, ready for counting. Schools, local authority buildings, open air booths and even inns are used as polling stations. The simple layout of the voting paper enables counting of the votes to proceed very rapidly, and the first results are announced within a matter of hours. All invalid and spoiled voting forms are forwarded to the district election commissioner for inspection. They do not amount to any considerable quantity, especially in Federal elections, whose procedure is slightly simpler than that of *Land* elections, and appear to arise mainly from misunderstandings of the voting process.

The *Bundestag* must meet within at most 30 days of the holding of the election. During this interval, the parliamentary parties (*Fraktionen*) will have formed and will have elected their party executive. Each member of a parliamentary party, which must be at least 15 strong, must belong to the same political party. Private members are virtually powerless, since most of the business of the house is organized by the *Fraktionen—e.g.* the making up of the parliamentary committees.

The first task of the new *Bundestag* is the election of its President and his deputies, who correspond very much to our Speaker and Deputy Speaker. The President is usually a member of the majority party, but some of the Vice-Presidents are usually chosen from other parties represented in the house. They sit for periods of two hours at a time. The next task of the new *Bundestag* is to elect its parliamentary clerks: they number fifteen at present, and are chosen from the parties in accordance with their relative strengths in the *Bundestag*.

The installation of a government proceeds as soon as a party leader emerges who commands a majority of the *Bundestag*. He is appointed Chancellor by the Federal President and charged with the nomination of his ministers, who must again be installed by the Federal President. It is usual for the leader of the largest party in the *Bundestag* to be chosen as Chancellor, but the office may go to some other politician capable of commanding a majority of the house, in the case of party coalitions, for example. In the event of a candidate proposed by the Federal President not obtaining the necessary vote of confidence from the *Bundestag*, the house may within 14 days elect another member who can command the necessary majority, even against the President's will. Failing this, the office goes to the candidate who receives the largest vote in a new ballot. If he commands no overall majority, the Federal President may either appoint him to office or dissolve the *Bundestag* within 21 days. The Chancellor lays down the guidelines of government policy, and is answerable to the *Bundestag* for them. The *Bundestag* has no power to dismiss a minister from office, only the Chancellor being directly answerable to it, but it can bring strong pressure to bear which has several times led to a resignation.

The parliamentary committees are composed of *Bundestag* members appointed in accordance with party representation in the house, their membership varying between 15 and 27. Since they discharge most of the important business of the house, their efficient functioning is vital. The chairmanships of these committees are allocated to the various parties on the basis of the d'Hondt system of proportional representation. When a parliamentary committee is presented with a draft bill for its examination, it appoints a councillor from among its members, who will be in charge of that particular bill's progress through the committee. He is expected to acquaint himself thoroughly with the implications of the bill and to gather all relevant information and views from interested parties, including government ministries. He will finally write a report on the committee's work on the bill, which is presented to the *Bundestag*, and will most likely speak on the details of the bill when it comes up for its second reading in the house. Committee meetings are private and free discussion is therefore much more the rule than in the plenary sessions of the *Bundestag*, which are public and where members are more concerned with their impact on the mass media and their own party leaders. The standard of debate in the *Bundestag* is not very high, and the content of speeches can frequently be anticipated.

5. *The Political Parties*

In 1957 there were still as many as sixteen different political parties contesting the West German Federal elections. In the event, few even qualified for admission to the *Bundestag*, for politics in the Federal Republic are dominated today by the giants among the political parties. The elections of 1969 left only three parties with seats in the *Bundestag*. A brief review of the more significant parties follows.

CDU The party with the largest following, and the one continuously in office from 1949 to 1969, is the *Christlich-Demokratische Union*, the Christian Democrats. As a party it came into being only after the last war, but it continues the tradition of the older Catholic Centre Party of the Weimar Republic and earlier. The most significant aspect of its policy since 1945 is the playing down of the religious basis of its appeal, for a party which spoke only to the Catholic element in West German society could not hope for a majority poll in a state where Catholics were in a numerical minority.[7] Today its support derives almost as much from the Protestant electorate as from the Catholic one and a number of its leading figures are Protestant. We must note, however, that even under the *Reich* it counted Protestants among its ranks.

The dominant personality in the history of the CDU is that of Konrad Adenauer, the man mainly responsible for its almost miraculous post-war rise to political ascendancy in West Germany. Emerging from a political retirement forced on him by the Nazis in 1933 (he was mayor of Cologne), he virtually appointed himself leader of the party and led it to victory in the first post-war Federal election of 1949. He remained leader and Federal Chancellor until 1963, when he was coerced into handing over power to a successor less elderly than himself: he was then 87 years of age.

The main policies of the CDU have been forged by Adenauer and his Economics Minister, Ludwig Erhard, who succeeded him in 1963 as Federal Chancellor, signalling the dominance of the right wing of the party. Economic stability and social security were the basis of the CDU's domestic policy, while foreign policy had the twofold aim of restoring Germany's sovereignty by the complete removal of Allied controls, and of ensuring the security of the new-founded state by associating it with West European defence and economic co-operation organizations. Part of the CDU's wide popular support is attributable to the attention which they paid to social benefits and welfare measures; to a certain extent they cut the ground from under the SPD's feet with these policies. Adenauer in particular had an obsessive fear of communism, and so long as he was in power a rapprochement with Russia was out of the question. A deep distrust of Russian intentions remains a strong element in CDU thinking. This is especially the case in the person of Franz Josef Strauss, the leader of the Bavarian faction of the CDU, which operates under the separate name of Christian Social Union (*Christlich-Soziale Union* or CSU), though the two campaign as a joint party.

Although the largest party in terms of electoral support, the CDU does not have a very large paid-up membership. Registered party members in 1970 totalled about 320,000 (to which we must add the 85,000 members of its Bavarian wing, the CSU) and its party funds derive more from large-scale donations than from members' subscriptions. It is estimated that in 1957 it spent thirty times as much on the Federal election campaign as it received in membership fees.

The organization of the party is remarkably democratic, but the party's relative financial independence of its members means that policy decisions can be taken without much regard for local party

[7] Catholics make up about 45% of the West German population.

feelings, and the individual in fact has little influence on party affairs. The Federal executive is elected annually and includes no paid party officials. The organization at *Land* level also enjoys considerable freedom from control from above. It has a youth section, the *Junge Union*, membership of which is not restricted to CDU members, and which discusses freely a wide range of topics of current concern. The CDU's wide electoral support is proof that it has largely succeeded in throwing off its image as a purely Catholic party. Support derives largely from the middle and professional classes, from the farming community, businessmen and the housewives; in short, those whose interest lies mainly in preserving the status quo or who are suspicious of radical change. In the *Länder*, principal support comes from the industrial areas, from the southern states and from Schleswig-Holstein, mainly in towns of less than 50,000 inhabitants. Of the age groups, $49 \cdot 4\%$ of those under 30, 45% of those between 30 and 60, and $50 \cdot 7\%$ of those over 60 voted CDU in 1965. Women (comprising $51 \cdot 7\%$ *of those eligible* to vote) were stronger supporters than men (42%), and Catholics slightly outnumbered Protestants.

SPD The Social Democratic Party (*Sozialdemokratische Partei Deutschlands*) is the largest party in West Germany in terms of paid-up membership; it has about 800,000 members. There are 7,500 local party organizations, compared with the CDU's 5,000. It is also the only party to have survived from pre-Hitler days. Since its inception in 1869, it has almost consistently been an opposition party. Its first leader, Ferdinand Lasalle, was a radical Marxist, and the basis of its thinking was consistently Marxist right up to its fission into two factions (a larger moderate and a lesser radical one, the Spartacists) in 1918. Its policies had caused it to be officially banned for two years by Bismarck (1878–1880), yet by 1914 it had become the largest individual political party in the German Reich. By 1919 it polled 45% of the vote and had an enormous paid-up membership and superlative organization. Yet, in spite of these facts, the Socialists were actually in charge of the national German government for scarcely more than three years between 1919 and 1933. Coalitions of their political opponents ruled instead.

The early post-war years of the SPD were, like those of the CDU, dominated by a figure of outstanding personality, the veteran socialist Kurt Schumacher, who emerged from a Nazi concentration camp to take over the party leadership. Physically maimed by his sufferings under the Nazis, he strove to reform his party according to its old Marxist principles, and ruled it with the same rod of iron that Adenauer used to control the CDU. They were bitter enemies, and Schumacher was at times led astray by the sheer personal desire to oppose Adenauer's policies. The efforts of the

SPD were concentrated on preventing the commitment of the Federal Republic to the Western bloc and the consequent re-inforcing of the division of the two Germanies. A consistently Marxist criticism was also directed at the economic policies of the CDU coalition government, and when the 'economic miracle' never-theless occurred, the SPD suffered a considerable loss of public confidence. With the death of Schumacher in 1952 the much milder Erich Ollenhauer took charge of the party's affairs. Like Adenauer, Schumacher had not suffered powerful personalities in his entourage, and the succession to the leadership fell into much less able hands.

The power of the traditionalists in the party had been revealed at the SPD convention of 1950, when 96% of the leading Federal officials were pre-1945 party members, and only 21% of the district delegates had joined since 1945. It was difficult for younger men with new ideas to make headway in the party, and many promising figures either left altogether or entered *Land* politics and local government. It was the election of Willy Brandt as party leader in February 1964 that was the sign of the final breakthrough of the 'new men', who had been working energetically to reform the party for some years. Their policy victory occurred in the year 1959, when at the party conference held in Bad Godesberg, the SPD tacitly dropped its demands for nationalization and spoke rather of a property-owning democracy in which the worker would receive new opportunities for bettering himself and his family with a promised reform of social services and education. The electoral fortunes of the SPD have improved progressively since 1957, and in 1966 they finally achieved governmental status when they entered into a coalition with the CDU under Chancellor Kurt Georg Kiesinger. The elections of 1969 were to bring them the chancellorship itself.

The power of the party organization is much stronger in the SPD than in the CDU. Being financed largely from members' subscrip-tions (though trade union donations also help), it must be run economically and under the close supervision of party officials and must take note of party members' views .The party executives tend to be self-perpetuating, partly because their critics have shown a reluctance to shoulder the burden of work which the former—often voluntarily and unpaid—regularly carry out. The fact that the party conference, for reasons of economy, meets only every other year, does not help to diminish accusations of authoritarianism or secretiveness. More recently, it has been attempting to increase its appeal to the younger generation and also to broaden the social basis of its electoral support—both with considerable success. The influence of men like Willy Brandt has been invaluable in these new endeavours. Electoral support for the SPD, besides coming from the traditional working-class sector, also derives from a fair proportion of the intelligentsia and from civil servants and pensioners. Chief support in the regions comes from the city states (by far the greater part of the large cities has an SPD administration) and the northern and central *Länder*, and from Protestants rather than Catholics. In 1965 and 1969, only 10% of the Catholic vote went to the SPD. Of the sexes, men vote more readily for the SPD than women, and the younger men more readily than the older. It is a remarkable fact, indeed, that if only the men had the franchise in West Germany, the SPD would have a majority over all other parties.

FDP Whereas the SPD can claim half of the total national membership of West Germany's political parties, the Free Democrats (*Freie Demokratische Partei*) have a party following of less than 100,000. Although a new organization formed after 1945, the FDP is really a continuation of the old German liberal parties, the National Liberals and the Progressives prior to 1914, and the People's Party and the Democratic Party of the Weimar Republic. They are sometimes referred to as the 'Liberal Democrats'. Much of the support for the old liberal parties has, however, flowed into the SPD or CDU, leaving the FDP a small party often torn by its own internal differences.

Fundamentally, the FDP is a champion of political, religious and economic freedom and distrustful of all seemingly unnecessary controls. It is decidedly lukewarm in its approach to the concept of the welfare state, but liberal in its cultural and educational views, and prepared to experiment in the field of foreign affairs. The old labels of Left and Right are not entirely appropriate to the qualifying of the FDP.

Following a nationalist rather than an internationalist line, the FDP has also tended to the idea of a unitary, centralized state rather than the present federal organization of West Germany. It favours a Senate rather than the *Bundesrat*, with increased powers for the Federal President. Its own organization, however, shows a strong federal character, and the *Land* groups are largely independent bodies. It is possible, indeed, to find almost every shade of liberalism represented in this very diverse party, and it has formed coalitions in various *Landtage* with parties of both left and right. In Bremen, Hamburg and Baden-Württemberg it is the left-wing forces that predominate; in Schleswig-Holstein, Lower Saxony and North Rhine-Westphalia, the centre or right wing faction is in the ascendancy. In the *Bundestag*, it resolved speculation about its political alignment by taking up seats to the right of the CDU. Though a small party, it has played a significant rôle in Federal politics since 1945, having been a member of almost every coalition government. During the years 1966–69 it constituted the sole opposition. It is also represented in the governments of nearly all the *Landtage*.

The inner tensions at play in the party have led at times to fundamental cleavages which have further weakened its political strength and prestige. In 1956, a group of 16 *Bundestag* members, including four members of the cabinet in Adenauer's coalition government, seceded from the FDP to found a new party, the Free People's Party, which shortly allied itself with the right-wing German Party (DP—see below). At the same time, by absorbing some of the membership of forbidden neo-Nazi parties, the FDP itself moved towards the right. Its electoral fortunes have declined considerably in recent years, though the defeat of the conservative-minded Chairman Erich Mende in 1967 and the assumption of the leadership by Walther Scheel was indicative of more enlightened policies and began a movement towards alignment with the SPD which was first symbolized by their joint support of the SPD candidate for the Federal Presidency in March 1969. The FDP has always looked for a rapprochement with the Soviet bloc and Scheel's appointment as Foreign Minister in the 1969 coalition of SPD and FDP is in line with this interest.

Support for the FDP comes almost entirely from the middle class voter, especially the small or medium scale entrepreneur, the farmer, and the professions. The South-West is the region of its strongest following. Protestants rather than Catholics, men rather than women, the young rather than the old is the pattern of support. They have yet to succeed in their aim of broadening the social basis of their electoral appeal.

Their entry into a coalition government with the SPD in 1969 was followed by severe reverses in *Landtag* elections early in 1970. It is debatable, however, whether these reverses stem from its alignment with the SPD, for in the *Land* (North Rhine-Westphalia) where it had been associated in the outgoing government with the SPD it actually improved slightly on the 1969 result (from $5 \cdot 4\%$ to $5 \cdot 5\%$ of the vote). Their reverses, however, unleashed a fresh spate of backstage plotting against Herr Scheel by Dr Mende and other right-wing members, and the FDP was threatened with yet another split. In June 1970 Siegfried Zoglmann, a leading FDP figure, founded a National Liberal Action (NLA) group, with the declared aim of leading the FDP back into its old ways. By September 1970 the movement had branches in four *Länder* and a membership of 1,700, and Zoglmann was threatened with expulsion from the FDP if he did not desist. His response was to cross the floor of the *Bundestag*, together with two other prominent party members (one of them was Dr Mende) who joined the CDU, thus reducing Willy Brandt's majority in the *Bundestag* by six. The electorate does not seem to have been impressed by this secession, however, for in the November 1970 *Land* elections in Hesse and Bavaria, the FDP share of the poll actually increased. It rose from 6·7% to 10·1% in Hesse, and in Bavaria (rising from 5·1% to 5·5%) even restored the FDP to a parliament in which they were previously without representation. The SPD were the principal losers in these fluctuations, but bore their losses philosophically, since they had given strong support to the election campaign of their FDP partners, whose loss of their right-wing faction actually strengthened their coalition relationship with the SPD.

NPD The National Democrats (*Nationaldemokratische Partei Deutschlands*) are a comparatively recent foundation, their party dating from November 1964. They are really, however, the heirs of a succession of extreme right-wing parties which have followed one another since 1945, several of them being banned by the Federal Constitutional Court on the grounds of their neo-Nazi, anti-democratic character. The NPD is of interest primarily as the channel of expression for various forms of discontent, frustration and resentment in the present-day West German public. Its rapid growth of support in the mid 1960s caused some alarm in both the Western democracies and the Soviet bloc, but after threatening for a time to oust the FDP as the third largest political party in the Federal Republic, it went into a decline once more at the end of the 1960s and is not even represented in the present-day *Bundestag*. Its membership is claimed to be as high as 40,000, with strong support in the armed forces. Many are ex-members of the Nazi Party and most of its party officers have an extremist right-wing history. Funds for the party derive mainly from membership subscriptions, collections at party meetings (often very generous) and the sale of its various periodicals. Donations from ultra-conservative industrial sources have also been strongly suspected—including certain foreign ones. Support at the polls comes from men (68%) rather than women (32%), from the age-groups 30–44 and 45–59 (28% and 30%, respectively, of the NPD voters), rather than the younger (26%) or older (16%), from small towns and rural areas rather than cities, from Protestants rather than Catholics, and from those with only the basic level of education rather than those with higher education. Support comes generally from all social classes.

The fortunes of the NPD declined significantly during 1969 and 1970. It lost all its seats in the six *Länder* which it contended in 1970, failing to qualify under the 5% clause, as in the 1969 Federal elections also. In November 1970 support fell in Hesse from 7·9% to 3% and in Bavaria from 7·4% to 2·9%. There were indications that in Bavaria the CSU collected many of the lost NPD votes, campaigning much to the right of normal CDU policies.

The call of the NPD is for an end to Germany's 'humiliation' by the victors of 1945, for a strong and independent German state, for

30

a thorough-going clean-up of all liberal and permissive manifestations of present-day society and a return to the good old German ways.

Some of its practices and the utterances of certain of its speakers have led it to be considered a newly-emergent form of the Nazi ideology, but this is a somewhat exaggerated and alarmist view. Chief tactician is the party leader, Adolf von Thadden, who was previously closely associated with other proscribed right-wing parties; he is a clever speaker and less extreme in his statements than certain of his followers. Indeed, he has been concerned to reduce the preponderance of ex-Nazis among the NPD's membership.[8] (The potential threat from the NPD is examined more closely later in this chapter.)

GDP (GB) The All German Party (*Gesamtdeutsche Partei*) or All-German Bloc was an amalgam of numerous small parties which grouped themselves together in an attempt to continue in existence, but which none the less failed to achieve representation in the 1961 *Bundestag* election.

The basic fusion which led to the formation of the GDP was that of the German Party (DP—*Deutsche Partei*) with the BHE (*Bund der Heimatlosen und Entrechteten*—the refugees' party) in April 1961. Each of these parties had based its support on a particular section of the German public, the DP principally on the conservative farming community of North Germany (in 1952, 35,000 of its 45,000 members came from Lower Saxony), and the BHE on the very considerable number of refugees from the East and certain ex-Nazi elements. In the event, their supporters drifted away to the larger parties, the refugees especially, as they became integrated into the West German community and ceased to regard themselves as a separate entity. Whereas the DP had been strengthened in 1956 by the adherence of the break-away section of the FDP, the BHE had itself been split in consequence of a dispute over its future policies: there were those who wished German integration policies to extend to Slavonic Europe, and the name of the party was adjusted to All German Union (*Gesamtdeutscher Block*). The split came in June 1955, when the two principal party leaders and six other members left the party to join the CDU. The remainder seceded from the CDU coalition, to form the nucleus of a new conservative, national party, joining up with a fragment of the DP in April 1961. For the DP had itself divided in 1960, when nine of its 15 *Bundestag* members broke away to join the CDU; the remainder

[8] He resigned the leadership in November 1971, in a gesture of despair at the dissensions within the party following upon its electoral disasters of the year.

joined up with the GB/BHE to form the GDP. Membership was in the region of 100,000 and financial support came also from industry; but electoral support failed to materialize. Their failure in the 1961 elections was followed by the rise of their heir, the NPD.

It is interesting to note that a co-founder of the BHE, Dr Gustav Heinemann, who had left the CDU cabinet in 1950 in rejection of Adenauer's plans for re-armament, resigned in 1957 from the GB in protest against its revanchist tendencies, and joined the SPD. He was to become West Germany's third Federal President in 1969.

KPD If the various right-wing parties can be said to have had a chequered career over the past 25 years, the Communist Party (*Kommunistische Partei Deutschlands*) certainly experienced a very curtailed one. Immediately after the cessation of hostilities in 1945 the prospects for the German Communists were good: the discrediting of the Nazi régime, the heroic struggle of the Russian people and their armies during the war, the fight conducted on many fronts by the Communists against fascism were all factors which counteracted the propaganda with which the Nazis had assailed the communist ideology. In the elections held in the American and British zones of Germany in the immediate post-war years, the Communist vote averaged 8–9%. But support fell away in face of the behaviour of the Russian occupation forces in Germany and then the political policies pursued in the East Zone. In the first Federal elections of 1949 the KPD polled $5\cdot7\%$ of the votes cast; four years later they were excluded from the *Bundestag* under the 5% clause, having obtained only $2\cdot2\%$ of the votes. They had also lost much ground in the *Land* elections: having initially been represented in all the provincial *Landtage*, by 1954 they held seats in only three.

Meanwhile the CDU coalition had contested, at the Federal Constitutional Court, the legality of the KPD on the grounds that its policy entailed the overthrow of the régime and the constitution, and in August 1956 the party was outlawed and its funds confiscated. In this way an issue was settled in a legal manner which the electorate had proved itself well able to deal with at the polling booths, and Dr Adenauer has been criticized for his unnecessary intervention.

With the more recent and highly successful emergence of the NPD, pleas were made on many sides for either the proscribing of this party of the extreme right, or else the legalizing of a Communist party once again, if charges of favouritism towards the NPD were not to stick. Accordingly, in 1968, a new Communist party was licensed under the changed title of German Communist Party (*Deutsche Kommunistische Partei*—DKP). Its following is as yet very small: it has attempted, unsuccessfully, to win the more extreme left wing of the SPD away from Willy Brandt, and has also sought to make common cause with the militant students' socialist organization (SDS), again without much success. As yet it manifests too doctrinaire a commitment to the Moscow line.

DFU The German Peace League (*Deutsche Friedens-Union*) is another comparatively recent arrival on the political scene, and another organization which has been courted by the Communists— perhaps rather more successfully, since it represented many of their aims during the years of their proscription. Founded in 1961 its policies include German disarmament and neutrality, a truly Socialist German society and a rapprochement with the Soviet bloc. It has not yet achieved parliamentary representation; in fact its electoral support is steadily declining, partly, no doubt, in consequence of recent Federal Government attempts to reduce East–West tension (607,000 votes in 1961, 430,000 votes in 1965).

6. *Post-war Election Results*

The first Federal elections in West Germany took place in August 1949, after the ratification of the articles of the Basic Law. Most of the parties were comparative newcomers to the political scene, having made their début in the local or *Land* elections of 1946–1948, and the occasion was rendered more difficult for the elector by his lack of the experience of choosing between parties and policies during the Nazi era (1933–1945). Observers waited anxiously to see how the democratic process would work under these circumstances. Participation was high, at $78 \cdot 5\%$ of the electorate, and the results were as follows:

CDU/CSU	7,359,000 votes	31%	139 seats
SPD	6,934,000 ,,	29·2%	131 seats
FDP	2,829,000 ,,	11·9% ..	52 seats
DP	939,000 ,,	4%	17 seats
KPD	1,361,000 ,,	5·7%	15 seats
Others	4,306,000 ,,	18·1%	48 seats

Support was almost equally divided between CDU and SPD, which already here emerge as the political giants, far outnumbering any other group (there were ten different parties in all)—a tendency which was to become even more pronounced in succeeding elections. The four years which intervened before the next Federal elections gave the voter a chance to see the parties in action and to judge the personalities of their leaders. The dominant, cohesive leadership exercised by Dr Adenauer, who had formed a coalition government of all parties except the SPD and KPD, combined with his success in putting West Germany back on her feet both economically and politically, contrasted sharply with the negative opposition of Kurt Schumacher in the SPD, and at the 1953 polls the electorate gave

C

their verdict in favour of Dr Adenauer, now fast becoming a kind of father figure for the West German, and personally associated with Germany's post-war revival. The Russian suppression of the East German workers' rising in June 1953 also made Germans in the west distrustful of left-wing tendencies. In a *Bundestag* enlarged by 85 seats and with 4 million more voters, the results of the 1953 Federal election were:

CDU/CSU	12,443,000 votes	45·2%	243 seats
SPD	7,944,000 ,,	28·8%	151 seats
FDP	2,629,000 ,,	9·5%	48 seats
GB/BHE	1,616,000 ,,	5·9%	27 seats
DP	896,000 ,,	3·3%	15 seats
KPD	607,000 ,,	2·2%	no seats
Others	1,412,000 ,,	5·1%	3 seats

Once again, the CDU had no overall majority and Adenauer proceeded to the formation of another coalition which included all but the SPD.

Another four years went by, with a continued upward climb in West Germany's fortunes, diplomatic successes for Adenauer (the attainment of full sovereignty for West Germany with membership of NATO in 1955, and membership of Western European Union, which was to lead to the EEC organization), and disarray—as we have reported—among the smaller parties. The 1957 elections were to bring the high watermark of CDU fortunes. The suppression of the Hungarian rising by the Russians in that year strengthened the appeal of a party with experience in governing and a record of toughness towards the East. Election results were as follows:

CDU/CSU	15,008,000 votes	50·2%	270 seats
SPD	9,495,000 ,,	31·8%	169 seats
FDP	2,307,000 ,,	7·7%	41 seats
GB/BHE	1,373,000 ,,	4·6%	no seats
DP	1,006,000 ,,	3·4%	17 seats
Deutsche Reichs-Partei	307,000 ,,	1%	no seats
Federalist Union	254,000 ,,	0·8%	no seats
Others	150,000 ,,	0·5%	no seats

The CDU share of the vote had increased by 5% and they held 26 more seats, giving them a majority over all other parties, although not the two-thirds majority required to effect changes in the constitution. The SPD was beginning its revival also, advancing from 151 to 169 seats. Only four parties remained represented at Bonn, and the DP only because it had succeeded in winning more than three constituencies. The German electorate was continuing to show its lack of interest in small, radical or neutralist parties.

Although in command of an overall majority, Adenauer proposed the renewal of his coalition with the FDP and DP, leaving the SPD in isolated opposition. The FDP declined his offer, refusing to serve under him as leader of the nation's policies; his scant regard for FDP views in previous administrations sparked off this particular revolt. They were soon to regret their departure into the political wilderness, and the 1961 elections found them looking forward to participation in a new coalition. Adenauer's coalition, then, contained only the DP, but gave him a comfortable majority of 77. He reduced the size of his cabinet to seventeen ministers (two from the DP) and at the same time instituted an inner cabinet for more efficient working—and tighter personal control.

The SPD meanwhile concentrated on winning increased power in the various *Land* elections that occurred in the succeeding years. They already held five of the *Länder* (Berlin, Hamburg, Bremen, Hesse and North Rhine-Westphalia) and hoped to gain Lower Saxony in 1959. This would have left the CDU with a majority of only one in the *Bundesrat*. But although the Social Democrats increased their vote, they did not win an outright majority, the balance of power being held by the DP. In other *Land* elections the SPD also increased their strength, usually at the expense of Dr Adenauer's party, but the balance in the *Bundesrat* remained in favour of the CDU.

It became plain at Bonn, however, that Adenauer was overreaching himself, and he committed a number of mistakes which were to cost his party votes at the next elections. He attempted to rush through a bill permitting West German conscription, and with such scant concern for parliamentary procedure that he alienated even some members of his own party. He also attempted to by-pass the *Länder* over the establishing of a commercial television service, and was rapped over the knuckles by the Federal Constitutional Court (1960–61). When the Federal Presidency became vacant in 1959, he decided to stand as a candidate, until he discovered how restricted the President's powers were. He promptly dropped his candidacy and decided to remain as Federal Chancellor, wrecking plans for the appointment of his successor. Nevertheless, the CDU had many strong cards to play in the election campaign of 1961. The West German Mark was now one of the hardest currencies in the world; the older citizens, remembering two inflations in the course of the previous thirty years, were not willing to risk experimentation and change. Further, unemployment had been virtually abolished, where only a few years previously 2 million workers had been without jobs. West Germany had climbed to third place among the world's manufacturing nations, after the USA and Great Britain. Half a million houses were being built annually to supply a crying social need—or, as one of the CDU slogans put it, a house a minute. Against this, the SPD could only offer plans—for social reform, for a more egalitarian distribution of the products of the economy and for attempts at an understanding with Eastern Europe. The appeal of the CDU to the electorate not to throw Dr Adenauer overboard, with all his years of experience, at a critical juncture in German history (the Berlin Wall went up five weeks prior to the polls) counted for a lot, and the SPD was played down as a party of inexperienced and inconsistent men. Nevertheless, the new leader of the SPD, Willy Brandt, fought a spirited campaign and spoke to more election meetings than any previous candidate. The elections of 1961 produced the following picture.

CDU/CSU	14,298,000 votes	45·3%	242 seats
SPD	11,427,000 „	36·3%	190 seats
FDP	4,028,000 „	12·7%	67 seats
GDP		2·7%	no seats
DRP		0·8%	no seats
DFU	607,000	1·9%	no seats

The decline of the CDU had imperceptibly begun. They no longer commanded an absolute majority of the *Bundestag*, and were once more dependent on coalitions with others. The percentual fall in their support was almost exactly equalled by the percentual rise in the SPD vote. The FDP increased their vote (deriving 40% from former CDU adherents), but all other parties were eliminated.

The inevitable coalition between CDU and FDP was formed after protracted wrangling between Adenauer and Dr Mende, the conservative-minded FDP leader, and several important cabinet posts were granted to the CDU's junior partner. The FDP went back on their election pledge not to serve under Adenauer, on the condition that he retired after two years in office. Their main joint concern was to keep the SPD in opposition.

Things ran far from smoothly for this administration. A serious blow to its public image was administered in October 1962, when the Defence Minister, Franz Josef Strauss, acted unconstitutionally in arresting the chief editors of the magazine, *Der Spiegel*, which had published reports highly critical of West Germany's armed forces. The resignation of Herr Strauss followed and the coalition was saved. Meanwhile, Adenauer was strongly resisting attempts to replace him with a younger and more generally acceptable successor in the person of his Economics Minister, Ludwig Erhard, architect of West Germany's post-war economic miracle. In the end, Adenauer reluctantly went, but the CDU was left far from united behind Erhard in October, 1963. Adenauer remained party chairman and continued to intrigue from behind the scenes. Erhard was a convinced democrat and believed in consensus government by his cabinet, in complete contrast to the 'chancellor democracy' of

Adenauer. Control of his party began to slip from Erhard's hands, just as economic problems in the form of trade union agitation for higher wages and shorter hours mounted and the spectre of inflation was distantly glimpsed by the experts. The formation, in November 1964, of the NPD party marked a new threat to the democratic stability of West Germany, while student unrest was also beginning to disturb the academic world. Erhard was nevertheless able to lead the CDU confidently into the next Federal elections of 1965, and his popularity with the electorate was an advantage to his party in their campaigning. In all, fourteen different parties or groups submitted themselves to public scrutiny, but few had any hope of emerging into the new *Bundestag*. The results of the 1965 elections were: –

CDU/CSU	15,392,000 votes	47·6%	245 seats
SPD	12,711,000 ,,	39·3%	202 seats
FDP	3,062,000 ,,	9·5%	49 seats
DFU	432,000 ,	1·3%	no seats
NPD	658,000 ,,	2·0%	no seats
Others	90,000 ,,	0·3%	no seats

Only three parties were now represented in the *Bundestag*, and the CDU and SPD between them held all but 49 of the seats, each having increased its popular support. The FDP had suffered a considerable loss of public confidence as a result of its ambivalent attitude to Adenauer and a CDU coalition. Dr Erhard remained in office, in charge of a new CDU/FDP coalition, but his hold on his own party was weakening under pressure from rivals for the leadership, and stern tests lay ahead in the form of economic and industrial disturbances. The struggle between the left and right wing in the CDU centred on the appointment of the 'Atlanticist' (*i.e.* pro-NATO) Dr Schröder as Erhard's Foreign Minister, the old guard (including Adenauer and even, it seems, the Federal President, Lübke) seeking to prevent Schröder's nomination. Erhard won the day, but the threat to his position remained, not least from the fact that his coalition partner, Dr Mende, was campaigning for co-operation with the East Germans as a means of bringing about a European détente, and was highly unwelcome to the right wing of the CDU.

The crisis came in 1966. West Germany's previously extremely favourable trade balance was slipping dangerously towards a debtor situation. Standing at £542 million in 1964, it had slumped to about one-seventh of this amount in 1965. Excessive home demand was blamed. A 1966 budget cut of £681 millions was made, but the government still found itself incapable of controlling the overspending by the *Länder*, whose financial independence is enshrined in the Basic Law. An amendment to the constitution, to curb this independence of the *Länder* and to control the granting of bank loans to local authorities, required a two-thirds vote of the *Bundestag*, which would necessitate the support of the SPD opposition. The SPD were strongly placed to put pressure on the CDU, especially as they had just defeated them in the July 1966 *Land* elections in North Rhine-Westphalia. The FDP were also reluctant to help out the tottering Dr Erhard, who had previously given them an undertaking not to increase taxes and dues, but was now proposing to increase the duties on tobacco, spirits and petrol and to reduce certain welfare benefits. A crisis in the higher command of the Defence Ministry further loosened Erhard's control over his own party and he found himself fighting for his political life. His idealistic attempts to bring France and the USA together in a European policy had foundered on the rock of Gaullism. Fortune seemed indeed to have turned her back on him. His warning of the possibility of an incomes policy having to be achieved by way of a wages and prices freeze was merely his attempt to secure support for a system of long-term economic planning which would also involve the *Länder*; but it served to alarm all parties, including his own. Behind the scenes, consultation took place between the FDP and the SPD on the possibility of a coalition: it would have been a perilous balance in terms of policy, and would have had a majority of only six votes. Discussions were also held between the CDU and the SPD, with a similar aim in view. The FDP quitted the coalition government on October 27th and the next day the *Bundesrat* rejected the government's draft budget for the following year. On November 30th, Ludwig Erhard resigned and was replaced by Kurt Georg Kiesinger as leader of the CDU and Federal Chancellor. In effect, the economic difficulties of the country had been used largely as an excuse for his party adversaries to get rid of Erhard. West Germany's economic position was far from serious and was presently to undergo a remarkable recovery. A coalition of the CDU and SPD parties followed, leaving the 49 FDP deputies as the only effective opposition in the *Bundestag*.

It is the view of many observers that an election should have been held to decide the issue of who was to govern, instead of the compromise coalition which emerged. But the CDU feared defeat at the polls in their present disarray, while the SPD appear to have been only too eager to seize the chance of serving at last in an administration and appearing before the public as men competent to govern. There was also the fear that fresh elections would produce a stalemate result, leaving the problem still unresolved and democracy discredited among certain sections of the community. There seemed little danger, in comparison, in a short-lived coalition of the two big parties, if it enabled them to sort out the crisis by means of firm co-ordinated action. The danger lay rather in prolonging such a coalition and turning parliament itself into a mere rubber-stamp body. The price which Kiesinger had to pay for SPD support was considerable and involved the sacrifice of a number of CDU sacred cows. Probably the most notable of those was the policy of no negotiation with the East. With the SPD leader Willy Brandt in charge of foreign affairs, a new *Ostpolitik* was cautiously inaugurated which aimed at an eventual détente between West Germany and the Eastern bloc and some form of association between the two Germanies. A more ambitious programme of social welfare and educational reform was also envisaged, as well as advances in industrial democracy. Considerable strains were placed on the alliance at times, as individual groups in both CDU and SPD took exception to proposals put forward by the other party: the association was essentially one of compromise, and this produced tensions which finally rendered the coalition almost unworkable. The Federal elections of 1969 were a welcome release to both parties.

The achievements of the Grand Coalition during these three years were none the less considerable. It carried out more liberal reforms than all five preceding administrations together. New emergency laws were approved, containing notable democratic safeguards; and the civil code was thoroughly revised and liberalized. State economic planning became a science instead of a heresy, and under the SPD Economics Minister, Karl Schiller, long-range estimates were made, enabling expansion programmes to be drawn up and investments carried out which soon produced an upswing in the German economy; while joint action by *Bund* and *Land* promoted such matters as university development, agricultural reform and regional finance. Welfare measures were greatly increased, the budget for the Ministry of Labour becoming second largest of the government's financial allocations, and such matters as vocational training, workers' benefits and social security were all radically improved.

Adverse reactions in the country during this period were the rapid growth of the NPD and the wave of student revolt and violent demonstration which brought university life to a virtual standstill. The rise of the NPD may to some extent be attributed to the existence of the Grand Coalition, which to certain people at least signified the absence of any effective opposition at Bonn—opposition, we may note, to a mainly liberal régime. For a time, the NPD vote at *Land* elections actually outstripped that for the FDP. But resentment and reaction feed on failure and a sense of insecurity, and the resurgent prosperity of the West German economy sounded the death-knell to NPD hopes. Having broken through dramatically at *Land* elections in the year 1967–68, they lost much of their support again in 1969, to remain what they basically are, a marginal party of malcontents, neo-fascists, nationalists and irredentists.

It has been said of the student rebellion that it, too, was a signal of protest against the massive government bloc of CDU and SPD, to which they constituted the 'extra-parliamentary opposition' (*Außerparlamentarische Opposition* or APO). To a degree this is true, but their rebellion was really directed at the age-old forces of tradition and hierarchical control which were preventing the universities and colleges from moving into the twentieth century, and which more enlightened politicians themselves (especially of the SPD and FDP) were seeking to reform. Swept for a time into extremes of utterance and behaviour by various anarchist and Maoist agitators, the APO finally came full circle and announced its own demise late in 1969. For most of its life, however, the student unrest constituted a serious problem of law and order for the coalition government of Dr Kiesinger. The general mood of rebellion still smoulders in the student movement.

Kiesinger was never entirely happy in his position as Chancellor. He was compelled to act as a kind of chairman-referee to his bi-party cabinet, yet controversial measures required a firm resolution on his part to push them through: this incurred the immediate danger of collisions with entrenched views in either party. The SPD found its own image suffering under the shadow of CDU leadership, and in a succession of *Land* elections it lost ground consistently to the CDU, where previously it had recorded an uninterrupted succession of increases in its vote in every *Land* election. The campaigning for the 1969 elections showed the relief experienced by SPD and CDU members alike at their release from this unnatural symbiosis. There was little indication of a desire to renew the coalition, indeed rather a determination not to contemplate a new one.

The results of this election were as follows:

CDU/CSU	15,203,000 votes	46·1%	242 seats
SPD	14,074,000 ,,	42·7%	224 seats
FDP	1,904,000 ,,	5·8%	30 seats
NPD	1,422,000 ,,	4·3%	no seats
Others		1·1%	no seats

The CDU, shaken by its further decline, proposed to the FDP the formation of a coalition, but the SPD and FDP were already embarked on negotiations for a coalition of their own. The CDU protested furiously that they were still the major party and had the right to rule. The FDP's reply was that in their campaign they had insisted on their refusal to govern with the CDU, and that the voters who had supported them therefore clearly wished an SPD/FDP alliance. It was also pointed out to the CDU that when they themselves stood in second place to the SPD in *Land* elections they had hardly applied the principle which they now invoked in their own favour. The new coalition of SPD and FDP under the Chancellorship of Willy Brandt took up office, with Walther Scheel, the FDP leader, as Foreign Minister, and a *Bundestag* majority of twelve. Brandt's position was far from secure, for the loyalty of certain FDP members to the coalition was a tenuous one, and CDU pressure was constantly exerted on them to defect, thus helping to bring about a CDU/FDP coalition. In September 1970 the FDP was compelled, as we saw, to take action against one of its members who had created a right-wing opposition group within the FDP, under the title of National Liberal Action. The defection of Zoglmann, Mende and another leading party member of the FDP left the Brandt coalition with a *Bundestag* majority of only six in November, 1970. No further defections occurred though there was a scandalous attempt by the CSU to buy over another FDP member in November 1970, a venture whose exposure resulted in some increased electoral support for the FDP in the Bavarian *Land* elections of that month.

Brandt's freedom to introduce the sweeping social reforms envisaged in the SPD programme was also severely restricted by his utter dependence on the FDP, which, while going along with him in his attempts at a rapprochement with the East, had reservations about domestic reform. The coalition has had remarkable success in its policies so far, especially in its approach to the Soviet bloc, and Brandt, who was once considered incapable of achieving wide voter-appeal, has won great popularity with the West Germans. Should the coalition with the FDP become seriously threatened, his most likely move would be to call for new Federal elections, in the anticipation that the SPD would emerge as the overall victor.

Summing-up. Certain general aspects of the political picture over the past 25 years are worth commenting upon. The continued trend towards a two-party system is most marked: the CDU and SPD between them controlled 60% of the votes in 1949; they netted 74% in 1953, 82% in 1957, 81·6% in 1961, 87% in 1965 and 88·8% in 1969. The German voter has thus declared his disinterest in small, particularist parties, which were in fact entirely eliminated from the *Bundestag* scene after 1961. It is also a fact, however, that the constitutional system operates against the smaller parties. In 1949, for instance, they received 39·8% of the vote and 32·6% of the *Bundestag* seats: in 1963, gaining 26% of the poll, they received only 19% of the seats. In 1957 they scored 18% of the vote but obtained only 11·67% of the seats. The 5% qualifying clause is also a hurdle they find hard to surmount.

The West German voter has shown a remarkably high and consistent level of interest in the Federal elections. Even if frequently left cold by the election campaigns, he has still turned out to vote on the day. Participation in the 1949 election was 78·5% of those eligible; in 1953 it advanced to 86·2%, and in 1957 it rose to the record level of 88·2%, continuing to remain high, at 87·7% in 1961, 86·9% in 1965 and 86·8% in 1969. Percentages for *Land* elections are not quite so high, but still impressive.

The success of both major parties in broadening the social basis of their appeal is illustrated by the results of public opinion surveys conducted during the 1961 and 1965 elections. Whereas in 1953 the catholic members of the electorate had voted 80% for the CDU, in 1961 only 75% did so. Whereas 69% of all trade unionists had voted SPD in 1963, only 64% did so in 1961. In the year 1957, in regions with small or medium-sized industries and a mixed Catholic-Protestant population, only one-fifth of the voters chose the SPD; in 1961 the SPD obtained one-third of these votes. In the *Land* elections of the Rhineland Palatinate (traditional CDU territory) the SPD vote was 34·9% in 1959, and 40·7% in 1963. In a survey conducted in 1961 roughly a fifth of those who voted CDU and a fifth of the SPD supporters regarded themselves as belonging to the lower working classes. The upper working class group provided the SPD with 55% of their votes and the CDU with 34%. Middle class voters produced 22% of the SPD vote, and 34% of the CDU. From the top levels of society the CDU drew 14% of its vote, and the SPD 3%. The CDU dropped their designation of the SPD as a 'party of class conflict' in the face of these statistics.

It is interesting also to take a look at the men and women who are elected to the *Bundestag*. The ratio of the sexes is decidedly out of balance, especially for a country where the female population outnumbers the male by almost three millions. In 1965 women deputies made up 8·1% of the membership of the *Bundestag*, and the 1969 figure was only 6·1%.[9] The SPD has more women deputies than the other parties. However, female membership of the parties themselves is very small, and a woman seeking to make headway in a political career has excellent prospects.

In the 1969 *Bundestag*, civil servants (31·5%) and white collar workers (27·6%) made up the majority of the deputies elected. More than half of the total had university degrees. The average age of *Bundestag* members is seen to be decreasing (1965, 54 years: 1969, 49 years), and this is also the case in the *Landtage*. SPD deputies tend to be younger on average than CDU members, though the discrepancy is not great and is becoming smaller. Length of ser-

[9] This is still better than the figure for Great Britain, which has never been higher than 4·4%.

vice statistics for the *Bundestag* are obviously conditioned by relative party strengths over the past 21 years, but in 1969 few members had sat for more than eight years (64 out of 518).

7. *Government in the Länder*

As we have seen, West Germany consists of eleven separate *Land* divisions (if we include West Berlin), each of which possesses its own *Landtag*. In each state, the system of election is a little different from that of its neighbours and even officials are sometimes at a loss to explain the details. Broadly speaking, however, the system resembles that for elections to the *Bundestag* and consists of some

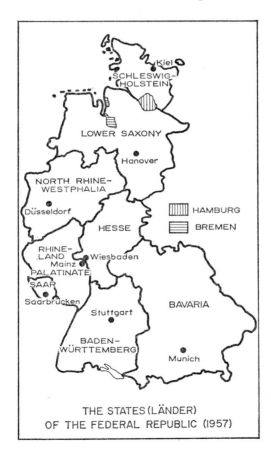

THE STATES (LÄNDER)
OF THE FEDERAL REPUBLIC (1957)

proportional representation combined with direct constituency voting. All the *Landtage* are elected for a four year period, with the exception of the Saar, where the parliament sits for a five year term. The *Landtage* are single-chamber assemblies except for Bavaria, which has an upper house also, known as the Senate. This Senate is an attempt at giving representation to a broad cross-section of the population, drawn from "the social, economic, cultural and local authority corporations of the *Land*" (Article 34 of the Bavarian Constitution). The Senate has little actual power however, and certainly no delaying or blocking control over Government legislation.

The size of a *Landtag*, and of the cabinet, depends mainly on the size of the individual *Land*, and ranges from fifty deputies in the Saar to two hundred and four in Bavaria and two hundred in North Rhine-Westphalia. In most of the *Länder*, various coalitions of the political parties are in control of affairs: indeed the sharpness of party rivalries seems to be felt less acutely at this level and a greater desire for administrations which are representative of the corporate identity of the region exists. This somewhat 'folkish' approach is now yielding to a more conscious attention to differences of party ideologies, mainly under the impact of the election campaigns mounted by the political parties themselves, and the increased significance of the balance of party power in the *Bundesrat*. Initially the CDU under Adenauer (seeking absolute control in the *Bundesrat*), and more recently the SPD, have infused a more partisan spirit into *Land* elections. The campaign in North Rhine-Westphalia in 1966 was especially high-geared, in terms of propaganda, ministerial speakers from Bonn and financial outlay. Spending by the SPD equalled 80% of the sum expended on their entire Federal election campaign of 1965.

Because of the uncoordinated pattern of Allied policy in the immediate post-war years, the holding of elections in the various *Länder* was instituted on a quite *ad hoc* basis, so that no one *Landtag* election coincided with another. This situation has been perpetuated down to the present, so that an election of some moment always seems to have just taken place, or to be about to take place. There were six in the course of 1970, all on different dates. This is disruptive of the regular pattern of political life and the smooth functioning of government at Bonn. Since the fortunes of the Federal Government cannot be divorced from the outcome of a *Land* election, an exaggerated degree of federal interest—and intervention—is generated in the political life of the provinces, and a synchronizing of at least some of the *Land* elections would seem to be in the best interests of all. Proposals are now under consideration for bringing about such a re-organization.

The pattern of *Land* assemblies and their coalitions at the end of 1970 was as follows (previous party strengths and government coalitions are shown in brackets):

Land	Year of Election	CDU/ CSU	SPD	FDP	NPD	Others	Government Coalition
Baden-Württemberg	1968	60 (59)	37 (47)	18 (14)	12 (—)	—	CDU/SPD
Bavaria	Nov. 1970	124 (110)	70 (79)	10 (—)	— (15)	—	CSU
Bremen	1967	32 (31)	50 (57)	10 (8)	8 (—)	— (4)	SPD/FDP
Hamburg	March 1970	41 (38)	70 (74)	9 (8)	—	—	SPD/FDP
Hesse	Nov. 1970	46 (26)	53 (52)	11 (10)	— (8)	—	SPD/FDP
Lower Saxony	June 1970	74 (67)	75 (65)	— (7)	— (7)	— (3)	SPD
North Rhine-Westphalia	June 1970	95 (86)	94 (99)	11 (15)	—	—	SPD/FDP
Rhineland-Palatinate	1967	49 (46)	39 (43)	8 (11)	4 (—)	—	CDU/FDP
Saar	June 1970	27 (24)	23 (21)	— (5)	—	—	CDU
Schleswig-Holstein	1967	36 (34)	30 (29)	3 (5)	4 (—)	— (1)	CDU/FDP
West Berlin	1967	47 (41)	81 (89)	9 (10)	—	—	SPD/FDP

The minor parties have tended, in the past, to achieve better results in *Land* rather than *Bund* elections, and several that were excluded from the *Bundestag* in 1961 (and even before then) actually featured as coalition partners in certain *Land* administrations. The main break-through of the NPD was achieved in the *Land* elections of 1967 and 1968, not at Bonn, where their vote has always been lower. It is the general experience that parties which are in opposition to the Federal Government do well in local and *Land* elections, but that the votes flow back to the government party when Federal elections take place—a common experience in western democracies.

By the end of 1970 it was clear that both NPD and FDP had suffered badly in that year's provincial elections. The fortunes of the NPD were particularly poor, for in the six *Land* elections in which it campaigned, it failed to achieve representation in any *Landtag*, falling consistently below the 5% hurdle. The FDP has not fared quite so badly. In June 1970 it disappeared entirely from the parliaments of the Saar and Lower Saxony, under the 5% clause, but it did manage to improve its position in the Autumn elections held in Hesse and Bavaria. The ability of the FDP to preserve its unity as a party and consequently as a member of the government coalition at Bonn now becomes crucial, for the fortunes of Willy Brandt's administration depend on its support. The divisive activities within the party (reported earlier) are bound to be accentuated by any further electoral setbacks, and are, in their turn, likely to have an adverse effect on the party's electoral chances. The effect of Herr Zoglmann's intervention, with his National Liberal Action, in the April 1971 elections in Schleswig-Holstein, was watched with close attention by all parties.[10]

Participation in *Land* elections is usually high, though between 5% and 15% lower than in Federal elections. Each *Landtag* is presided over by a Prime Minister (*Minister-Präsident*) who also draws up the list of his cabinet ministers. Hamburg and Bremen call their assemblies the *Bürgerschaft* (Civic Assembly) and their cabinet is known as the Senate: the chief minister has the title of First Burgomaster. Cabinets in the *Landtage* tend to be smaller than the Federal cabinet, and ministers sometimes hold two appointments, for the business of a *Landtag* is necessarily less onerous than that of the *Bundestag*. Much of the work connected with legislation is carried out in committee, as at Bonn, the members of the committees being appointed according to party strength. There is a more comradely spirit and sense of communal purpose to be found here than among the *Bundestag* deputies and the proceedings are usually less formal. Members of *Landtage* are free to vote according to their conscience and are not bound by party dictates, just like their counterparts in the *Bundestag*. They enjoy a fair measure of social prestige and often exercise considerable influence as leaders of interest groups within their *Land*. Not a few progress to membership of the *Bundestag*. Technically speaking, they are not paid a salary, but receive compensation, which is related to the earnings of civil servants, with additions for attendance at committees and plenary sessions. This is not enough for their needs, however, and most of them either derive money from another occupation or else serve their party in some official capacity, for which they are also paid. Their average age is slightly lower than that of *Bundestag* members, but there are fewer women in the *Landtage* than at Bonn. Neither *Landtag* nor *Bundestag* members receive a pension. The social composition of Federal and *Land* Parliaments shows a large degree of similarity. One notes in particular the preponderance of professional men.

The business of a *Landtag* is of necessity less momentous than

10 In the event, both FDP and NPD were eliminated from the *Landtag* and the SPD/FDP coalition was replaced by a CDU administration. Later, in June 1971, Herr Zoglmann announced the formation of a new party, the *Deutsche Union*.

that of the Federal Parliament. Legislation on major matters and federal issues is, as we saw, the prerogative of the *Bundestag*, but the *Landtage* do have discretion in the case of 'framed' legislation, where they operate within guidelines laid down by the Federal Assembly (*e.g.* town and country planning, conditions of service for officials, press and film laws). In the sphere of 'concurrent' legislation they deal with economic matters which primarily affect themselves rather than the *Bund* (*e.g.* local taxes and levies, income and property taxes) and the administration of justice and maintenance of the courts of law. Their own particular field of legislation, in which they enjoy exclusive rights, is that which includes education, broadcasting, culture, religious affairs, police, local government and *Land* administration. In a sense, one could say that the basic purpose of the *Länder* is the assumption of the administrative responsibilities of the central government (a burning topic of our times!). By far the greatest number of civil servants work for the *Land* administrations, not for the Federal authority. It has been calculated that, excluding the railways and post office, only about 10% of public officials work for the Federal Government, about one-third are employed by local government, and well over a half are serving a *Land* administration.

There is a tendency latterly, however, for the Federal Government to intrude upon the authority of the *Länder* and to seek increased powers of direction. This is one of the consequences of attempts that have been made, under the CDU/SPD and SPD/FDP coalitions, to lay down a national plan for education and in particular university development, and also to develop long-term economic planning for the whole country and bring spending by the *Länder* under stricter budgetary control. Already a Federal Minister for Education and Science has been appointed (1969) to promote and supervise national educational planning, where previously no such Federal Government post existed. The ultimate authority rests always with the *Bundestag*, which in cases of obstruction can, with the approval of the *Bundesrat*, compel any *Land* or local authority to do its will.

The matter most likely to cause friction between the regions and the *Bund* is that of finance. This has therefore been most carefully regulated in the Basic Law, which sought to prevent the usurpation of regional funds by the central authority which had been such a feature of German government in the days of the *Reich*. The details are spelled out in unambiguous terms[11] in Article 106:

[11] The author of these particular clauses of the Basic Law was a former Prussian finance minister, and the precision of his formulations has been much admired as an example of Prussian thoroughness.

47

I   The yield of fiscal monopolies and receipts from the following taxes shall accrue to the *Bund*:
  1. customs duties
  2. such excise taxes as do not accrue to the *Länder* in accordance with paragraph II
  3. turnover tax (a 4% levy on most business transactions, now replaced by Value Added Tax)

II   Receipts from the following taxes shall accrue to the *Länder*:
  1. property tax
  2. inheritance tax
  3. motor vehicle tax
  4. taxes with localized application.

III Receipts from income tax and corporation tax shall accrue . . . to the *Bund* and the *Länder* in the ratio of 35% to 65%.

IV   . . . . The requirements of the *Bund* and the *Länder* in respect of budget coverage shall be coordinated in such a way that a fair equalization is achieved, any overburdening of taxpayers precluded, and uniformity of living standards in the Federal territory ensured.

The *Land* governments' 65% share of corporation and income tax constitutes their main source of revenue. In consequence of the much increased yield of these taxes since 1960, the relative balance of revenue shifted in favour of the *Länder*, and the Federal Government therefore advanced its share to 40·5% for 1963 and 41·5% from 1964 onwards. Of receipts from local taxation, the *Bund* in 1961 initially collected 55·6%, the *Länder* 32·6% and the local authorities 11·8%. Local authorities depend on the *Land* for much of their finance, but do possess sources of their own, such as the real estate tax and local business taxes. In an attempt to equalize the burdens carried by the various *Länder*, some of which are obviously much richer than others, the Federal authority makes use of two devices. In its budgets it provides for welfare payments and subsidies to refugees, war victims and the like who are the charge of the *Land* governments: this accounted for 2·6% of the tax yield in 1961. Secondly, use is made of a 'horizontal' equalization of burdens arrangement, whereby the richer *Länder* must contribute a certain proportion of their tax receipts towards easing the burden of the poorer ones. In 1961 the following payments or receipts took place:

Land	*Received*	*Land*	*Contributed*
Schleswig-Holstein	305·2 Million DM	North Rhine-Westphalia	752·5 Million DM
Lower Saxony	446·6 Million DM	Baden-Württemberg	191·1 Million DM

48

Land	Received	Land	Contributed
Rhineland-Palatinate	332·8 Million DM	Hesse	155·3 Million DM
Bavaria	219·3 Million DM	Hamburg	333 Million DM
Saar	127·9 Million DM		

To avert the danger of straying too far apart in policy or procedure, the various *Länder* maintain liasion with one another through periodic meetings of ministers from the various states, sometimes followed by the setting-up of a committee to study a common problem. Perhaps the best known of these committees is that concerned with education, which meets regularly and has done some extremely useful work.[12]

8. *Local Government*

The smallest unit of administration in the Federal Republic is, as we saw, the *Gemeinde*. Between *Land* and *Gemeinde* there is a midway authority, that of the *Landkreis*. These vary greatly in size and population, but on average contain about sixty *Gemeinden* and 75,000 inhabitants. The administration of a *Kreis* (district) is partly autonomous and partly in the control of the *Land*. The executive organ is the committee of the *Kreistag*—an elected body—and the chief official is known as the *Landrat* or, in North-West Germany, the *Oberkreisdirektor*. The activities of the *Kreis* authorities are concerned largely with supervising the affairs of a group of *Gemeinden*, and include road-building, the provision of public transport services, the care of youth, hospitals and welfare services. The President of the *Landtag* supervises the activities of the *Landkreise* and of any large size towns or cities lying outside the competence of the *Kreis*, which are themselves usually designated *Stadtkreise*.

The *Gemeinden* are self-administering units, drawing their finances from the product of local property and trade taxes: in 1962 the trade taxes brought in 77% of the total revenues of the *Gemeinden*. These sources are not, however, sufficient for their needs, and they also receive grants and loans from the *Länder*.

There are in all 24,503 *Gemeinden* in West Germany, and 11,284 of them have less than 500 inhabitants, while 790 have a population of less than 100. The designation *Stadt* (township) is applied to 1,349 of these *Gemeinden*, but only 800 have more than 5,000 inhabitants. Roughly a quarter of the West German population lives in these *Gemeinden*.

The Basic Law lays down and guarantees the self-administration

---

[12] See p. 186.

49

of these smallest units of government. This tradition of local self-administration is firmly rooted in some regions, going far back into history, and in particular to the system instituted by the Prussian ministers Stein and Hardenberg early in the nineteenth century. The continuing force of local tradition has led to a considerable diversity in local government patterns throughout present-day West Germany ranging from the collective council type of administration prevalent in southern Germany to the principle of a dominant mayor or city manager who bears prime responsibility, as in parts of the north and west. Each local authority or parish has its own elected council, with a local chief (sometimes a *Bürgermeister*) plus other elected paid officials, in addition to the honorary representatives of the citizens. The activities of the latter most usefully supplement those of the paid officials.

Local government activities are directed to four principal spheres: building, education, cultural affairs and social welfare. Libraries, adult education, museums, permanent and travelling exhibitions, municipal theatres, amateur theatricals and orchestras—all these are supported and helped, as well as water, gas and electricity supplies and the upkeep and development of the local roads and communications networks.

The control of the *Land* over the *Gemeinde* is a stricter one than that of the Federal Government over the separate *Länder*. Each *Land* can legally dictate to the *Gemeinden* the kind of self-administration they are to exercise: it can scrutinize their budgets and finances, alter their boundaries and grant or withhold its approval for local statutes. The *Gemeinde* authorities, moreover, have no representation at *Land* level, whereas the *Länder* are powerfully represented in the *Bundesrat*. There is, therefore, some discussion and debate on the allocation of functions and the share of charges between the two, since the local authorities are, for instance, called upon to execute the laws and to follow the directives of the *Land* authority in many matters, such as school building. The *Gemeinden* have therefore been asking for a bigger share of the public income, as well as in the preparation of laws and regulations. In 1949, the amount of aid received from *Land* governments by local authorities amounted to 29% of their expenditure, but it fell away rapidly up to 1953. New measures to improve the subsidy and regulate the sharing of taxes between *Länder* and *Gemeinden* led in 1958 to an improvement to the level of a 20% contribution. From 1962, the contribution rose to 27% after further deliberations, and fresh reforms are envisaged.

For greater ease of administration the larger cities are further sub-divided into districts (*Bezirke*),[13] which again have their own local council, executive committee and burgomaster, all standing under the ultimate authority of the city council. Hamburg has seven such *Bezirke*, West Berlin twenty, and Bremen fourteen, each with a differing pattern of organization.

9. West Berlin

A few words must be devoted to the territory of West Berlin and its special relationship to the Federal Republic. As we have seen, although this *Land* is represented at Bonn both in the *Bundestag* (22 deputies) and the *Bundesrat* (4 seats) these delegates are not allowed to vote in plenary sessions, though they may speak in debates and vote in committees. Neither is the city a full legal member of the Federal Republic.

The restrictions on West Berlin's political freedom arise from the terms of the London agreement of September 1944, according to which it stands under four-power Allied jurisdiction until such time as this agreement is replaced.[14] Nevertheless, the Basic Law defines it as a constituent *Land* of the Federal Republic of West Germany and its enjoys a large degree of self-government having its own Parliament. It may not be governed from Bonn, however. The House of Representatives has 140 members, and there is a governing council (the Senate) which consists of a chief burgomaster, a burgomaster and eleven senators. All legislation passed in Bonn which has reference to West Berlin must also be approved by its own Parliament before coming into force.

When the Basic Law was drawn up, and the question of a capital for West Germany arose, the decision was taken to make Bonn the provisional Federal capital, until such time as the city of Berlin could be fully restored to its traditional role. The *Bundestag* in February 1957 actually declared Berlin to be the capital of Germany, for the hopes of nearly all West Germans are centred on the eventual reunification of their country. A symbolic gesture of the West Germans is the election of their Federal President in West Berlin. The East Germans, for their part, regard this as provocation. Isolated and surrounded as the city is by the territory of an antagonistic régime, with highly vulnerable lines of communication, and

[13] Not to be confused with the *Regierungsbezirke*, purely administrative areas into which *Land* authorities divide their territories.

[14] Berlin is not mentioned in the Potsdam Agreement of 1945, despite Russian claims which are based on it.

with the military presence of Russian forces, West Berlin is at present ill suited to operate as a Federal capital.

One consequence of its special situation is that the Communist party of East Germany, the SED, is allowed to campaign in West Berlin's elections, but it has met with very little support from the electors who have consistently given a majority to the SPD, turning out to vote with a level of participation that is even higher than that for Federal elections. West Berlin is, in fact, energetically committed to the Western alliance; as well it might be, for apart from its utter military and physical dependence on support from the West, it must also be heavily subsidized in order to continue to function. The Bonn government had by 1963 already paid to the East German authorities 400 million DM in dues for the transportation of goods by road and waterway to West Berlin, and these charges are increased every time there is a major difference between the two régimes: the most recent increase, of between 20% and 30%, was in May 1970. An even heavier load on the Bonn government is the financial subsidy required to keep the economy of West Berlin solvent. Even so, the city's rate of industrial growth has been slower than that of the Federal Republic. With a large proportion of its population drawing pensions or social benefits, the city is also economically unbalanced: the average age of its inhabitants is higher than in the rest of the Federal Republic. Between the years 1951 and 1962, Bonn's subsidy amounted to 11,300 million DM. The subsidy for 1970 was 2,820 million DM and in 1971 rose to 3,410 million DM. A postal surcharge (*Notopfer Berlin*) raised 413 million DM in eight years, through a two-Pfennig levy on all stamps.

West Berlin, with its 2·2 million inhabitants, is still the biggest city of West Germany and is a major industrial centre, employing more labour than any other city of the republic. Principal industries are electrical and mechanical engineering, and the vast majority of its products are exported to West Germany. Its isolated situation is once again a handicap, for almost all raw materials have to be imported over a 110 miles gap and the balance of trade works out unfavourably. As an outpost of western democracy it is regarded as well worth these sacrifices by the *Bund*.

Tensions were eased somewhat by the conclusion of an agreement on West Berlin by the four control powers in September 1971, followed by successful negotiations between the East and West German governments in December 1971. West Berlin's political independence and access rights from the west are now fully guaranteed and visits by West Berliners to East Germany have been rendered very much easier, with a maximum of thirty days' stay per year.

B. EAST GERMANY

1. *Constitution*

The constitution of the East German state, in contrast to the Basic Law of West Germany, has no provisional character, being laid out as the basis for the realization and perpetuation of an East German community founded on Marxist/Leninist principles. Indeed, in the East German view there exist today two quite separate and sovereign German states, namely the Workers' and Farmers'[15] Socialist Republic of East Germany, and the bourgeois-capitalist Federal Republic of West Germany. There is no provision for an eventual reunion of the two parts of the former Reich by means of a possible amending of the constitution. The political, social and economic ideals of East Germany are clearly enunciated, and a larger Germany would only be conceivable to them on such terms. The national emblems proclaim the identity and striving of the German Democratic Republic (DDR—*Deutsche Demokratische Republik*): the symbols on the state coat of arms—a hammer, a wreath of corn and a pair of compasses—denote the united striving of workers, farmers and intellectuals. (The traditional eagle in the West German coat of arms is viewed as a symbol of the old imperialism). The state flag, a rectangle with horizontal black, red and gold stripes, represents the tradition of the German struggle for civil liberties: these colours originated between the years 1813 and 1832, being first identified with the students' associations of those times, and then finding adoption by the liberals and the movement for German unity. It was the flag of the 1848 rebellion, and it became the state flag of the German republic that was proclaimed in 1919. The present West German flag comprises the same colours, that of the East Germans being differentiated from it by the addition of the state coat of arms.

The East German constitution was framed in the year 1949, and therefore dates from the same period and sequence of events as that of West Germany. Until this date the authorities in the then Soviet zone of occupation had been reluctant to take measures which would lead to the division of Germany into two opposite camps and had

---

[15] The German word *Bauer* which is used in this formulation is difficult to match with a suitable English equivalent: the word 'peasant', frequently employed, is not really appropriate, for it suggests primitive and depressed conditions; 'farmer' on the other hand tends to suggest ownership or tenancy of the land. We shall nevertheless use it here, since 'peasant' hardly seems fitting in these days of mechanized, scientific farming (where does one find 'peasants' in Britain?), and in a sense the East Germans are the owners of the farms on which they work.

therefore allowed the continuation of the traditions of Weimar, in an endeavour to keep in step with the democratic practices of the western-occupied zones. The failure of the Allied powers to find a satisfactory basis for a unified Germany and the continued allegiance of the majority of German voters to the liberal-democratic parties, rather than to the Communist alliance, provided the grounds for the Russian break with the Western occupation powers and the setting up of an independent East German state. In actual fact, the West German state was called into being before the East German one.

The constitution of 1949 represented an attempt to legislate for the situation then prevailing, but the changed political realities of the 1960s necessitated a new formulation, and the 1949 constitution was replaced by an amended one drafted in the winter of 1967/68 and submitted to a plebiscite in April 1968, when it was approved by a 94·5% majority. This new East German constitution of 1968 provides a clear definition of the state, its function and powers, and its relationship to the individual citizen.

The republic is defined as a "socialist state of the German nation" (Article 1)—an interesting evolution of the old imperial formulation of "Holy Roman Empire of the German Nation" that emerged during the medieval power-contest in Europe. All power in the East German republic is exercised by the worker; for "man is the centre of all efforts of socialist society and its state" (Article 2). The democratic character of the representative political bodies is laid down (Article 5): "Citizens of the German Democratic Republic exercise their political power through democratically elected popular representative bodies", whose activities are based "upon the active participation of citizens in the preparation, implementation and control of their decisions."

There is general acceptance of the rules of international law (Article 8). The private citizen is assured of his civil rights, freedom from exploitation, oppression and economic dependence, and the protection of the freedom and dignity of his person (Article 19). No exceptions are made on the grounds of nationality, race, creed or social status. Freedom of conscience and belief is guaranteed. All citizens are equal before the law, and the equality of the sexes is insisted upon (Article 20).

The right to work (Article 24), to a full and appropriate education and training (Article 25), to freedom of expression (Article 27), and of peaceful assembly (Article 28) are also written into the constitution. The person and liberty of the citizen are inviolable (Article 29). Further articles deal with corporate ownership of the means of production, the role of private enterprise, the division of administrative responsibility and the structure and management of the state, parliamentary procedure, regional and local government, the judicial system and the courts of law.

This constitution, for all its wide range of clauses, remains rather a declaration of principles and ideals than a detailed prescription of the organization, order and control within the state: the 'small print' is often missing. This becomes especially clear if we compare it with the West German Basic Law, which painstakingly spells out the powers and functions exercised at each level of the administration and defines in detail the democratic and legal safeguards that operate. The East German constitution rather gives the impression of seeking to enunciate principles which are internationally recognized democratic ideals, in its own quest for international recognition. There are even instances where the proclaimed ideal is at variance with actual practice. Thus, freedom of expression is guaranteed (Article 27), yet there have been innumerable instances of arrest, following upon criticism of the authorities or of state policy. We also note that Article 14 of the 1949 Constitution, which asserted the workers' right to strike, has not been taken up into the 1967 Constitution, and that strikes are, in fact, illegal and their organizers liable to arrest. People who have quoted the Constitution in support of their actions have at times even been characterized as enemies of the state.

2. The Rise of the Communist State

It is interesting to trace the stages by which the Soviet Occupation Zone of Germany turned into the East German Democratic Republic. Shortly after the conclusion of hostilities in 1945, the Soviet military administration authorized four political parties as being representative of the will of the people. These four parties were the Communist Party (KPD), the Social Democratic Party (SPD), the Christian Democrats (CDU) and the Liberal Democrats (LDP). The first three we have already identified in our West Germany section: the LDP corresponded roughly to the West German FDP. The first elections were local ones and took place in September 1946; but in the April before this event, the merging of the KPD and the SPD had been effected, to produce a new party of the left, the SED or Socialist Unity Party (*Sozialistische Einheitspartei Deutschlands*). Already, in June 1945, the two parties had agreed to work in close co-operation and set up a joint committee composed of 5 representatives from each party. (In West Germany, the SPD leader Schumacher turned down a similar proposition). In addition to these political parties, other groups were also allowed to participate in the election, under the collective title of "anti-fascist democratic mass-organizations". They included the Farmers' Mutual Assistance Association, the Free German Youth (FDJ), the Free German Trade Union Federation (FDGB), the Democratic Women's Association and the League of Culture for a Democratic Renewal of Germany.

The results of these local government elections gave the SED alliance 52·4% of the vote, the CDU and LPD together 39·9%, and the mass organizations 1%. Obstacles had already been put in the way of nominations of CDU and LPD candidates for the September elections, allowing the SED to win many seats uncontested, and in the five provincial (*Land*) elections of October 1946 similar harassment of the bourgeois parties occurred. In the event, the SED and allied groups obtained 50·96% of the vote, while the CDU and LPD polled 49·04%. These results clearly showed that the impetus towards the creation of a socialist East German state would have to be given by the SED and that it would need to operate outside the confines of the traditional western democratic system. At this stage of its career, it was considerably assisted and advised by officials of the Soviet military administration who were not averse to using their powers to impede the opposition parties.

In November 1947 the SED leaders called for the summoning of a German People's Congress, and on 6th and 7th December an assembly of more than 2,000 Communist delegates from all parts of Germany met in Berlin, with the declared aim of preventing the division of Germany. A second All-German People's Congress was held on March 17th and 18th of the following year, and elected a German People's Council (*Volksrat*), comprising 400 members; already the controlling hand of the SED leadership was shown in the allocation of 300 of the seats to East Germany. By April of 1948, committees of this Council were drawing up proposals for a German constitution and a system of national economy, justice, social policy and culture in conformity with communist ideology. An all-German plebiscite on re-unification was demanded, but the Western powers rejected this proposal, after its acceptance by the Russians.

The Third People's Congress met in May 1949, being attended only by East German delegates, since the Western powers refused to allow the election of delegates in their own part of Germany, and laid down their own requirements for German reunification. Already Russia and the West were following divergent courses in Germany, each side guiding the development of their zone in accordance with their own political traditions. For the East German elections, all the parties were instructed to submit a joint list of candidates, and the allocation of seats was pre-determined. This situation was brought about by the creation of the so-called National Front (January 1950), a parent body for the various political parties and mass organizations. Its very composition gave the SED and its

Communist partners an outright majority, enabling them to direct policy and practice along lines desired by them. Instead of the individual parties drawing up separate lists of candidates for elections, the decision was now made to draw up a joint list of candidates from all the parties and organizations campaigning. This would, so the argument ran, produce a list which could be unanimously approved by the electorate, since it would represent the combined striving of the national parties and organizations. Its effect was to eliminate all candidates who were not acceptable to the SED alliance, since all those whose names appeared on the list had first to be approved by a committee of the National Front, which looked closely into their dedication to the ideals of the new socialist movement. Each campaigning party was then allocated the number of seats which it was felt corresponded to the population-sector whose interests it represented. The SED was awarded 90 seats, the CDU and LDP 45 seats each, two new parties which had not previously campaigned—the National Democratic Party and the Farmers' Party—were granted 15 seats apiece, and then the SED-led "mass organizations" were allocated the remaining 120 seats. The fate of the 32·7% non-Communist minority was sealed, and East Germany was firmly launched on a Marxist/Leninist course when, on October 7th 1949, the People's Council was renamed the Provisional People's Chamber, on the authority of the Russian military government. On September 7th, the Western powers had authorized the installation of a Federal government in West Germany, and the Russian response was to recognize the constitution drawn up by the People's Congress and call the East German Democratic Republic into being, transferring to it all administrative functions. Wilhelm Pieck, a founder of the KPD and now chairman of the SED, was elected President of the new state by a special chamber composed of 34 members from the SED-dominated *Land* assemblies and the SED-led national assembly; while Otto Grotewohl, a leading functionary of the SED, became head of the new provisional government with Walter Ulbricht, secretary-general of the SED, as his deputy. The holding of national elections for a central parliament was fixed for October 1950, on the basis of an all-party single list of candidates, a list which was then approved by 99·7% of the electorate, with a participation of 98·5%. The attainment of complete sovereignty came on March 27th 1954, when Russia restored full rights to the DDR.

3. Parliamentary System

The People's Chamber (*Volkskammer*) is the supreme organ of state power. Its 500 members are elected by a national poll and its normal period of office is four years. The *Volkskammer* must be convened not later than thirty days after an election. Its sessions are public, but private sessions can be decided upon by a two-thirds vote of the members. The attendance of more than half of the deputies is required to constitute a quorum. Decisions are made on the basis of a simple majority vote, but amendment of the constitution requires at least a two-thirds vote of all the deputies. The *Volkskammer* can dissolve itself by a two-thirds majority decision but it can be dissolved only by its own decision. It must be assembled on the request of one-third of its members.

The most important function of the *Volkskammer* is the appointing of the State Council and Council of Ministers (see below) and also the president and judges of the Supreme Court and the state procurator-general; it also has the power to dismiss all elected officials at any time. In effect, it is largely a rubber-stamp body, the real source of power and policy-decision lying with the Council of State and the Council of Ministers.

The Council of State (*Staatsrat*) was established in 1960, on the death of President Pieck. The office of President was then abolished and was replaced by the principle of collective leadership, on the model of post-Khrushchev practice in Russia; the *Staatsrat* remains the highest organ of the state. This Council of State consists of a Chairman, six Deputy Chairmen, sixteen other members and a secretary, all of whom must be approved by the *Volkskammer*. The Chairman is virtually head of state and deals with all foreign relations of the Republic; the post has been Walter Ulbricht's since its inception in 1960.[16] The Council makes the fundamental decisions on defence and national security (it can mobilize the nation in a state of emergency), ratifies and cancels state agreements, appoints its diplomatic representatives abroad and receives the accredited representatives of foreign countries in East Germany. It also discusses the national economic plans and passes on its recommendations to committees of the *Volkskammer* for consideration. Herr Ulbricht has characterized its main concern as the relations between the people and the state authorities. It has important discretionary powers of its own, of an administrative, legislative and judicial character. It has the right to issue decrees which are then submitted to the *Volkskammer* for confirmation; it can also make decisions having the force of law and it can declare how existing legislation is to be interpreted. The six Deputy Chairmen include

[16] In May 1971 Ulbricht retired from the post of First Secretary of the SED, but retained his supervisory role of Chairman of the Council of State.

the Chairman of the Council of Ministers (Willi Stoph), the President of the *Volkskammer* and the leaders of the four political parties which make up the National Front. The sixteen other members represent various sectors of German industry and national life, and include five women.

The Council of Ministers (*Ministerrat*) is likewise elected by the *Volkskammer* and is answerable to it and to the Council of State. It bears full executive responsibility for government policy and operates on the principle of collectivity, though individual members can be questioned, censored and even dismissed for failure in their duties. This Council deals, on behalf of the *Volkskammer*, with the execution of government business (political, economic, cultural and social) and is responsible for the economy. It submits to the Council of State and the *Volkskammer* the drafts of long-term plans and annual labour plans, the budget and other bills whose adoption is sought. It supervises the activities of the various government ministries and the regional and local government bodies. It controls the State Planning Commission, the industrial and special ministries and the Agricultural Council, and other organs with central tasks such as the Research Council. Its chairman is proposed to the *Volkskammer* by the Chairman of the State Council and is then himself responsible for forming the Council of Ministers. They hold office for a period of four years—*i.e.* one Parliament's life. The number of ministries has varied with successive Parliaments, as has also the division of responsibilities. Since 1952 a *Praesidium* of twelve or thirteen of the senior ministers has been in existence, more or less replacing the more cumbersome Council of Ministers and creating the possibility of more co-ordinated action.

In a state where all production is state-managed and the material resources state-owned, the planning of the economy is an enormous responsibility. The duty is assumed by a number of state commissions or councils, such as the State Planning Commission, whose task is overall planning, both long- and short-term, and the industrial and agricultural production councils. The chairmen of these councils are also members of the *Praesidium* or inner cabinet, and discussion of their work takes place here. Another member of the *Praesidium* is the Chairman of the Control Commission, whose task is to ensure that the administrative authorities act in accordance with their mandate to make no unauthorized use of their resources.

Legislation Parliamentary bills may be submitted to the *Volkskammer* by the Council of Ministers, by the political parties or the mass organizations, by the Council of State or by the Trade Unions. Before becoming law every proposed bill must be approved by the *Volkskammer* (Article 65 of the Constitution).

A draft law usually receives two readings, between which the expert committees of the *Volkskammer* examine it in detail. Really important proposals are also discussed with the electorate outside parliament, the deputies explaining and discussing at constituency gatherings the details and implications of the bill, and bringing back with them the views of their constituents, who can propose amendments to be incorporated into the final draft. The draft of the Labour Code, for instance, was only finally submitted to the *Volkskammer* after it had been debated in a joint commission made up of the central committee of the SED, the national executive of the Trade Unions Confederation, and the Council of Ministers, and had been discussed by seven million citizens in 325,000 meetings, which produced 32,000 suggested amendments.

The Council of State assesses all bills for their conformity with the constitution, and after approval they become law within one month, coming into force 14 days later, unless otherwise specified.

Standing committees of the *Volkskammer* exist (*e.g.* health, justice, education, foreign affairs, defence), and there is also a Committee on Citizens' Petitions, a body which scrutinizes all matters brought to the notice of the *Volkskammer* by private citizens, who possess the right to petition in this way. (It is estimated that 600 people present themselves monthly during the public office hours of the Chairman of the Council of State.) Individual deputies can also be petitioned by their electors.

The *Volkskammer* is also empowered to hold plebiscites on fundamental issues, when these are considered necessary (Article 53).

The principle of the separation of powers is not observed in the DDR. All ministers and officials are appointed by and answerable to the *Volkskammer* and can be removed from their offices at any time. This includes members of the higher judiciary also. The reason given is that "neither the government, as the executive, nor the judges of the Supreme Court, as the organ of the administration of justice, can or want to dissociate themselves from the mission with which they are entrusted by the people". This principle extends down to even the smallest community organizations.

Although the *Volkskammer* is, in theory, an extremely powerful body, providing the citizens with an ultimate control over all executive, administrative and judicial policy, it is in effect little more than an elaborate shop-window, possessing the trappings but not the substance of power. It meets about eight times a year normally, to approve the nomination of ministers and officials and to give its assent to bills which the government leaders have passed to it. On an average, the number of bills approved by the *Volkskammer* in the course of a year is little more than ten; the Council of State and Council of Ministers find it simpler to bring new legislation into force in the guise of administrative ordinances, which require no *Volkskammer* approval. Many of the far-reaching legislative changes of 1953 were effected in this way, and the practice has become almost standard since 1958. The *Volkskammer* serves principally as a communication channel between the government and the people, for the deputies are kept busy with the task of informing their constituents of official policies and reporting back constituency reactions.

4. *Political Parties and Elections*

There are currently five political parties in the DDR: the Socialist Unity Party (SED), the Democratic Farmworkers' Party (DBD), the Christian Democrats (CDU), the Liberal Democrats (LDPD) and the National Democrats (NDPD). The basis of their existence is quite different from that of Western political parties (which generally represent differing political ideologies), in that they represent specific social and economic groups within the East German state.

As we have already seen, the SED came into being in April 1946, when the Socialist SPD and Communist KPD joined together as one political body, seeking to create a new social order out of the chaotic collapse of Hitler's totalitarian state. This link was fostered by the Soviet authorities, who saw in the SED the spearhead of their drive to create a Communist East German state. At first the key positions within the new party were divided equally between SPD and KPD members, both parties having voted unanimously for the merger. Presently, however, the chief posts came to be entrusted to dedicated Communists, and close liaison was maintained with the 'anti-fascist democratic mass organizations', a parallel force in the drive for a Communist-aligned state. The SED claims to be capable of leading society, because it is the party of the most progressive force of the people, the working class. It is guided in its thinking by the principles laid down by Marx and Engels. Claiming to represent the largest group of the people, it appropriately claims the largest proportion of seats in the *Volkskammer*. Its fortunes have paralleled those of other East European Communist Parties, and it has undergone like them a sequence of internal upheavals and policy wrangles, perhaps at their worst during the period 1951–2 when the Stalin era came to an abrupt end. Despite all this it has remained the dominant power (occasionally supported by Russian arms in the East German state).

The Democratic Farmworkers Party of Germany (DBD) represents those who work on the co-operative farms or are associated in other ways with agriculture and forestry. Its aim is to help integrate these people into the structure of the socialist economy and the new order of society.

The Christian Democratic Union (CDU) draws its support principally from members of the Catholic and Protestant churches and other free-church communities, and likewise seeks to integrate them into the new social order. The older party leaders soon resigned from office when the new trend of events became evident and the Russian military authorities had characterized them as antagonistic forces.

The Liberal Democratic Party (LDPD) is the party of small businessmen, craft workers, retail traders, intellectuals and office staff—the traditional middle classes, in effect, and represents the effort to associate them with the socialist reconstruction of Germany. A similar function is discharged by the National Democratic Party of Germany (NDPD), which also includes former members of the Nazi party or the armed forces of the Reich, who have rejected their allegiance to the totalitarian régime of the past. Among the principal tasks of these parties has been the winning-over of the intelligentsia, the small industrialist and the independent farmer to the new form of society. The DDR yearbooks proudly list the numbers of entrepreneurs whom they have persuaded to accept state control, and of farmers who have been induced to join agricultural collectives.

To these political parties we must add the names of the mass organizations, which also participate in parliamentary elections and are allotted seats in the *Volkskammer*: the Confederation of Free German Trade Unions (FDGB), the Democratic Women's Federation of Germany (DFD), the Free German Youth (FDJ) and the League of Culture (KB).

There are no opposition parties in the *Volkskammer*, all groups combining in the collective effort of furthering the development and efficient running of the Workers' and Farmers' Republic. Thus, all parties are represented in the administration and, as we saw, four of the Vice-Chairmen of the Council of State are the leaders of the CDU, NDPD, LDPD and DBD. Collective responsibility is the keynote in this classless republic. Any necessary discussion, criticism and objection takes place in the preliminary examination of proposed measures, and the logical outcome of such discussion is held to be inevitable agreement on collective policy, since the fundamental goals of all groups are commonly shared. The necessity for an opposition is not seen to arise, for it could only mean opposition to the very essence and common striving of the community.

The principle of 'democratic centralism' is propounded as the basis on which the system works—either at party or national level. It requires that all members shall be participants in the formulation of policy and the election of leaders and officials, but also demands in return that all members conscientiously carry out the decisions that have been made and obey the instructions of the elected leaders. The sense of solidarity is the uniting force: all members of society are bound together and find common cause in the fight to realize the communal goals that have been set. To be an opponent of such a system is to be an enemy of the state and the people.

5. *Election Procedure and Results*

All citizens who have reached the age of 18 years have, since 1950, been entitled to vote, without restriction of class, sex, creed or status. Candidates who have reached the age of 21 may be elected to the *Volkskammer*. Those aged 18 can be elected to local representative bodies. (Article 22 of the Constitution).

The country was originally divided up into 24 multi-member constituencies, which ranged in size from 130,000 to 240,000 electors, but in 1963 their number was increased to 67, in order to ensure that no one constituency had more than 100,000 voters. In the district council elections of 1965 the number of constituencies was increased from 1,404 to 2,509, to facilitate contacts between deputies and their constituents, as well as to enable deputies to survey local conditions more accurately. In every election, at least one third of the serving members must be replaced by new delegates, thus maintaining a constant stream of new energies into parliament and the regional assemblies.

The nomination of candidates proceeds in a manner markedly different from that of the Western democracies. Candidates are selected by election commissions, which are composed of representatives chosen by the parties and mass organizations of the district concerned. Each candidate undergoes a close scrutiny at public meetings, in which he must render account of his political convictions and detail the contribution which he has made and proposes to make to the national programme. Electors may ask him whatever questions seem appropriate and he is often set specific tests which are designed to assess his acceptability for office. The process is an exhausting one for the intending candidate, as he moves from meeting to meeting in factory workshops, collective farms, housing blocks, institutes and public gatherings.

This system of local election commissions has been in force since changes in the electoral law effected in 1963 and 1965. Previously the list of candidates was drawn up by the central body, the National Front of Democratic Germany, a successor to the People's Congress and established in January 1950. The new system in force since 1965 thus marks a degree of democratization in the nomination process: the end result, however, is still a single list of candidates approved by the collective committee of the election commission. The voter simply has the option of approving or rejecting the list of names submitted to him, and since to reject them would merely set in train the same operation once more, the voters take the easy way out and thus provide the authorities with the massive votes of confidence which are regularly reported. A slight element of choice was introduced for the first time in the 1965 elections, when it was possible for more nominations to be received than there were seats to be filled, but all candidates had still to be approved in advance by the election commission. Those candidates who are not elected are placed on a reserve list, from which any vacancies which arise during the life of the parliament are filled. To be elected, a candidate needs a simple majority of the votes cast.

Campaigning is obviously in a much lower key and infinitely more restricted in scale than in West Germany, and the extra effort made at election times hardly seems necessary, for here there is no clash of ideologies, no intervention by vested interests and no suspense as to the outcome. The state organs of propaganda are regularly in operation and no extra effort is therefore necessary at election times. The essential choice is made with the nomination of the candidates, and polling-day itself becomes merely a setting of the seal on what has previously been decided. Many electors therefore do not bother to vote in secret in the booths provided, but cast their vote publicly, often marching to the polling station in large groups of factory workers, co-operative members or residents of large housing blocks. To vote in secret is itself a suggestion of opposition, and somehow those who cast a negative vote are identified and subsequently sought out for intensive efforts to convert them to the party viewpoint. The vote of confidence for the national coalition has been overwhelming on each occasion. In 1950, 99·7% of all votes were cast for it in the *Volkskammer* elections, and the figure for 1954 was 99·46%. In the 1957 local elections, 99·52% of the poll, and in the 1958 *Volkskammer* and district elections 99·87% of the poll went in its favour. In 1961, a record 99·96% vote was returned in regional elections, the *Volkskammer* election of 1963 produced a 99·95% peak and the local elections of 1965 yielded a 99·86% vote of confidence. Participation in these polls was consistently high, the figure of 98·5% for 1950 being characteristic.

The delegates, once elected, take their seats for four years, whether at national, regional or local level. They do not sever their connections with the factory or enterprise from which they have come, but continue to be paid by it, for they are regarded as being on leave and return to their jobs in the intervals of this part-time parliamentary service. They receive in addition a tax-free allowance to cover expenses. They enjoy free use of public transport and are accorded full immunity. Their prime responsibility remains that towards their own constituents, to whom they must report regularly on parliamentary matters, and for whom they must provide regular consultation hours. A deputy who is found to be neglecting his duty of representing his constituents can in fact be recalled by an electors' meeting, as a result of legislation of 1958. As guardians of the public welfare, deputies may submit oral or written questions on the work of any of the state organs and representative bodies, and are entitled to take part in the meetings of lower-level representative bodies in an advisory capacity.

The allocation of seats among the parties takes place before the holding of the election, on the basis of what is estimated to be their relative strength in the population as a whole. In the first national elections, in May 1949, for the Third Peoples' Congress, the SED were allotted 90 seats, the CDU and LDP 45 seats each, the NPDP and the DBD fifteen seats each, and the "mass organizations" 120 seats. For the election of October 1963, the allocation was:

SED —	110 seats	Trade Unions (FDGB)	— 60 seats
LDPD —	45 seats	Youth Movement (FDJ)	— 36 seats
NDPD —	45 seats	Women's League (DFD)	— 30 seats
CDU —	45 seats	Cultural League (KB)	— 18 seats

The general balance was thus preserved.

In the general election for the 5th *Volkskammer* in July 1967, there were 581 candidates in the field for 434 seats (the remaining 66 seats out of the total of 500 are filled by deputies elected from Berlin). The following break-down of their social status was given:

61 skilled workers and foremen in industry	15 physicians
44 agricultural workers	5 physicists
66 engineers and technicians	3 chemists
43 chairmen of agricultural co-operatives	21 chairmen or members of craft co-operatives
12 factory managers	14 retail traders
30 graduate economists	4 clergymen
5 writers and artists	17 graduate sociologists
28 teachers	17 jurists

192 (33%) of the candidates were women, and 43 were under 25 years of age.

The age groups in the *Volkskammer* in January 1959 were as follows:

up to 25 years— 20	41 to 50 years—116
26 to 30 years— 23	51 to 60 years— 96
31 to 40 years—103	over 60 years— 42

E

6. Regional and Local Government

As in the case of West Germany, political life in East Germany was first resumed at local level and the political parties made their first appearance here. Local elections took place in September 1946, and *Land* elections in October 1946—thus actually anticipating similar developments in West Germany. The division of the country into five *Länder* was at first retained (Mecklenburg, Brandenburg, Saxony-Anhalt, Saxony and Thuringia), each *Land* possessing its own parliament and government. The five *Länder* were also represented in an upper chamber, the *Länderkammer*, which did not however possess any legislative powers; it had 50 *Land* representatives and 13 from Berlin.

In July 1952 radical administrative changes brought about the abolition of the *Land* units; they were replaced by 14 Districts (*Bezirke*), plus East Berlin. By some strange anomaly the *Länderkammer* itself was not abolished until December 1958. The *Bezirke* were initially presided over by non-elective committees, all of whose chairmen were members of the SED. At the same time the number of county authorities (*Landkreise*) was increased from 121 to 194 and the number of independent city authorities (*Stadtkreise*) was reduced from 143 to 23. Closer supervision and control were thus facilitated and many old traditions were broken down. In addition, it was decreed that resolutions passed by a District Assembly (*Bezirkstag*) could be overruled by the *Volkskammer*. East Germany is since 1968 divided into 15 *Bezirke*, which comprise 26 *Stadtkreise* and 191 *Landkreise* which are again sub-divided into 9,021 *Gemeinden*.

Each *Bezirk, Kreis*, town, borough and community has its own elected assembly, with an executive committee at its head. Elections for the national, regional and district assemblies are normally held on one and the same day, and the term of office is four years in each case. The system for selecting the candidates resembles that for *Volkskammer* nominees. The size of the regional assemblies varies with the significance of the area represented, the *Bezirke* and largest towns electing between 140 and 200 delegates. The executive committee is usually about 20 strong, half of whom are full-time members and receive a salary. Local authorities with a population of less than 10,000 elect a council of up to 35 members, with an executive committee of from six to eleven, all serving on a part-time, unpaid basis, with the exception of the Chairman. These councils meet between four and nine times a year, the responsibility for administering the area resting with the executive committee, and especially the Chairman and Secretary. Special committees of these councils also exist and usually include co-opted, non-elected persons who can

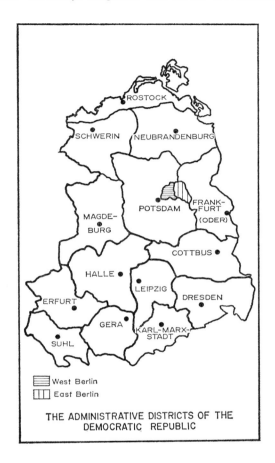

West Berlin

East Berlin

THE ADMINISTRATIVE DISTRICTS OF THE
DEMOCRATIC REPUBLIC

provide specialist advice. Article 83 of the constitution reads: "The committees organize the expert co-operation of the citizen in the preparation and implementation of the decisions made by the popular representative body". In the community of Badeborn (Kreis Quedlinburg) for instance, 24 members were elected in the 1965 polls, but there were 162 people, the equivalent of 10% of the population, who participated in the work of the eight standing committees. The larger authorities usually appoint Deputy Chairmen in charge of specific services.

The various councils carry out at *Bezirk*, county, city, town or village level the tasks of administration, which include the maintenance of law and order, civil defence, the raising of revenues, the local implementation of the economic plan, consumer supplies, town and country planning, housing, public works, highways, transport, education and training, health and welfare service, youth and sport. Authorities in rural areas have a special responsibility for furthering agricultural production.

A greater measure of autonomy has been accorded to the local councils in recent years, particularly by the Council of State decree of 1967, which gave them greater financial rights and powers of planning decision. Towns and communities are now themselves responsible for their own revenues and expenditure, including investments, and for the planning and development of their area of competence. Delays caused by the long chain of command from the top have in this way often been eliminated. In addition, any income raised by their own initiative may be spent on local schemes, without any consequent cut being made in their statutory share of the state budget.

Each authority is accountable to the one above it, whose officers may, if they wish, attend its meetings, and also have the power to annul its decisions and enforce specific requirements on it. It is estimated that more than 206,000 people serve in some form of representative capacity in the DDR, which gives a ratio of one to every 50 adult citizens. Their main function is not to legislate but to assist in the detailed organization and management of the national plans and state administration. They lighten very considerably the burden of the bureaucracy, help appreciably, through their local expertise, in the solution of many minor problems and at the same time create a sense of public participation and surveillance in the affairs of the state. An example may suffice. In the municipal assembly of Karl-Marx-Stadt (formerly Chemnitz, population 295,000) there are 180 deputies and a council of 16 members. 42% of the members are workers in industry, 22% are office employees, 25% are classed as 'intellectuals', 7% are craftsmen and private businessmen, 4% are farmers. One third of the deputies are women. There are seventeen standing committees and 55 working groups, comprising 820 people. In addition to this, about 100,000 people are involved in the activities of the National Front, in its municipal committee, borough committees and residential committees. Municipal assembly and National Front work in close collaboration in solving the problems of the city. Even the city budget is discussed at the various committee levels, before the municipal assembly takes the final decision.

The financing of the municipality in 1967 was shared between a state budget grant (46%), the yield of taxes and profits from state-controlled enterprises, community taxes and private sector income (35%), and profit shares from enterprises and the product of various municipal taxes (15%). (It is claimed that no town or community in the DDR has a debt). In 1951, out of a budget of 59 million marks, 14·2 millions were spent on education, culture, youth, and sport, 20·8 millions on health and social services; in 1959, the figures were 37·9 millions and 42·1 millions respectively, and for 1967 the allocations were 57·3 millions and 60·8 millions, out of a total budget of 210 million marks.

7. *Summing-up*

The picture that emerges from the foregoing survey is that of the undisputed dominance in East Germany of the SED. The central committee of the party includes all the most important functionaries of the state—the leaders of the political party itself, the leading figures in the government, the heads of the mass organizations and the top men in the key economic and security agencies. Moreover, its power reaches down through the regions and the local authorities, as well as the various levels of the economic planning agencies and administrative committees, in all of which its members hold key positions. All aspects of the state's activities are thus encompassed by this one political movement. Through the years the SED has faithfully reflected policies and events in Soviet Russia, its initial hard-line doctrinaire approach during the Stalin era (which sparked off the workers' rebellion in June 1953) giving away to a more liberal attitude during the Krushchev period, especially in 1955 after Krushchev's denunciation of Stalin's methods; an improvement in living standards was then undertaken, with greater attention to the production of consumer goods, and a liberalization of the administration was promised. But the wave of free ideological discussion which ensued unnerved the party leadership, as it found the very basis of its policies in dispute, and the Hungarian uprising of 1956 was the signal for a fresh tightening up of controls and the arrest of many free-thinking citizens. The alternation of leniency and toughness has continued through the years, the problem clearly being that of discovering a means of liberalizing the régime and granting more democratic control to the citizens, without sacrificing ultimate control of the shaping of national policies— a problem in all Communist states to-day. The most recent example of liberalism leading to revolt was that of Czechoslovakia in 1969; Ulbricht and his government were among the first to hurry to the suppression of this latest outbreak in the Communist camp. He has even been seen as the prime mover in the crushing of the revolt, out of fear of its implications for his own country.

Throughout the ups-and-downs of the past twenty-five years a few astute and resolute men have remained at the head of the party, and *ipso-facto,* the state. Prime among these stands the figure of Walter Ulbricht, First Secretary of the SED until 1971 and head of the Supreme Council of State. Like his predecessor Wilhelm Pieck, and his faithful lieutenant Hermann Matern, Ulbricht is a long-standing member of the Communist Party (he was a Communist member of the Reichstag from 1928 to 1933). All three spent the wartime years in exile in Soviet Russia. Another figure who loyally followed Ulbricht throughout is the present Prime Minister Willi Stoph (a Communist Party member since 1931). The SED has a considerable membership, but members have little control over the party machinery. The $1\frac{1}{2}$ million members belong to 50,000 local party organizations, but the movement of influence is from top to bottom rather than from the local party upwards. Since the party convention meets only once every four years, its ability to influence party decisions is minimal and the conventions are mainly the occasions for demonstrations of solidarity. The real decisions are made by the party Secretariat and Central Committee, and reported to the party convention, which always accepts them unanimously and without criticism. The Central Committee consists of between 100 and 150 members and is advised by the Politburo, which is author-ized to conduct affairs between plenary sessions, and by the party Secretariat, the body responsible for the whole national administra-tion. That the Central Committee is not itself the crucial decision-making body is demonstrated by the fact that it has at times published its approval of proposals for new measures which have actually been in application in the country—sometimes for a matter of years.

The vital power lies in the hands of the party Secretariat, whose First Secretary was until 1971 Walter Ulbricht;[17] there are six other secretaries also, some of them members of the Politburo. Each sec-retary is at the head of a vast network of control organizations which ultimately take account of every facet of the national life. The formal government organs are all paralleled by Secretariat sections, which are staffed by experts who provide suggestions for, and guide the activities of the various government ministries. The various state and mass organizations are similarly controlled, as is also the party's own organization and personnel throughout the state. There are sections which deal with such matters as propa-ganda, culture and science, which supervise the official party paper, *Neues Deutschland,* and the rest of the press and organs of publicity, and, particularly important, concern themselves with education.

---

[17] Ulbricht retired in May 1971 from this office, being succeeded by Erich Honecker, one-time head of the Free German Youth organization and another veteran Communist.

There are 25 such sections in all. The pattern is, moreover, repeated at regional level, where 16 Secretariats exist, and again at local level. Thousands of committed experts thus make up a vast bureaucracy which supervises and directs the entire life of the East German state; they are all dedicated members of the SED. In addition there is the National Front, which includes in its membership all those organizations which are not a part of the SED, such as the Trade Union Federation, the allied political parties, the Women's Democratic Federation, the Free German Youth and so on, and all of which are either under SED leadership or allied to the SED. It is through this channel that propaganda and influence from the SED is exerted over the vast majority of the population—for almost every citizen of East Germany has been encouraged into becoming a member of one of these organizations. The National Front is the organizing power and four members of the SED sit on its executive council, together with four from each of the constituent organizations. Here decisions are made which again accord with SED policies, and the decisions are unanimous.

The ramifications of the National Front are nation-wide and extend down to the level of the individual household. At local level, the principal officers of the National Front councils are usually SED members, with the secretary of the local SED maintaining a tight liaison. Its lowest level of operation is that of the housing block, where it reckons to have 350,000 voluntary part-time workers who carry out all manner of jobs, from the distribution of official documents to the collection of complaints about the functioning of the administration. In this way the entire population is brought into contact with the functioning of the state. Citizens are helped to acquire a sense of participation; at the same time, the voice of the SED permeates everything with which they are concerned. The party is indeed the state.

Section II

Management and Labour

A. WEST GERMANY

1. *The Trade Unions*

(a) Origins and early development

The history of the German trade unions reaches back a long way, almost as far, in fact, as that of their British counterparts. The more militant branch of the German labour movement has always, however, been the political party, the Social Democratic Party of Germany (SPD), and the unions have had a lesser role to play. This is rather the reverse of the situation in Britain, where the trade unions were the pioneers of the labour movement in the nineteenth century and today still make quite a lot of the running.

The first German trade unions were constituted in the late 1860s, thus making Germany the first country to follow the example of the British workers. The forming of trade unions was, in fact, forbidden by the constitution until 1869, otherwise they would most likely have been organized sooner. The political movement of socialism had already begun by this time, based on the teachings of Karl Marx and led by Ferdinand Lasalle, who had, in 1863, founded the *Allgemeiner Deutscher Arbeiterverein* (General Union of German Workers) which was to give rise in 1875 to the SPD. Although there was, inevitably, a considerable identity of interests between the trade unions and the political labour movement, they differed on one vital issue, which right down to modern times remained a principal distinguishing feature between them and is probably the reason why the trade unions remained the less militant group. The Socialist party held the Marxist theory of the progressive decline and break-up of the capitalist system, and sought to accelerate the advent of the worker's emancipation in the proletarian revolution. The trade unions, on the other hand, took a more pragmatic and less ideological view of their function: they were to safeguard and improve the rights and interests of the worker. They did not necessarily believe in the progressive decline of the capitalist system, but looked rather to an increase in their own power to increase their members' security and well-being. These divergent views have weakened the hand of the Left on numerous occasions in the past, and a closer identity of the two forces only became a realizable prospect when the SPD, at their Bad Godesberg conference of 1959, threw overboard much of their Marxist credo. The interest of the trade unions in recent times has been directed, as we shall see, more to the issue of co-partnership and co-determination with management in industry.

(b) West German Trade Unions after 1945

Union groups began to reform soon after the cessation of hostilities, the lead usually being given by veterans of the pre-1933 period, many newly released from concentration camps. These groups were among the prime movers in the starting up of Germany's post-war economy, and industry owes them a considerable debt for their enterprise and dedication. The scope of their activities was at first greatly restricted by the Allied military governments, which would allow no centralized organization to operate in the country, and they could consequently only establish themselves at District (*Bezirk*) level. In 1947 organization at *Land* level was permitted, and authorization was given in 1948 for organization on a national basis. In the three years that had passed, membership had already risen to the 1932 level of over 6 million workers.

Attempts were made, in the early post-war years, to work against the impending division of Germany into two states, the West German unions seeking in consultations with their East German counterparts to create a national organization of trade unions. These attempts proved futile, however, when it became clear that the Soviet Zone authorities were using the trade unions of East Germany to further their own political purposes, and no basis for agreement could be found. The negotiations, begun in 1946 and pursued at three-monthly intervals, were finally broken off in 1948. The formation of the West German DGB in 1949 was an acknowledgment of the failure to achieve a nation-wide trade union association.

A central Secretariat was established at Frankfurt-am-Main to make the necessary arrangements for a national organization of West German trade unions, and in October 1949 over 400 delegates from sixteen trade and industrial unions met in Munich and voted to create the German Federation of Trade Unions (DGB—*Deutscher Gewerkschaftsbund*), which came into formal existence on 1st January 1950. It was joined, in the summer of 1950, by the 'independent' unions of the western sector of Berlin. Total membership of the DGB todays stands above the $6\frac{1}{2}$ million mark, or about 28% of the total labour force. This compares rather unfavourably with Britain which, with a similar-sized labour force, had a registered trade union membership of $8\frac{1}{2}$ millions in 1967. The onset of Germany's post-war economic miracle has clearly led many West German workers to believe that they do not need to belong to a trade union in order to secure good wages and conditions of work.

The organization of the West German trade unions today is

geared to the realities of twentieth century industry and technology. The agreement of October 1949 brought a uniting of three hitherto independent trade union movements.[1] A certain weakening of their old alignments was one consequence of this fusion, as well as a less partisan political approach. The unions have, in fact, proclaimed their neutrality towards all political parties, based on a common appeal to all of them to protect their interests and further their causes. (Not unnaturally, the SPD has shown itself the most willing to respond.) This neutrality clause was seized upon by the astute Konrad Adenauer, in the 1957 election campaign, to frustrate the proposed donation of campaign funds by the DGB to the Socialists, thus denying the SPD a substantial benefit. The real gain, however, has been in the new structure of the West German trade union movement. There are today sixteen trade and industrial unions. (Compare this with 345 British trade unions registered in 1967.) The multiplicity and diffusion of the past have disappeared behind these industry-based organizations, which have spared the West German economy endless demarcation and comparability disputes. All workers in a particular sector of industry and all those employed by a particular group of trades are organized on the basis of their employment. Thus all workers in the steel industry, be they furnacemen, clerks, engineers or storemen, belong to the same trade union, which negotiates on their behalf. A national wages policy and long-term economic budgeting are thus greatly facilitated, conciliation is more readily managed, and the number of individual labour disputes very considerably reduced; the bargaining power of the unions is also strengthened.

The sixteen unions, in order of size, are (1966): —

IG Metall[2]: metalworkers including motor industry (1,900,000 members)

Gew. Öffentliche Dienste, Transport und Verkehr[3]: public services and transport (972,000 members)

Gew. Chemie, Papier, Keramik: chemicals, paper and pottery (534,000 members)

IG Bergbau und Energie: mineworkers and power industry

Gew. Textil, Bekleidung: textiles and clothing

Gew. der Eisenbahner Deutschlands: railwaymen

IG Bau, Steine, Erden: building and construction industry

[1] The Socialist unions had had a membership of 4·6 millions in 1932, the Christian unions 1·3 millions, and the right wing Hirsch-Dunker group had claimed 600,000 members. There had also been a small Communist group with 36,000 members.

[2] IG is the abbreviation for *Industriegewerkschaft* ('industrial union').

[3] *Gew.* stands for *Gewerkschaft* ('trade union').

IG Nahrung, Genuβ, Gaststätten: food, catering and entertainment
Gew. Holz: woodworkers
Deutsche Postgewerkschaft: postal workers
IG Druck und Papier: printing and paper workers
Gew. Gartenbau, Land- und Forstwirtschaft: horticulture, agriculture and forestry
Gew. Leder: leatherworkers
Gew. Handel, Banken und Versicherungen: commerce, banks and insurance
Gew. Erziehung und Wissenschaft: education and science
Gew. Kunst: fine arts

In addition to these affiliated groups of the DGB there are two other organizations of considerable proportions, which were unable to make common cause with the DGB: they are the organizations of the civil servants, salaried staffs and white collar workers. The DAG (*Deutsche Angestellten-Gewerkschaft*—Union of Salaried Employees) has nearly half a million members, and the DBB (*Deutscher Beamtenbund*—Civil Servants' Union) has 720,000 members.[4] Since the end of 1955 there has been a recrudescence of the Christian Trade Union (*Christlicher Gewerkschaftsbund*—CGB), with a membership of about 200,000. A teachers' association (GDL—*Gemeinschaft Deutscher Lehrerverbände*) and a senior management union (ULA—*Union der leitenden Angestellten*) have also made their appearance.

The DGB holds its central congress every three years. This congress is the highest organ of the movement and its affairs are conducted by a Federal Committee made up of nine executive members and the Presidents of the 16 individual member unions. The membership of the DGB has been analyzed into $80 \cdot 4\%$ workers, $11 \cdot 3\%$ salaried employees (*Angestellte*) and $8 \cdot 3\%$ civil servants. This can give a misleading impression however, for, looking at things from another angle, we discover that whereas only 40% of industrial workers belong to a trade union, and as few as 25% of salaried staffs, the figure for civil servants is 75% (statistics of 1957).

The West German trade unions are organized on a thoroughly democratic basis. All officials and delegates must be nominated and elected by the workers or their nominees, whether at factory, area, regional or national level. They also come up for re-election at frequent intervals. Each union is organized at *Land, Kreis* and

[4] In point of fact, the DBB has no individual members, being an umbrella-body for a number of federated groups of permanent, semi-permanent and retired civil servants. Its economic affairs are handled by the German Public Servants' Economic Federation (BWB—*Beamten-Wirtschaftsbund*).

Bezirk level; the DGB itself is a member of the International Federation of Trade Unions.

The Munich Conference of 1949 had set forth the policy of the trade unions under four headings:

1. They demanded an economic policy which would give full employment to all, with full utilization of the national resources and the satisfying of the economic needs of everyone—but in conformity with human rights and dignity (this last with an eye on East Germany!).

2. They demanded participation in economic planning and direction, where personal, financial and social issues were involved (co-determination).

3. They demanded the transfer to public ownership of the key industries, especially mining, iron and steel and the key chemical industries, the power industries, the main transport undertakings, the credit institutions and banks. (In theory, they were thus becoming more radical than they had ever been.)

4. They called for social justice and equality: to be achieved through the appropriate sharing, by all workers, in the products of the national economy, and the guarantee of a proper standard of living for those who were prevented from working by old age, disability or sickness.

In 1955, demands were pressed for a five-day working week—first requested in 1952—with parity of wages and salary, an eight-hour day, greater social security and an improved degree of participation in decision-making. Since the five-day week is now almost universally in force, a new claim was made in May 1965 for a yearly holiday of at least four weeks, plus one month's bonus pay.

An ideological volte-face nevertheless took place at the special convention of the DGB which met in Düsseldorf on November 21–22, 1963. The programme evolved here replaced the Munich manifesto of 1949, and was the outcome of four years' discussion and compromise. The declared purpose of the new policy was to bring the trade unions "within the concept of a modern democratic state"; the intention was also, we may guess, to bring them into line with the recently modified aims of the SPD, as set out in its 1959 programme. The nationalization clause of 1949 was dropped, and acceptance was announced of the system of a social market economy (the *Soziale Marktwirtschaft* of Ludwig Erhard), linked to national planning and controlled investment. There was much opposition from the older diehards of the union movement, and considerable wrangling took place, but in the end this compromise proposal was accepted. The main seeking of the unions since then has been to improve the degree of co-determination enjoyed by their members on industrial boards of management, and to encourage co-partnership and profit-sharing schemes. In these fields they have had a fair measure of success (see next section). There has, nevertheless, been considerable agitation by the left-wingers in the movement recently against the union leadership, whom they have accused of collusion with the forces of reaction.

The interests and activities of the West German trade unions range over a wide field. In the social sphere they have sought improvements in welfare arrangements, pressing for better invalid, accident, sickness, disability and unemployment insurance schemes, and their public ownership and management. The increased post-war employment of juveniles and women workers has also created new problems, to which constant attention is given. Committees of the DGB also examine such problems as the impact of automation on industry and employment, the planning of the use of extra leisure time arising from shorter hours of work, the implication of German membership of EEC, aid to the under-developed countries and so forth. Separate agencies of the DGB have been established to cater for the special interests of office workers and officials. The unions have also joined in the post-war building campaign, and have themselves erected a large number of homes for workers: between 1945 and 1965, 200,000 such homes were provided. They have also called back into existence the Union Savings Bank, which the Hitler régime had confiscated.

Education is a considerable field of activity for the West German unions, who have set up schools and institutes of their own. These offer excellent training facilities in all branches of vocational schooling: some are even boarding schools. The teaching of trade union history and principles is also actively pursued. Financial support for study at universities and institutes is also provided for members of the unions. Much adult education work is also carried out, especially in evening classes. The arts are not neglected, either, for the unions are concerned with widening the cultural horizons of the workers. The use of films and the theatre have greatly assisted these efforts, and one enterprise in particular has now become world-famous. This is the annual festival of the arts in the Ruhr town of Recklinghausen. Here workers from all parts of Germany (and Europe!) can attend theatre performances given by Germany's leading artistes, and also join in the discussions connected with these events. The institution of the Gutenberg Book-Guild has enabled broad sections of the public to gain easy access to works of literary merit.

The German trade union movement was 100 years old in 1969, and the DGB twenty years old. Observers were beginning to question the continued effectiveness of the organization in the present-day West German state. Its membership still accounts for a minority of the working population; and although the past fifteen years have seen an increase of 8% in its membership, the number of employed persons has increased by 50% during that same time. Recruitment has been poor among the salaried workers, and there has been a marked growth in the strength of the professional organizations, testifying to the failure of the DGB to appeal to these sectors. It is even being asked whether the system of 16 industrial unions is really effective any more, since so many people in each industry look elsewhere for representation. The relationship of the DGB to individual unions is also under scrutiny, and it is pointed out that the DGB is a mere umbrella organization without power to fix subscriptions or take part in wage negotiations. In May 1969 the veteran DGB chairman, Ludwig Rosenberg, retired from office and was succeeded by Kurt Gscheidle, an SPD member of the *Bundestag* and assistant general secretary of the postal workers' union. In an interview with the journal *Volkswirt,* on 17th January 1969, Gscheidle demanded a more determined effort to enlist the support of the salaried and professional worker; this would be achieved partly by a clearer definition of DGB aims, structure and social philosophy. He complained of the tendency to 'go it alone' exhibited by certain unions, and of the clumsiness of the decision-making mechanisms of the DGB, which made it virtually impossible for the Central Committee to react swiftly to events and speak authoritatively, in the knowledge that it had the backing of all the unions. Herr Gscheidle hoped for a pruning-out of unnecessary business from the vital central organs of the DGB and the investing in them of authority to speak and act on behalf of all unions on certain agreed matters, in particular social policy, political education, youth work and public relations. It has yet to be seen how far individual unions are prepared to go in surrendering some of their new-found independence to the parent body.

2. *Co-determination and Partnership*

Already under the Weimar Republic the German trade unions enjoyed a small measure of co-determination, in the Works Councils established in 1920 in all firms with more than twenty employees. It is this aspect of their policies that has grown most in significance since 1950. They are concerned in particular about the great concentration of German heavy industry in a few hands, especially in the Ruhr: in no other country of Europe is so much power controlled by so small a circle of industrialists. Conscious of its power to govern their lives, and remembering in particular the support of Hitler by certain big business interests, they are seeking increasingly a voice of their own in policy decision-making and social affairs.

The pattern of what has been achieved to date is a varied one. The principal gains were achieved in the immediate post-war years, for by 1951/2 the employers had stiffened their resistance to such an extent that little more headway has been made since; even the achievements of those early years were only finally clinched under the threat of a strike by the trade unions, before the prospect of which the employers, and the CDU, finally acquiesced. It had even been claimed in some circles that the unions were seeking to coerce parliament and were therefore to be resisted at all costs, in the name of democracy. The promulgation of the Law on Co-determination, in April 1951, removed the threat of a general strike.

Basically, there are three levels of workers' participation: that of the *establishment or workshop*, that of the *company or enterprise*, and that of *public administration*. We shall begin with the first of these, *participation at works level*. The most important legislation here is the Works Constitution Law of October 11th, 1952. The point at which workers' participation becomes effective is defined as the Works Council. This is elected by all workers above the age of 18, in a free and secret ballot; workers who have been employed in the establishment for at least a year and have reached the age of 21 may stand for election. The size of the Works Council depends on the size of the establishment; where between 5 and 20 workers are employed, only one representative, known as the *Betriebsobmann*, is elected. Works Councils of between 25 and 35 members exist in factories with over 9,000 workers. As far as is possible, manual and non-manual workers must be proportionately represented, likewise the balance of the sexes. Juvenile employees have a representative of their own. Delegates normally hold office for three years.

The Works Council has the right of consultation with the employers on matters of *general interest*, and also enjoys certain defined rights of co-determination and consultation in *social, personnel* and *economic* matters. Matters of *general interest* include proposed improvements to benefit staff or establishment, supervision of regulations concerning the employees, dealing with complaints and safeguarding the interests of any particular individual. Co-determination and consultation rights exist in the sphere of *social policy*: the Council enjoys parity with the management in deciding such matters as hours of work, work-breaks, time and place of payment, holiday-taking, internal welfare arrangements, work rules and individual workers' conduct, piece work and bonus rates and methods of payment. No employer may resist the wishes of the workers on these matters, and provision is made for a Conciliation Board in the event of their failure to agree. In *personnel* matters, the Works Council has no powers in an establishment where less than 20 people are employed. In larger concerns, certain rights are accorded to the Council. These include the right to object to new appointments, where there is reasonable cause to suspect the acceptability of the appointee (a matter dificult to prove, and seldom attempted). Re-grouping and transfer are other personnel matters which come within the competence of the Works Council: here again, the Council must show just cause for objecting to a management proposal, but the employer may not proceed in face of the Council's justified opposition. In the case of senior staff, it is usually only required of the employer that he notifies the Council of the intended appointment. The final personnel matter involved is that of dismissal. The Works Council must be consulted before a dismissal notice is issued, so that justice can be seen to be done. However, the terms of this requirement are so imprecise that it is virtually worthless; indeed, it is not sufficient to prove that an employer did not notify the Works Council of an intended dismissal, it must be proved that he actually had no intention of so doing. Only in cases of bulk engagements or mass dismissal is the obligation laid on the employer to consult with the Works Council to avert any consequent hardship which might arise.

Economic matters are the third of the spheres in which consultation must take place at works level. In enterprises employing more than 100 people the law provides for the setting up of a Joint Works Committee (*Wirtschaftsausschuß*), of between 4 and 8 members, one half supplied by the workers and one half by the employers; all must be employed in the concern, and one at least must be a member of the Works Council. The Works Committee must receive information about business matters that affect the concern, including manufacturing and working practices, the production programme, the financial standing of the enterprise, the state of production and the order book and any other matters vitally affecting the interests of the workers. The annual balance sheet must be explained to the Committee and the Works Council. It would appear, however, that there are still many firms which have not yet established a Joint Works Committee.

The Works Council enjoys further rights of consultation on proposals to change the structure of the enterprise. These include: reduction in size; complete closure, or closure of important branches; mergers; fundamental changes in the object of the enterprise, or of plant and equipment, not arising from marketing conditions; basically new working practices. Provisions are made for arbitration in the event of a failure to reach agreement on these matters, and an employer who persists in his intentions in face of an adverse ruling by an arbitration court is liable to a payment of twelve months'

F

earnings in all cases of redundancy. These payments for redundancy are, however, the only legal consequences of the failure to reach agreement between employer and Works Council in economic matters.

Once every three months a Works Meeting must be held, which all employees may attend, and to which the Works Council must submit a report of its activities. This meeting may submit resolutions to the Works Council and pass comment on its activities, but it has no other statutory rights. The employer, or his representative, must be invited to the Works Meeting, which he has the right to address. In the case of concerns employing between 20 and 100 people, and therefore having no Joint Works Committee, an obligation is laid on the employer to inform his staff, either verbally at a meeting, or in a works magazine, of the progress of the enterprise at three-monthly intervals. This applies also to larger concerns.

Public service employees are covered by separate legislation, but they too possess rights of co-determination and consultation. The equivalent to the Works Council is here the Personnel Council which represents established officials, non-permanent officials and manual workers in proportion to their numerical strength. Its operations resemble those of the Works Council, though in personnel matters the discretion of the individual is given greater play in the raising of private issues (*e.g.* suspension, transfer, retirement).

Leaving the sphere of establishment or works legislation, we proceed to the second category of co-determination and consultation. This brings us to *company and enterprise level.* It is only Joint Stock Companies (including co-operative societies and mutual benefit insurance companies) that are affected here; legislation does not apply to private companies, whatever their size. In all such companies employing more than 500 people, the Board of Supervision (which supervises the conduct of the Board of Management) must contain a one-third representation of the workers. The size of the Board of Supervision must therefore be divisible by three. The workers' representatives are elected in the various branches of the company in general, secret, direct elections and sit, like other members of the Board, for a period of five years. Trade union officials may be elected to the Board also, once the basic representation of one manual and one non-manual worker has been achieved. All workers' representatives enjoy the same rights as other members of the Board of Supervision, not only in labour matters but in all aspects of company affairs.

The greatest degree of control is granted to workers in the mining and iron and steel industries, when the firm employs more than 1,000 people, is a joint stock or limited liability company, or a unit company (*i.e.* one created by the Allied attempt to split up the heavy concentration of industrial power after the 1939-45 war). The effective law for these institutions, passed in May, 1951, provides for *equal* representation of workers and management on the Boards of Supervision. The Board normally consists of eleven members, four representatives of the shareholders and one "further member", four representatives of the workers and one "further member", plus an eleventh person, also referred to as a "further member". The workers' representatives are normally one manual and one non-manual worker, both elected by the Works Council, and two representatives nominated by the relevant trade union headquarters. Where a company's nominal capital exceeds 20 million DM, the Board may consist of 15 members; where the capital exceeds 50 million DM, a Board of 21 members is permitted; the principle of equal representation still applies. The presence of the "further members" on the Board is designed to provide an element of neutrality in its dealings; these people may not, therefore, be representatives of a trade union or an employers' association, nor in any sort of connection with such organizations for at least twelve months before election; neither must they have been connected with the firm, either as a worker or employer, nor must they possess any financial interest in it.

The shareholders may select their representatives as they choose, but the workers' representatives must be nominated by the Works Council and the principal trade union in the company. The eleventh (or fifteenth or twenty-first) member cannot be elected against the votes of three members of either the shareholders or the workers. On the Board of Management, which is responsible for the conduct of business by the company and is its representative in law, the workers' interests are represented by a Labour Director, who not only watches the administration of social and personnel matters, but has an equal voice with the other members of the Board of Management on all company affairs. He is appointed by the Board of Supervision, but cannot be removed from his post except with the approval of the majority of the workers' representatives on this Board. Legislation of August 1956 excluded Holding Companies (*i.e.* not direct producers, but merely groups which administer the interests of the shareholders in subsidiary companies) from the terms of the 1951 Act, with the result that workers in this section of mining and coal and steel production only possess the right to one-third representation on Boards of Supervision, except where the subsidiary companies are predominantly concerned with coal and steel production. They are then still subject to the terms of the act, and equal representation, on the basis of 15 members, 7 drawn from either side, plus one "further member", must be practised (21 members in the case of firms with over 50 million DM capital).

In addition to this statutory legislation, there also exist certain voluntarily negotiated co-determination agreements in various sectors of German commerce and industry, ranging from iron and steel groups to insurance firms, banks and co-operative societies.

The third sphere of operation which we listed is that of the *organs of public administration*. Certain of these state institutions have almost the nature of independent, self-administering bodies, and it is here that the unions have also achieved a small measure of consultation and participation. In the 81 *Chambers of Industry and Commerce* distributed throughout Federal territory, the trade unions are permitted to assist in the shaping of vocational training; no other rights have been accorded. Types of apprenticeship, the structuring of courses and the design of the qualifying examinations are matters on which they may speak. Half of the members of the vocational training committee are appointed by the workers or the trade unions (Law of December 18th, 1958). Under the terms of legislation passed in September 1965, *Handicrafts Establishments* must provide a measure of supervision and control by the worker. This includes the maintenance of a good relationship between masters, journeymen and apprentices, the regulation and supervision of apprentice training and the conduct of passing-out examinations for journeymen. The workers are allocated equal seats on the committees of these bodies that deal with journeymen's and apprentices' training. There must also be a special journeymen's committee to look after the interest of those in training. The local Chambers of Handicrafts, which represent the interests of all handicrafts undertakings in their area, must elect one-third of their members from the ranks of the journeymen.

Social insurance is another field of public administration where the worker is allowed some representation. Insurance in West Germany is, as we shall see, split up into a wide range of differing schemes, but all social insurance institutions are, in public law, corporations or institutes, and many of them must admit workers' (or beneficiaries') representatives to their control bodies. Legislation of August 1952 provides that, in health insurance, the administering bodies shall be made up of one-half representatives of the insured persons, and one half from the employers' representatives. In agricultural accident insurance schemes, the workers make up one-third of the controlling board. Unemployment insurance is covered by legislation of April 1957, which provides for one-third representation of the workers on Labour Exchange committees, and where insurance is concerned, a 50% share in the voting with the employers. In the administrative committees of regional and local exchanges, workers, employers and public bodies each have a one-third share of the votes. Certain other public corporations, such as the Post Office and the Federal Railways, the Federal Bank, radio and television corporations, as well as *Land* administrations, also provide a small measure of worker representation.

We must bear in mind, incidentally, that wage negotiations and collective agreements do not fall within the sphere of competence of the Works Councils or Boards of Supervision, but are dealt with directly by the unions and the employers' associations—as in our own country. The aim is to preserve the principle of neutrality on these joint bodies, which operate "within the framework of existing wage agreements", as the law puts it. The Works Council must similarly remain neutral in the event of a strike, and its facilities may not be used by the strikers. Some trade unionists have seen a danger of deflecting workers' interests and allegiances away from the unions and towards a politically neutral body; the trade unions themselves have no direct say in company affairs.

It is perhaps too early yet to judge the effects of this co-determination legislation. Certainly there is little to distinguish between the productivity levels, wage trends and strike records of firms affected by this legislation and those which still stand outside it. Many workers in the steel industry seemed ignorant of the working of the system when a recent survey was conducted, and even tended to regard their representatives as 'bosses' men'; the sense of democratic participation would hardly seem to have been engendered here. And the very industry where parity of representation has been achieved, iron and steel, has had a very unsettled period of labour relations in the last few years.

The West German trade unions are far from satisfied with their achievement today; they have nevertheless achieved more than their British counterparts. They are now pressing for the extension of equal representation to all spheres of industry. They have called also for the setting up of a national economic council, with equal representation for workers and employers, which would study the planning of national production and advise the government on economic and social policy. They are also calling for similar bodies to replace the existing chambers of commerce and agriculture and other such trade bodies. A particular interest of the CDU unions is that of expanding profit-sharing and co-partnership schemes. At their annual conference in September 1970, they called for an extension of co-determination in industry and accused the SPD of being as reluctant to act in this matter as had been the CDU/FDP coalition. A state secretary of the Ministry of the Interior was, however, at this very time informing a DAG meeting in Bonn that the government were already preparing such legislation. Its appearance will be eagerly awaited.

The employers, meanwhile, are far from enthusiastic. They are determined, as far as possible, to reserve to themselves control of economic affairs—the Works Councils have little power here. Employers' organizations have made it clear that investment, price policy, publicity and market planning are their special preserve, based on expert knowledge and experience. They also take exception to the fact that, although only one-third of all German workers belong to a union, 83% of works councillors are members of one of the 16 trade unions. They object further to the arrangement which enables the workers to appoint to advisory boards representatives who have no connection whatsoever with the firm, and point out that this has led to certain union leaders collecting as many directorships as retired British generals!

3. Negotiation and Arbitration

The Basic Law contains no recognition of the right to strike or to make collective agreements; neither does it forbid lock-outs. Regulation of these matters is transferred to those concerned, namely the workers and employers, through their representative bodies. Constitutional powers are reserved for legislation on matters such as co-determination and co-management.

Such issues as terms of employment, wages, hours of work, work practices and the like are the subject of agreements between workers' organizations and the individual industries concerned, though there must be no infringement here of established social legislation. By law, all parties—workers, employers and officials alike—are guaranteed the right to organize in defence of their interests, and their right to conclude agreements is affirmed. The foundation on which West German production rests is the institution of collective agreements, and since the passing of the appropriate legislation in 1949 (*Tarifvertrag-Gesetz*) 76,321 such agreements had been concluded by the end of 1966. Most of them concerned wages and salaries; the rest conditions of work, leave, sickness benefits etc. These agreements are legally binding on all parties, and their infringement can lead to prosecution. Wage agreements are normally negotiated over a period of years, the arrangement being that no new terms may be negotiated until the expiry of the agreed period. The problem of inflationary trends is usually dealt with by allowing for intermediate adjustments to the agreed wage rates to take into account any significant rise in the cost of living index. By this means industry is better able to draw up its budgets and to make long-term plans. Unofficial strikes are illegal, and Labour Courts have even ruled that workers on unofficial strikes must make good any damage which they cause.

When disputes occur, the organizations representing both sides have the right to conduct their own negotiations for a settlement. There is no provision for compulsory arbitration. When arbitration fails, each side has the right to collective action: the workers to strike action, and the employers to a lock-out. A strike leads to the suspension of labour agreements; a lock-out cancels them completely. Little resort has been necessary to either in the past 25 years.

Trade union tactics when calling a strike usually consist in selecting a particularly vulnerable sector of industry for concentrated action, in the hope of wresting from it concessions which can then be used as a precedent for agreements with the rest of the industry in question. This was the procedure adopted in West Germany's first really big strike after the war, that called by the metal workers' union in the shipyards of Schleswig-Holstein in 1955. This was a particularly bitter and protracted strike, in which both sides dug in their heels in this their initial major confrontation; it lasted six months and cost both unions and employers a large amount of money. The unions finally gained most of their points. Usually, however, strikes are infrequent and of short duration, for the employers place great importance on the maintenance of good relations and unbroken output in the factories. The wave of prosperity in post-war Germany has also made it possible to grant most of the unions' requests without managerial misgivings. West Germany's statistics of work days lost through industrial strikes are most impressive in comparison with those of almost any other nation. The following table illustrates the point:

Year	Days lost through Strikes, per 100 employees.						
	West Germany	Belgium	France	Italy	Holland	UK	USA
1955	5·0	39·6	25·1	60·6	4·3	17·4	54·5
1960	0·2	12·9	8·4	50·3	14·1	13·6	34·2
1963	4·1	9·0	43·9	91·1	1·1	7·7	27·4
1964/8 (Averages)	0·5	11·4	14·7	87·3	0·7	10·9	44·7

A long spell of industrial harmony was broken in 1969, when unofficial strikes (*wilde Streiks*) broke out among miners and metalworkers during the September election campaign for a new Federal Government. The 'English sickness' was said to be spreading to Germany at last. Matters were quickly put right, however, when the employers granted substantial increases in pay, 11% for the metal-workers and 14% for the miners. The immediate consequence was a rush of new pay demands from the railway, paper and printing and leather workers' unions, and sounds of alarm from industrialists and economists at the prospect of a wage and price spiral. A state of flux is certainly replacing the earlier tradition of stability and respect for legality.

Workers' pay is covered by a number of official acts. The employer is bound to pay the agreed rate for the job, public holidays included. The payment of overtime rates for work-periods in excess of the agreed norm is also obligatory. The right to further payments from social funds (e.g. marriage and child allowances) is also guaranteed to the worker. The employer is responsible for the continuation of certain wage payments in cases of illness or injury (as we shall see in Section N, p. 171–2). In addition to their compulsory payments to employees, many employers also provide special gratuities, at Christmas for instance, or on special anniversaries. They are bound even here, however, to observe the principle of equitable distribution. A scheme introduced by legislation of July 1955 makes it possible for an employer to invest on behalf of a worker certain tax-free sums at the rate of 624 DM per annum, yielding a benefit of 20% and more, depending on individual circumstances. The same tax relief applies to workers who invest money themselves. These funds may be invested in savings institutions, building societies or industrial concerns. The worker is spared the payment of income tax on this amount, and the employer the social insurance contributions.

Certain firms have instituted bonus and profit-sharing schemes of their own, and some workers are even allocated blocks of shares in their company. The pottery firm of Rosenthal is a pioneer in this movement towards co-ownership in industry. A property-owning category of workers is the ultimate aim of such policies.

The legal obligation is also laid on the employer physically to protect the worker as far as possible. This not only covers the worker's person, but also his possessions (such as bicycle, work-clothes) and the regular payment of his social insurance contributions. Any additional social benefits voluntarily accorded by the employer must be equitably distributed. Annual leave is another statutory right of the worker, and must be granted with full pay. The minimum annual leave for all workers above the age of 18 is fixed by law at 15 working days. From the end of their 35th year of age workers are entitled to 18 working days' holiday. Six months' regular employment with a firm gives a worker entitlement to leave. Pay-levels during leave are based on an average of earnings received over the preceding 13 weeks, and holiday wages must be paid before the leave is taken. It is the employer who usually determines the dates of such leave, normally after ascertaining the worker's wishes. Length of leave usually considerably exceeds the statutory minimum, for most collective agreements include provision for extra leave, according to length of service, seniority, age, medical history and so forth, and can often amount to 28 working days per year. Office workers usually receive more leave than manual workers, and civil servants and officials receive up to 36 days. Physically handicapped workers have the right to an extra six days leave in the year, and victims of Nazism also receive extra leave, the amount depending on the *Land* in which they are employed. On average, the West German worker has considerably more time off than his British counterpart.

The dismissal of workers is also regulated by the law. A minimum of fourteen days' notice must be given to industrial workers who are to be dismissed; in the case of salaried employees the period of notice is a minimum of six weeks, although this can be reduced to four weeks by arrangement. Those suffering from disabilities or with a long service record in the firm are entitled to longer notice, while elderly workers must receive anything up to six months' notice. Good cause must be shown for the person's dismissal (Law of 10.8.1951): bad conduct, faulty workmanship, unsuitability for the type of work, or else the economic necessity to reduce output are typical valid reasons. This legislation protects only workers in firms with more than five employees, who are at least 21 years of age and who have been employed by the firm for at least six months. Members of Works Councils can only be dismissed on very special grounds.

Complaints may be taken to the Labour Courts, which are distinct from the ordinary courts of law. These act as adjudicators in disputes arising from the interpretation of industrial agreements or in differences between employer and employee; in certain cases they have the right to impose a settlement. The vital legislation was passed in September 1953, setting up three levels of operation for these courts: the *Arbeitsgericht,* the *Landesarbeitsgericht* and the *Bundesarbeitsgericht.* The first two operate at *Land* level; the third is the supreme instance, operating at federal level, under the auspices of the Ministry of Labour and Social Security. Its seat is at Kassel. The first recourse is always to the *Arbeitsgericht,* which adjudicates in the matter; the *Landesarbeitsgericht* is an appeals court, and the *Bundesarbeitsgericht* a revisionary body, concerned mainly with the shaping of new labour legislation and maintaining a watch over the activities of the lower courts. Both professional and lay magistrates sit on the Labour Courts, which are not concerned with industrial conciliation as such; the presiding judge is a professional, and he is assisted by two honorary judges, one of whom must be an employer and one an employee. Lawyers may only take part in the proceedings if it seems "necessary for the protection of the rights of the parties involved", and the atmosphere of the court is usually relaxed and friendly.

Cases must be brought to the attention of the Court within three weeks of the alleged offence or dispute. In addition to investigating complaints by individuals, the Labour Courts also pronounce on the legality of collective agreements and on their detailed interpretation. Even disputes between unions and employers can come before it for adjudication (*e.g.* the permissibility of strikes or lockouts).

Conciliation (*Schlichtung*) itself is handled privately by the interested parties, and there is no official enforcement of the procedure. Legislation of 1946 specifically provides for private conciliation. A network of mediation boards has been created, each containing two representatives from management, two from labour and an impartial fifth member. They meet privately and can settle matters by a simple majority vote. The mediation process must be speedy and has to reach a conclusion within 22 days of the breakdown of collective bargaining. If the board's proposals are unacceptable to the disputing parties, the matter goes to a formal court of arbitration, whose decision is binding.

Negotiation is rendered very much easier in West Germany because of the existence of only sixteen unions, each representing a particular sphere of industry. The unions have also shown considerable readiness to accept rationalization and automation in industry; there is, of course, no unemployment to worry them at present! The German worker is also rendered more adaptable by the nature of his training; there is usually a period of three years' industrial training for a new recruit, and the broad instruction in basic skills acquired here suits him for a variety of jobs, so that industrial reorganization is less of a threat to his livelihood. Promotion also comes readily and the social standing of technicians is high—both guarantees of a good labour supply and of willingness to pursue higher qualifications through study and further training.

4. *Employers' Organizations*

West German industry is centred principally on steel and iron, machinery, electrical goods, chemicals and instrument production. The firms are distributed over a wide geographical area and vary greatly in their size. In 1961 there were about 94,200 industrial concerns, of which only $1\cdot3\%$ employed more than 1,000 people, and $6\cdot5\%$ between 200 and 1,000 people. 48% came into the category of small firms, with between 10 and 199 employees, while 44%

of the total was made up of firms employing less than 10 workers. On the other hand, this last group only employed 1·9% of the working population and accounted for a similar percentage of national industrial production. 81% of all those engaged in industry were employed by firms with more than 100 workers. The process of concentration into larger units is well under way, but efforts are being made at restricting this movement in the interests of the smaller firms, of competitiveness, and the principle of individuality. Official taxation policy and company law are now framed to assist these efforts, which are actively encouraged by many of the employers' organizations themselves.

An umbrella organization of West German entrepreneurs came into being in 1950, as a counter to the growing influence of the trade unions and increasing government intervention in the industrial field. This was the *Gemeinschaftsausschuß der Deutschen Gewerblichen Wirtschaft* (Corporate Committee of German Commercial Enterprise). This great parent body is made up of a number of collective organizations which are themselves of considerable size and significance, principally associated with specific sectors of the economy and variously comprising industry, banking, commerce, retail trading, catering and entertainment, insurance, foreign trade, shipping, transport and handicrafts. We shall report on the main associate bodies.

The general collective organization of German employers' associations is the *Bundesvereinigung der Deutschen Arbeitgeberverbände* (founded in 1950), which co-ordinates the activities of 750 regional associations, themselves organized into 41 separate groups, and 14 *Land* organizations. From its headquarters in Cologne it maintains contacts with *all* forms of business enterprise throughout the Federal Republic, that is to say industry, commerce, handicrafts, banking, insurance, agriculture and transport. It represents 90% of all such private enterprises. The BDA is thus the employers' counterpart of the workers' DGB. Whereas the trade unions have no legal status the employers' associations usually have. They also possess the power of concluding collective agreements on behalf of their constituent members.

Like the trade unions, these employers' associations came into being at the end of the war on a local basis at first, until organization at zonal level was permitted. Some were representative of one category of industry only, while others represented a cross-section of industrial enterprise. The present parent body was created in November 1950, after the French zone associations had joined the organization created in the British and American zones in 1948. It was needed as a partner-body to the trade unions' DGB in the framing of industry's labour and social policies.

91

The central assembly of the BDA is composed of members drawn from the constituent employers' associations, in proportion to the number of workers employed in their firms. The central committee consists of the presidents of the member-associations or their deputies, plus the presidents of two industrial research institutes, and sixteen other co-opted members. The President and Vice-President of the BDA are nominated by the committee and confirmed in office by the assembly. Individual groups are not bound by BDA control, but are free to conclude their own agreements with the workers' organizations.

Responsibility is laid by the law on the employer to ensure that the terms of industrial, labour and social legislation are observed in his firm. He is responsible for the protection of the workers' rights— especially women and adolescents (payment of wages, hours of work, holidays, Sunday rest, etc.), and of their persons (against accident, or bad hygienic and moral conditions). Where more than fifteen people are employed, there is an obligation to provide work for severely handicapped persons, in a proportion of at least 6% of the labour force. The BDA attends to all such matters and negotiates with the trade union organizations as the official representative of the employers.

BDI   More important perhaps than the BDA is the organization specifically created to represent the industrialists, the *Bundesverband der Deutschen Industrie e.V.* (BDI). This is active as an economic and political force, seeking to promote the interests of the entrepreneur and to exert pressure on governments in pursuit of its aims. More than 90,000 firms belong to the BDI, representing 39 different branches of industry. It maintains a number of full-time committees, which produce regular reports on the most important sectors of the economy and the impact of government policies on industry. There are twelve BDI associations also at *Land* level. Membership is voluntary. The central body is composed of representatives selected on the basis of the labour force employed in each industry. Committees of particular significance include those on sales promotion, agriculture, foreign trade, works administration, energy and power, overseas development, European integration, finance and credit, justice, taxation and insurance. The BDI is particularly attentive to the interests of medium-sized concerns and campaigns actively for their protection, regarding them as vital incarnations of the German industrial tradition. As can be imagined, its reactions to the imposition of any restraints on free enterprise are of a very prickly character. It was a joint action mounted by the BDI and BDA that heavily subsidized the employers' side in the long drawn out metal workers' strike of 1955/56.

Mostly, however, the nature of its activities is by no means negative. It assists the Federal authorities in conducting foreign trade missions around the country and organizes a constant flow of information to its members on the state of foreign markets and export prospects for particular goods. Foreign enquiries are introduced to the right quarters in German industry, through the latter's link with the BDI. Foreign orders and advertisements are scrutinized as to their genuineness, and a translation service is also maintained. Lists of advertising possibilities in the trade papers of nearly half the world are also prepared, while trade and industrial films have been regularly sent abroad by the BDI as part of the industry's publicity campaign.

A central Bureau of Industrial Research is maintained, to investigate and advise on problems of industrial production. It is designed principally to help the small firms, which cannot afford large research staffs and experimental schemes of their own. A card index enables many questions to be answered by return of post. 50% of the firms making use of this scheme are of intermediate size, and 27% are small concerns. The trade fairs held in Germany and abroad are also heavily subsidized by BDI members, policy being decided by a co-ordinating committee.

The BDI is especially active in the field of education—not least, out of the desire to ensure itself an adequate supply of recruits with appropriate skills, in a period of acute labour shortage. It was a pioneer in demands for the raising of the school leaving age, and has regularly called for closer co-operation between schools and local industry, so that appropriate emphasis can be given to particularly useful subjects. Career advice in schools is also strongly supported, to avoid wasteful misplacement of talent. Funds have even been provided for the further education of instructors, to improve the quality of apprentice training. An education institute, run jointly by the BDI and BDA, concerns itself with these policies. The universities and technical colleges have not been overlooked either, and the BDI is pressing for a greater influence of industry in their policy-making and for a more practical, industrial bent to some of their courses. Scholarships are also provided for needy students wishing to follow university courses. The permanent committee which handles these matters includes a number of university principals. Some industrial concerns make a voluntary contribution of 1% of their profit to assist these efforts (tax concessions increase the scheme's appeal).

The BDI's concern for standards is exemplified in the attention which it pays to industrial design. In December 1951 it set up its own Committee of Industrial Design, whose activities include the promotion of training facilities in this field and contributions to the display of industrial exhibits at fairs and exhibitions.

Altruism and charity are also a part of the BDI's image. At the time of the Hungarian uprising of 1956 it voted an immediate sum of 14 million DM for relief work. It is also a very considerable patron of the arts, and through its cultural section donates about ¼ million DM a year to various branches of the arts. Grants of money are made to painters and sculptors, to composers, instrumentalists and architects. Exhibitions are arranged to show the work of young artists; musicians are invited to give concerts in the factories and to talk about their work. Promising authors are subsidized, and grants of money are made to museums. Works of art are purchased and sent on travelling exhibitions to factories and offices, where lectures are also held in connection with them, to increase artistic appreciation among the public. Of particular interest is the Regensburg Foundation, established in 1964, a town-planning seminar for young architecture students, which seeks "a method of preserving and renovating an old city and adopting it to a new economic situation". In the same year, 100,000 DM were donated towards the restoration of the Benedictine Abbey at Ottobeuren. The Germans, we are reminded, are an artistic as well as a commercial nation.

Chambers of Commerce and Industry

The oldest representatives of commercial association are the chambers of industry and commerce, which derive from the merchants' guilds of the middle ages. In 1848 those in Prussia were officially recognized as the legal representatives of the commercial interests in the regions, and in 1861 they formed the *Allgemeiner Deutscher Handelstag* which continued in being (if not quite in name) down to 1933, when they were incorporated into the Nazi bureaucracy.

They re-emerged in the autumn of 1949, under the central *Deutscher Industrie- und Handelstag* (DIHT) with its seat in Bonn, parent body of all eighty-one West German chambers of industry and commerce. They are legal bodies, of which membership is obligatory, and provide guidance to the courts, local authorities and legislators on all commercial matters. They are responsible for the supervision of commercial and vocational training in their area and for certifying the place of origin of local products. The DIHT itself co-ordinates the activities of the individual chambers and is their Federal representative. It is the sponsor of much study and research in the commercial field. Plenary sessions of this organization in which all regional chambers are represented, take place several times a year. The interests of individual enterprise, free competition and private property are stoutly defended here. A particular concern is that with foreign trade, for the promotion of which twenty-seven special bodies are active. It is also a member of the International Chamber of Trade in Paris and of the Conference of the Chambers of Trade of the EEC countries.

The Handicrafts Chambers (*Handwerkskammern*) perhaps deserve a brief note. They are an essential part of the organization of the handicrafts in the Federal Republic, for there are 686,000 concerns embracing 125 different trades and crafts, spread throughout the towns and villages of West Germany. These are grouped into 9,600 *Innungen*, a kind of guild, representing one type of craft in each given town or *Landkreis*. These groups are co-ordinated into 56 craft corporations (*e.g.* painters, carpenters etc.). The *Handwerkskammer* is the official regional body which supervises their activities, and there are 45 such chambers in West Germany, established by legislation of 1953. All handicraft firms must belong to their local chamber, their legitimation consisting in their presence on its membership list. One-third of the seats on the administrative organs of these bodies are allotted to journeymen-workers, and one of the two vice-presidents is also chosen by the journeymen.

The responsibilities of the Handicrafts Chambers include the implementation of legislation relevant to their sphere, and in particular the training and examination of apprentices, the supervision of journeyman and master's examinations, arbitration in cases of disputes between workers and employers and the issuing of certificates of the quality and value of goods. Much attention is also paid to sales promotion and guidance. There is an umbrella organization at Bonn for both the craftsmen's guilds and the handicrafts chambers, the *Zentralverband des Deutschen Handwerks*.

5. *Company Structure*

There are several types of company in West Germany, designated by such familiar abbreviations as AG, GmbH, KG and OHG. Their structure is perhaps not so familiar to English readers.

The *Aktiengesellschaft* (AG), of which there were 1,171 in 1962, is very similar to an English Public Company. Its shares may, but need not be, quoted on Stock Exchanges and there are certain publication requirements. The minimum share capital of an AG is 100,000 DM, which must be divided into shares of a minimum nominal value of 50 DM. The share certificates are normally freely negotiable without the need for registration. The Articles of the company can, however, require the consent of the company to any transfer of shares. The quoted share capital of these companies in 1962 was 24·71 milliard DM.

An *Aktiengesellschaft* must have a *Vorstand* (Board of Management) and an *Aufsichtsrat* (Board of Supervision). The *Vorstand* has the authority to decide all matters related to the conduct of the company's affairs, and is appointed by the *Aufsichtsrat*. It is responsible to the latter and to the shareholders at their general meeting. The AG must publish its annual profit and loss account and balance sheet, with other details of its affairs, in its annual report. It must also be registered in the official Commercial Register which is kept by the Court of Law for the area in which its Head Office is located. The Articles of Association must be laid before a court or a notary public by no less than five subscribers to a proposed AG, before it can be officially licensed.

The *Gesellschaft mit beschränkter Haftung* (GmbH), the limited liability company, is roughly the same as a private limited company in the UK. Its shares may not be quoted on stock exchanges and there is no requirement for it to publish its accounts. A GmbH must have a minimum of 20,000 DM for its inauguration, its capital being the total sum subscribed in cash or in kind by the members. Each member must subscribe a minimum of 500 DM and amounts must be in multiples of 100 DM. There is no limit on the number of members of such a company. A holding in the company may be inherited, or transferred to another person subject to the company's consent in writing; there are no share certificates.

A GmbH must appoint one or more managers, who need not be members of the company. These are the only persons entitled to represent and bind the company. They conduct the company's business within the terms of the company's articles of association, or as specified by the members. Company decisions can only be reached at a special meeting of the members, whose voting rights are determined by the extent of their share in the company's capital.

The constitution of an *Offene Handelsgesellschaft* (OHG) is governed by a special section of the West German Trade Act (*Handelsgesetzbuch*). It is comparable to a partnership in England, in as much as the liability of the partners is unlimited. Each partner must take an active part in the running of the business, unless the partnership agreement specifies otherwise. One partner may at no time act independently of the others and must at all times have their consent to any transactions outside the normal scope of the company's business.

The constitution of the *Kommanditgesellschaft* (KG) is likewise laid down by the Trade Act. The KG is a type of partnership, but has two different kinds of partners: (1) the *Komplementär*, whose liability is unlimited, including his own personal assets, and (2) the *Kommanditist*, whose liability is limited to his nominal holding in the company. There is no restriction on the number of either type of partner.

The management of the KG is the sole right and responsibility of the *Komplementär*, the *Kommanditist* being excluded from the conduct of the company's affairs. The latter may, however, raise objections to actions of the *Komplementär*, where these are outside the objects and normal business activities of the company. He is also entitled to receive a copy of the annual accounts and to verify them against the books.

West German company law requires that all companies, whether limited or not, and any individual conducting a business, must be entered in the Commercial Register held by the local court (duplicates are usually held by the local Chambers of Commerce). Applications for registration are not normally considered unless a stated minimum turnover can be expected. In the case of trading and industrial companies, this figure is 100,000 DM per annum.

6. *Co-operatives*

The co-operative movement in Germany has almost as long a history as that in Britain, and a considerable impetus was given to the German movement by pioneers of the British Labour and Co-operative Movement, like Robert Owen, W. King and Sidney and Beatrice Webb. We can trace the beginnings of the German co-operative movement to the savings societies which started up in 1850. By communal saving, these groups were able to obtain at lower prices bulk quantities of food and domestic goods. Other groups were presently formed, which made contracts with particular traders for discount rates on foodstuffs and household equipment. The growth of these groups was discouraged by Lasalle, the Socialist leader, who had a bolder idea—the formation of workers' production co-operatives, a very active one being started in Hamburg in the 1890's. A split in the movement came in 1903, when the Socialist wing of the movement founded, in Hamburg, the *Zentralverband deutscher Konsumgenossenschaften* (Central League of German Consumers' Co-operatives). The other faction was incorporated in 1908 as the *Reichsverband deutscher Konsumvereine* (Imperial League of German Consumer's Unions), which allied itself to the Christian trade unions. In 1933, however, all groups were liquidated, bringing the dissolution of 72 great co-operative organizations.

After the war things began anew, with all the retail co-operatives joined into one central organization, the *Zentralverband deutscher Konsumgenossenschaften*. By 1955 it had 303 groups, with a membership of 2¼ millions and an annual turnover of 2,167 million DM. It manufactures certain of its own products for sale. It has no special political interests, and certainly does not put forward parliamentary candidates, as in Great Britain, though it has links with the trade unions.

There is today considerable variety in the West German co-operative moment, and besides the consumers' co-operatives we find commercial co-operatives (organizations of traders and small craft firms), agriculture co-operatives, building co-operatives and co-operative banks. Each of these groups has its own parent organization. The commercial co-operatives had, in 1969, a strength of 2·7 million members, and 1,300 individual groups, and represented a potent force in middle-class mercantile activity. They are the oldest commercial co-operatives in Germany, having been founded in 1859, with the name *Deutscher Genossenschaftsverband* (League of German Co-operatives), and have eleven regional associations. They are financially self-supporting and maintain liaison with other branches of the co-operative movement, as well as assisting members with the re-designing and modernization of their premises, financing extensions and new branches and guiding the training of personnel.

A vital part of the co-operative movement are the 715 *Volksbanken* (literally 'people's banks'), from whose funds extensive loans are granted to co-operative members. That these are not merely short-term loans is shown by the fact that in 1967 38% of all advances came under the category of long-term lending. Total loans in 1967 amounted to 13·3 milliard DM, a potent shot in the arm for small-scale business enterprise.

The agricultural co-operatives are named after their founder, Fr. Wilhelm Raiffeisen, who inaugurated them in the 1850s with the aim of helping small farmers to continue in business through collective buying and the sharing of materials. There are today over 3 million individual members, who are organized in regional and specialist co-operatives (*e.g.* dairy, poultry, egg-farming, wine-growing) in addition to being centrally represented in the *Deutscher Raiffeisenverband*. There are over 22,000 agricultural co-operatives in all.

B. EAST GERMANY

1. *The Trade Unions*

The East German trade unions came to life after the war even before those of the western occupation zones. They were called into being by the Soviet military government in June 1945, and their first National Congress took place in Berlin in February of 1946. They were clearly intended as the spearhead of the new socialist order in East Germany. Germany's division into two parts was already taking on a permanent character. Since the vast majority of East German industry and commerce is now in state hands, the trade unions play a much more important role than is the case in West Germany today.

One consequence of the intensive organization and promotion of the worker in East Germany is a very high membership of the trade unions. The Free German Trade Unions Confederation (FDGB) has $6\frac{1}{2}$ million members, out of a working population of about $7\frac{1}{2}$ millions, and includes industrial workers, office staffs, professional people, the intelligentsia, in short, all those engaged in any sort of production or administration. The industrial unions (IG) are those of the building and woodworkers, mineworkers, chemical workers, printing and paper workers, workers in the railway, energy and power, postal and transport industries, metal industry, textile, clothing and leather workers. In addition there are the trade unions of trade, food and related products, agriculture and forestry, the teachers' and scientific workers' unions, those of state administrative employees and health service workers, and finally even the union of artistic workers, for writers, painters and the like.

Besides the role which the trade unions play in industrial, commercial and social life, they are, of course, also represented at the legislative level in the state, through their allocation of 68 seats in the Volkskammer—the second largest parliamentary group. All proposed legislation which has a bearing on the workers' interests is intensively discussed in trade union branches before being submitted to the Volkskammer, so that a double supervision is here exercised.

The basic local unit of trade union activity is the factory or works committee. This is elected by the body of the workers, normally for a two-year period, at a mass meeting. It remains answerable to this mass meeting for its achievements and pronouncements. The duties of these committee members, as described in the Labour Law of 1950 are those of being "the legal representatives of the workers, entrusted with the task of safeguarding their right as workers, and their interest in the sphere of production, labour safety, the observation of working conditions and wage scales stipulated by the law". But the preamble to this section, in an official report of 1959, hints at the other function of their two-fold character: "as schools of Socialism their main task is to make all workers take an active interest in socialist construction as an essential condition for the solution of the central economic task set by the Fifth Congress of the SED". In other words, the trade unions are servants of the state, as well as servants of their members. Again we see the same attempt to identify worker and state which the parliamentary system revealed.

The statutes of the FDGB proclaim: "The Free German Trade

Unions form a social mass organization which is not tied to any political party. The organization plays its full part in the class struggle, from which a truly socialist order of society will eventually emerge". The sphere in which the trade unions carry on their struggle for socialism is in the place of work. It is from their ranks that the 'pioneers' or 'pacemakers' usually emerge, who boost production levels by outstanding feats of individual dedication to their tasks, thus hoping to fire their colleagues with a similar spirit. These are the new heroes of the East German state, and their personal achievement is often rewarded with medals and bonus payments.

For over twenty years now trade union committees have functioned in all concerns in the DDR, whether privately owned or not. In the election held for these committees in 1967/68, 83% of the trade unionists took part; of the 366,627 members elected, 149,251 were women and 29,066 young people. Almost a third of the committees are chaired by women.

The Central Congresses of the FDGB are held in Berlin, the seventh taking place in May, 1968, and here the delegates discuss such matters as co-determination, the responsibility of the unions, and social welfare at the national level. But each factory or establishment is concerned with its own plans and welfare arrangements, and these are handled by the factory committee. Article 45/I of the new Constitution states: "The trade unions have the right to conclude agreements with government authorities, enterprise managements and other leading economic bodies on all questions concerning the working and living conditions of the working people."

The example has been quoted of a steel rolling mill in the town of Hennigsdorf. Here 7,600 workers are represented by 400 trade union shop stewards on the various factory committees. These include the Women's Commission and the Social Insurance Council; 34 workers belong to the factory Production Committee (see below); three are delegates to the Social Council for all the state steel rolling mills; 150 "act on behalf of workers' control" and "are responsible to the trade union for seeing that irregularities and differences in their department are quickly removed"; 14 are members of the mill commission of the Workers' and Farmers' Inspection (a state board which investigates the economy).

Another sphere in which the trade unions are active is that of social insurance, which is controlled and administered by the FDGB (see Section IV).

2. *Co-determination and Partnership*

Since 1967 Production Committees have been functioning in all large state-owned factories. Their purpose is to associate the worker closely with the firm in which he operates, to induce him to take a personal interest in the achievement of the factory's targets, and ultimately to feel a sense of personal commitment to the local and then the national economic goals. The Production Committee embraces as wide a range of interests and experience as possible: 'pioneer' workers, workers selected by their colleagues, foremen, professional economists and production experts, representatives of the trade unions, the Free German Youth, women's committees, the Workers' and Farmers' Inspection and other social groups. This committee is elected by all the employees, and it is accountable to them.

Each year a factory collective agreement is drawn up, within the terms of which the concern is to operate. All are held responsible for the achievement of the annual target, for it represents the outcome of joint discussion at all factory levels. The managers are open to criticism from the shop floor for their policies and decisions, and in cases where a manager has ignored justified recommendations from the Production Committee, he can be reported to the manager of the association of nationally-owned enterprises. It has been known for miscreant managers to be removed from their posts in this way. At the same time the individual worker is also held responsible for his own personal contribution. Since almost the whole of East German industry and commerce is now state-directed, these Production Committees are obviously an integral part of the machinery of national economic planning.

Not only are industrial targets set in this factory plan. Measures are also proposed for the improvement of workers' welfare, of work conditions and even of the domestic circumstances of the worker. A decree of January 1968, laying down the kind of topics that come within the competence of the Production Committees, shows the extent to which co-determination applies: "The works manager is required to place before the Production Committee important material such as recommendations for the factory plan, the rationalization scheme, variants for solving important scientific and technical tasks, measures for applying the principle of the new technology—new norms, distribution of wage increases and the economic report at the end of the year" (Paragraph 34 of the decree on nationally-owned enterprises).

Several of these themes need to be enlarged upon. Security of employment is a matter very much in the minds of workers and trade unions, yet—in the process of rationalization now taking place in East German industry—the threat of unemployment is an inevitable by-product. It is, in fact, welcomed as a sign of increased efficiency, but at the same time measures are provided for humanizing it. No worker may be dismissed, especially under rationalization schemes, without the consent of the trade union committee. Approval is in fact only forthcoming if a new job is guaranteed for the threatened worker, which must come as near as possible to meeting his interests, capabilities and needs. This, incidentally, is greatly facilitated by the acute labour shortage that prevails at present.

Hours of work and conditions of pay for the worker are carefully regulated by the state in its labour legislation, and so the management of these is not left to be determined by shop-floor discussion. Wages are, however, assessed on the basis of the amount of work done and its quality (such matters are taken into account as the physical effort required; the level of skill and learning needed; the degree of responsibility carried, and the element of danger, dirt or unpleasantness involved in the job). In each case the basic element is the 'technical work norm' (TAN). This usually amounts to about 60% of a worker's effective earnings. Workers on piece-rates, or performance pay, receive a basic rate which is 15% above the TAN level. In the case of 100% work-norm fulfilment, an employee draws a wage which consists of the basic rate plus a further 15%. Then for each degree of production in excess of the set work-norm the worker is paid extra wages on an ascending scale. The work-norm is set for each job by a factory committee, which includes the workers themselves; it is reviewed from time to time, to take account of changes in costs or productivity, and also through comparison with achievements in similar concerns. The 'labour pioneers' are in danger here of raising work-norm levels and thus depressing the wages of their colleagues—unless these too stir themselves, in emulation, to similar production rates.

The work-norms do not represent peak performances, but lie somewhere between average output and the upper limit. The fact that they are not too high is shown by the average worker's regular exceeding of them. Extra pay goes to workers engaged in dirty, heavy or dangerous jobs, ranging from 15% to 25% normally, but it can rise as high as 50% for particularly dangerous work. Women receive the same rate for the job as men and enjoy the same privileges, as stipulated in the Labour Law. They must in return undertake work hitherto reserved for men.

Another matter which comes within the purview of workers' committees is that of training, advanced instruction and promotion. All workers are offered facilities for improving their knowledge, through state or factory schemes and grants in aid; and in each factory there exist promotion schemes, which form a part of the collective agreement drawn up by management and workers. A shopfloor worker can thus advance to the managership of the concern.

Holidays with pay are guaranteed to all workers, calculated on the basis of a scheme which takes into account their age, sex and the demands of their job. Factory and office workers receive a basic holiday of 12 working days in the year (disabled workers receive three extra days); but workers in more exacting or unhygienic jobs get 18–24 days' leave. People in managerial or technical positions of responsibility are awarded 18–24 days; young people between the ages of 14 and 16 get 21 days, and those between 16 and 18 get 18 days' holiday. In many industries long service gives entitlement to extra days of leave.

And then, of course, there are bonus-premiums for record output achievements; not just for individuals, but for whole factories. A factory bonus must be shared out equitably among all workers, from the managers downwards, for it is the fruit of their combined efforts. The incentive character of these policies is reflected in an increase in labour productivity of 82% between 1950 and 1957. Another consequence was an increase in the supply of consumer goods and the possibility of price reductions. (See Section III, p. 165.)

In all these matters the trade unions have a crucial voice. The factory plan may not be passed on to the superior economic authorities until it has been vetted by a meeting of the shop stewards. In addition, there are trade union committees which deal with labour laws, wages, social insurance, health, safety measures, holidays, education and culture, labour supply, housing policy and building, and the disputes commission. All are sub-committees of the factory trade union committee.

The manager's responsibilities are defined in no uncertain terms. The works manager of a nationally owned enterprise must inform all his employees of the exact economic state of the enterprise and must encourage their participation in solving any planning difficulties. He must announce whether production is up to schedule, compare the enterprise's achievement with those of national and even international standards, report on the progress of scientific research in the plant and so forth. The factory manager also has the individual responsibility of making fundamental decisions on production policy, such as choosing to put a particular article into production to meet current demand and where to place the main concentration of effort. Such questions demand highly specialized knowledge and experience and cannot be answered by a factory Production Committee meeting. Visitors to East Germany who have talked to these industrial managers have reported them as being very little different, in type, from their West German counterparts.

That things have not always been as de-centralized as this is freely admitted by the East German authorities. Co-determination and factory policy-making were luxuries that could not be afforded in the early days of the regime, when in the entire East German state there were for example only four blast furnaces in existence. Then the central organs of government issued the directives, and the vital requirement was the *exact fulfilment of plans* which had been prescribed in detail from above.

3. *Private Enterprise and the State*

Although the eastern part of Germany has never been so heavily industrialized as the west, there was before the war a quite considerable degree of industrial and commercial enterprise centred in private hands, above all in Saxony and Thuringia. An initial cutting-down of this force was brought about by Russian confiscation, reparations and demolitions in the immediate post-war years. Since that time the process of nationalization and state control has steadily reduced the extent of the private sector, until today it scarcely counts as an economic force. Soviet companies, employing half a million East German workers, were finally returned in 1953 to the Germans and state ownership.

The most traditional manifestation of private ownership in Eastern Germany was probably the great agricultural estates of the landowners known as the Junkers. It was here that the East German authorities made their first symbolic incursion. Soon after the cessation of hostilities, in September 1945, the 'democratic land reform' was set in train. In the ensuing two months, 2,517,357 hectares of land were removed, without compensation, from 7,160 big landowners or prominent Nazis and distributed to 335,990 agricultural workers, small farmers, refugees and even non-agricultural workers. All landed estates of over 100 hectares were expropriated and village life was transformed as a consequence. (One hectare = 2·47 acres.)

The rural revolution was not yet complete however. Independent farmers are not easily constrained into a pattern of rigid planning and exact fulfilment of delivery commitments; and some of the newly established small farmers proved inefficient in their changed role. The move to collectivization, begun in 1952, was stepped up in April 1960, and was increasingly intensified, until today all farmers belong to some form of agricultural collective or co-operative. They have surrendered land, property, stock and machinery to varying extents, but all accept some degree of state control and communal ownership of the means of agricultural production. Each agricultural production unit is now a further extension of the economic planning system, and the customary meetings of trade union bodies, Production Committees and review bodies draw up the annual plan and targets here too, and help regulate matters arising from the terms of industrial and social welfare legislation. The state/party is very much a partner here.

It was the industrial sector, however, which was of vital importance to the economic fortunes of the new state. Here much large-scale industry was brought under state control, simply by expropriation. In many cases the owners had already fled westwards, or had Nazi records and their enterprises were simply transferred to national ownership. In other cases industrialists remained at their posts after accepting a form of state partnership, in which they became trustees of their establishment, which they managed in the interests of the national economy, keeping back a small financial return as their reward. The main impetus towards this form of establishment came in 1955 and the years that followed. By its power to control the supply of raw materials, of labour, of investment capital and many other services, the state has been in a position to compel compliance with its wishes from such semi-independent employers. By investing capital in the firm, the government becomes a sleeping partner, whose interests are in the charge of the owner-manager of the enterprise. The state's share of the profits is re-invested in the enterprise. The owner-manager is answerable to party and state for his actions. A similar policy has also been adopted towards the mercantile world, including retail business, the latter usually grouped into *Arbeitsgemeinschaften* ('work-collectives'). On all sides the visitor to East Germany is confronted with enterprises which are VEBs (*Volkseigene Betriebe*)—'communally-owned concerns'.

The proportion of national production currently in private hands is very small indeed: it consists principally of small businesses engaged in highly specialized or craft work, or of one-man concerns. It is a steadily declining proportion, as the following figures for national income distribution show:

Year	State Enterprises	State Partnerships	Private Sector
1950	56·8%	—	43·2%
1960	84·9%	6·1%	9·0%
1968	85·1%	8·6%	6·3%

or the occupational comparisons for 1955 and 1968, expressed in percentages of the working population:

	1955	1968
Private farmers and smallholders:	12·6%	0·1%
Private craftsmen:	3·9%	2·1%
Private wholesalers & retailers:	1·8%	0·4%
Independent professions:	0·4%	0·2% [5]

[5] *Statistisches Taschenbuch* of the DDR for 1969.

The trade union groups are equally active within private industry, and ensure that the terms of co-determination are applied here also. The factory agreement, labour safety, the payment of the agreed wage rates are all covered by their supervision, and especial attention is paid to the employer's obligations in respect to deliveries to nationally-owned enterprises and co-operation in the area economic plan. This strict supervision, plus the lure of lower commodity rates and cheaper services, have been the chief instruments in bringing ever more private industry into national partnership.

4. *Arbitration*

Disputes Commissions have existed in nationally owned enterprises and state-partnerships, in health, education, culture and administrative institutions since 1953. According to an official pronouncement of 1959, "disputes between workers and management may also arise in nationally-owned factories, although these are not irreconcilable differences between two opposing hostile factions, because contradictions of this type would find no fertile ground in a nationally-owned factory". Differences of opinion affecting the factory as a whole, or a part of it, are ironed out between the factory trade union committee and the management. If agreement is not reached the matter is referred to the next-higher trade union committee. In such cases the dispute is settled by negotiation between the Central Board of the trade union concerned and the particular Association of Nationally Owned Factories (VVB), or if need be, by the appropriate Labour and Wage Committee of the State Planning Commission. "Unfair decisions against the workers," we are told, "are never taken". The self-assurance of this last statement is quite breathtaking.

In the lesser instance of a difference arising between the management and an individual worker, the matter is handled by the factory Disputes Commission, consisting of two workers' representatives (nominated by the trade union committee) and two representatives of the management. If no agreement is possible here, the dispute is taken to the Labour Court for decision. The presiding magistrates in these Labour Courts are for the most part trade unionists of long standing.

In 1967, there were 21,000 industrial Disputes Commissions in operation, with 190,000 people working on them, elected in the various enterprises on the initiative of the trade unions. They consider many other matters besides labour disputes and violations of industrial or social legislation in the factory. They can have referred to them cases from the civil law courts, such as minor first offences and simple civil disputes. The Disputes Commissions, as 'social organs', can also propose corrective or 'educative' sentences, and offending parties may be called upon to apologize to their fellow-workers or to make good damage which has been done. Similar arbitration bodies operate in Production Co-operatives, private enterprises and even in residential areas, dealing with minor civil offences. 55,000 people served on arbitration commissions in 1967.

The civil courts themselves convene at times in the place of work of an accused person, where the case is of considerable public significance. The legal decision then has a more exemplary effect. Even the outcome of a trial may be analyzed and discussed, for educative purposes, in a factory or residential group; and magistrates often explain the law in public meetings, in order to deter potential offenders. The place of work thus becomes a location for much social activity, instead of the old concept of a 'sweat-shop'; at the same time the worker is drawn into an ever-increasing range of commitments to party and state.

5. *Commercial and Agricultural Co-operatives*

State-owned wholesale and retail trading is broadly the concern of two separate organizations, the Consumer Co-operatives (KG—*Konsumgenossenschaften*) and the national Trade Organization (HO—*Handelsorganisation*). In 1966 there were 36,258 consumer co-operative shops covering the whole range of retail trade, almost half of them being of the self-service type. Food, tobacco, sweets and alcohol accounted for the majority of sales by these establishments. Bulk-buying from state industry, close connections with the producer, the rationalized transport of goods and national market research render these concerns efficient and enable them to operate economically on low profit margins, with consequent advantages to the cost of living index.

The HO was instituted in November 1948, as a counter to inflationary pressures from a growing black market in scarce commodities and in order to mop up excess money that was in circulation. Scarce goods were sold here by the state, at high but not inflated prices. As this particular function grew increasingly unnecessary, the HO broadened its activities to become a vast state-owned trading combine which soon embraced all aspects of retail business. By 1966 it possessed 28,877 shops, as well as restaurants and multiple stores. By this date, it was even threatening the trading position of the Consumer Co-operatives. The opening of stores in rural areas has been a particular feature of the development of HO and co-operatives. A considerable development in mail-order business has also taken place in recent years, the co-operatives being very active in this field. On January 1st, 1965 a central trading enterprise with the name of *Konsument* came into being, comprising twelve co-operative department stores and a central mail-order house in Karl-Marx-Stadt (Chemnitz). On the same date the six largest state-owned department stores also merged under the name *Centrum*. All of these organizations have their workers' and trade union committees, and participate in the drawing up of work plans and enterprise agreements. Members of the public are also represented on these bodies, through their various corporate organizations.

Practically all farms are today organized into one of the two types of co-operatives, the LPG or the VEG. The LPGs (*landwirtschaftliche Produktionsgenossenschaften*) were created in 1952, but grew enormously in number in 1960 under Ulbricht's all-out drive for state organization of the rural economy, and brought all hitherto independent farmers together into groups, in which their assets were pooled in a common enterprise. The extent of each farmer's commitment may vary: some place only their land in the common pool, but cattle and poultry, vehicles and equipment, and even the farm buildings themselves can be similarly committed. There are three types of LPG, depending on the extent of collectivization. Type III is that of total commitment, whereby the farmer becomes the equivalent of an agricultural worker on the collective. Drawings from the trading profit of these co-operatives are made in proportion to each member's degree of commitment. This was the measure whose introduction led to the flight of many farmers to the West and left much of East Germany's farmland untilled for some time. Altogether, 51,000 farmers are estimated to have fled from East Germany between 1952 and the end of 1961. There were 11,513 LPG's in 1968, of which 5,759 were of Type III; their combined membership totalled 957,410. They accounted for 86·1% of East German acreage in 1968. Of their 5,434 million hectares of land, 4,851 millions were jointly owned. Only 6% of the land remained in private hands in 1967, being either church land or allotments.

The VEG type of co-operative farm represents only 6·9% of the agricultural acreage, there being 644 of them in 1968, with 435,700 hectares of land and 50,120 working members. They derive principally from the confiscation of the big estates in 1945, which brought 3,298,000 hectares of land into the government's hands. Much of this land went into the 210,000 new farms that were created, or into the enlargement of 120,000 small farms. The rest became VEG land. The VEG workers are treated in the same way as industrial employees: they are set work-norms (AE) which they must fulfil, and are paid a bonus wage if they achieve their target. They can also earn additional bonuses by over-fulfilment of their work-norms. For adult workers, the week is one of 48 hours, for those between 16 and 18 it is 45 hours, and for those between the ages of 14 and 16 it is 42 hours. In addition to their wages the farm workers receive certain quantities of produce at reduced prices for their own consumption and a share of any bonus profits.

The farms play their part, also, in the formulation of the state's annual economic plan, and a careful watch is kept on the production targets which they set themselves. Fixed amounts are paid for the produce which they are committed to deliver, but considerable bonus payments are made for any deliveries in excess of these totals.

The number of those engaged in agriculture has declined steadily over the years: in 1955 there were 1,225,000 people engaged in the various forms of agriculture; in 1965 there were 1,178,000, but by 1969 the figure was only 1,067,000. This still makes it the second largest sector of the East German economy, after industry. Nearly half of those employed are women. There has been a steady rise in productivity which has more than compensated for this manpower loss, though in the early years after the war, before the full collectivization of farming, agricultural policy was fraught with disaster.

Section III

The Economic Scene

A. WEST GERMANY

1. *Natural Resources*

The Germany of 1937 was not entirely self-supporting; but she came nearer to self-sufficiency than either of the two parts into which she is now divided. The total land area of 183,000 sq. miles is now parcelled out, in the arbitrary way of peace treaties, into the West German Republic's 97,000 sq. miles, the DDR's 42,000 sq. miles and the 44,000 sq. miles ceded to Poland and Russia. The Federal Republic, more than twice the physical area of the East German state, has been left with an unbalanced apportionment of resources, retaining a major share of the former Germany's industry and natural reserves, but losing much agricultural production; while the preponderantly agricultural eastern regions have been incorporated into an East German state sadly lacking in raw materials and industrially underdeveloped. The West Germans have had to concentrate on building up a substantial export market in finished industrial goods, in order to import their requirements in food and certain raw materials. The East Germans, while nearly self-supporting in food, have likewise had to build up an export trade in industrial goods, in order to obtain supplies of the basic materials without which their industry could not function. They have also shown considerable ingenuity in inventing and devising substitutes.

As a result of the 1945 partitioning and subsequent refugee movements, the western part of Germany is now only 70% self-sufficient in foodstuffs, compared with a pre-war figure of 80%. Her food imports now account for roughly one third of her total import figures. The area of 1937 Germany that lies east of the Oder-Neisse line had in the past produced 25% of her total food supply, 16% of her coal and approximately 7% of her industrial output; the Silesian coalfield alone had yielded 80 million tons of high quality coal annually. Today neither of the two German states has access to these resources.

West Germany is certainly better endowed than her eastern counterpart. Her iron ore deposits supply about 30% of her annual needs, and lie mainly in the Ruhr, Harz and Jura regions; Sweden and Spain are her principal foreign suppliers of ore. Probably her greatest natural asset is her possession of large deposits of

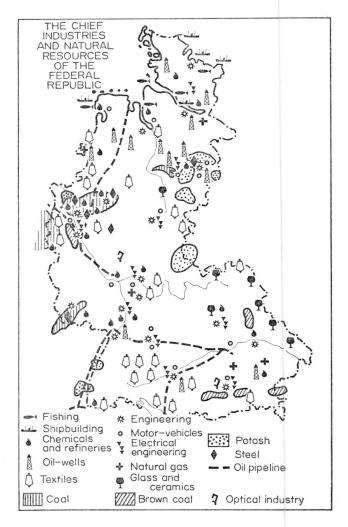

THE CHIEF
INDUSTRIES
AND NATURAL
RESOURCES
OF THE
FEDERAL
REPUBLIC

⊶ Fishing	❋ Engineering	
⊥⊥ Shipbuilding	○ Motor-vehicles	
◆ Chemicals and refineries	▼ Electrical engineering	▦ Potash
		◆ Steel
▯ Oil-wells	✛ Natural gas	— — Oil pipeline
◊ Textiles	⚘ Glass and ceramics	
▥ Coal	▨ Brown coal	ꀠ Optical industry

coal: the Saar and Ruhr coalfields are said to be large enough to
supply demands for another four hundred years. A certain amount
of coal is actually exported. About two-thirds of her coal is mined
in the Ruhr district, and most of the remainder in the Saar and the
Aachen area. Output in 1961 reached a peak level of 142·7 million
tons, but had sunk to 133 million tons by 1967 (see also p. 127).
Soft coal (*Braunkohle*) occurs plentifully in the central regions along

the southern edge of the North German Plain and is usually obtained by open-cast mining; supplies are estimated to be adequate for another seventy years. In 1961, 97·2 million tons were extracted. Coal still provided 91% of the power produced in 1961, and supplied 83% of the generating stations' requirements, though other sources of power have been developed in the meantime. By 1969 coal only supplied 32% of the total consumption of primary energy.

One alternative source of energy, though less plentiful in supply, is petroleum. Native West German oil production covered a fifth of her internal requirements in 1961, reaching a figure of 6·2 million tons; output rose to 12¾ million tons in 1968. Reserves lying in the Emsland area (north of Hanover) and along the coast of Schleswig-Holstein are estimated at 73 million tons. Recent exploration of the bed of the North Sea may well reveal greater reserves.

Magnesium chloride is found in large quantities in the Dolomitic rocks of Germany, but otherwise she is poorly endowed with non-ferrous metals. The moribund silver and lead mines of the Harz were brought back into production before the 1939–45 war, and Germany was then able to supply 32% of her lead requirements. Zinc and lead are also found in the Rhineland in fair quantities.

Of particular significance for West German agriculture are her vast reserves of sodium and potassium salts. In earlier times, German production totalled 96% of world output, and in 1960 West Germany was still producing one quarter of the world total of potash, mainly in the Harz region. Common salt is mined in the area of Lüneburg, output being increased in recent times to supply the needs of the rapidly expanding plastics industry.

Slate is quarried in Thuringia and the Rhineland, graphite is obtained in S.E. Bavaria, there are limited supplies of ferro-manganese in the Ruhr area, and there is abundant quartz. Reserves of ferro-alloys are otherwise negligible.

West Germany's timber reserves are very considerable. Her forests, two-thirds of which are coniferous, cover 17 million acres of land, and their timber content is estimated at twelve times that of Great Britain. The bulk of the saw-wood comes from the coniferous forests, especially those of the south-west (Baden and Württemberg), much of it being state-owned. A considerable part of state income is, in fact, derived from the timber industry.

On the textiles front, West Germany is less well supplied. She produces less than one tenth of the wool, and only about one eighteenth of the flax, hemp and jute that she requires. She is, however, self-supporting in sugar, thanks to her extensive sugar beet cultivation.

In south Germany, especially, considerable hydro-electric

H

exploitation of the mountain rivers has been a major source of power, producing a total of $11 \cdot 2$ million megawatts of electricity in 1961. Nuclear power stations on the other hand still contribute comparatively little: $5 \cdot 4$ million megawatts in 1969 out of a total of 150 million megawatts. However, they are expected to supply one quarter of the national need by 1975.

One resource which is threatened with severe shortage today is water. With an estimated annual increase of 3%, industrial and domestic consumption of water is causing official headaches and massive capital investment to ensure adequate supplies. Most of West Germany's water is derived from wells, but this is being increasingly supplemented by the building of reservoirs and dams.

2. *Official Economic Policy*

The end of the last war inevitably found Germany's economy very seriously impaired. Damage caused to industrial plant, communications and housing accommodation by aerial bombing, plus the impact of the long sea blockade on foreign supplies, was succeeded by stagnation under the Allied military occupation, with further depletion of her industrial potential through demolitions and reparation confiscations. Apart from her manpower losses as a result of wartime casualties (estimated at between six and seven millions, inclusive of civilian losses) Germany was in 1945 also deprived of essential manpower through the internment in prisoner-of-war camps of twelve millions of her most able young men. To complicate matters further, between 1945 and 1950 eight million refugees from the eastern part of Germany and Poland, most of them destitute, fled to the west, seeking shelter and employment. The majority settled in the Federal Republic.

The extent to which aerial and land bombardment had reduced the efficiency of Germany industry is not as great as we might imagine, however, thanks largely to the wide geographical distribution of much of her industrial plant. It is estimated that the loss of productive capacity was no more than 20% from these causes. And allied dismantling and demolition policy was less severe in the west than in the Russian zone of occupation. In the three western zones, only 8% of industrial plant was dismantled, compared with 45% in the Russian zone.

The main problems were those of supplies and finance. With three quarters of Germany's former population living within her boundaries, West Germany had only retained half of the agricultural area of the former Reich. The victorious powers themselves were mostly compelled to operate a strict rationing of supplies in their own countries and there was little to spare for German needs. The winter of 1945/46 was a particularly severe one and there were cruel shortages of food, fuel and clothing and even shelter for the vanquished Germans. The winter of 1946/47 was even harder, and was preceded by a poor harvest. In the towns and cities the average daily calorie intake was often at the 800 level (2,000 being regarded by health experts as the minimum requirement), and mass epidemics threatened to break out. Other supplies were also desperately short: in 1947 in the British zone only one person in forty could buy a suit each year, and only one in ten a shirt; only one person in seven could buy a plate, one in five a toothbrush and one in 150 a washing-up bowl. And only one in three of those who died could be provided with a coffin.

With the loss of her total merchant fleet and a ban on new building, West Germany could import little of her own, and in any case most important rail and road bridges were destroyed and her rolling stock seriously depleted, so that distribution was a major problem in itself. The first three years were years of despair, and many Germans concluded that the Allied powers were indeed bent on the total destruction of Germany. Morale among the civilians was low, and a black market in scarce commodities flourished on all sides. Children with no schools to attend became black market operators; to steal and rob was no longer regarded as a moral crime where one's very existence was at stake; and instead of money, cigarettes became the unit of currency. The Reichsmark no longer had any real purchasing power.

Some industry managed to continue in operation, and up to June 1948 production varied from just under a third to just over a half of the pre-war figures. But what was really needed was a vast injection of finance and a meaningful organization of the country's affairs. Altogether it is reckoned that Britain and the U.S. between them were spending 700 million dollars a year on their occupation of Germany. The remedy clearly was to assist Germany to stand on her own feet. Soviet policies were seen to be aimed at a take-over of the whole of Germany, and the West Germans had therefore to be encouraged with Western support and made to feel that they were welcome partners in Europe. West Germany was to be recruited into the Atlantic camp.

A start was made through West Germany's participation in the Marshall Aid programme, financed by the Americans with the aim of restoring the shattered economies of western Europe. West German participation in Marshall Aid began in April 1948, and it proved a veritable blood transfusion. By 1955, when American aid schemes came to an end, a total of 3,298,400,000 dollars had been pumped into the West German economy in various forms and guises. Agriculture was one of the first beneficiaries, and food production increased rapidly: by 1951 the output figures were better than those of the pre-war years for this part of Germany. The Federal Ministry of Food, Agriculture and Forestry, established in the autumn of 1949, had taken charge of national policies and the steady upward climb in food production was unabated from then on. One of its primary aims was that of keeping down the cost of food to those with little money, where necessary with the assistance of subsidies.

Industrial production also began to increase, as imports of raw materials purchased with Marshall Aid reached the factories, many of which had been rebuilt and equipped from the same financial sources. The dedicated effort of German labour and management resulted in figures for 1950 which were already 13% above the pre-war level in this part of Germany. In 1951 they rose to 35%, in 1952 to 45%, in 1953 to 58% and in 1954 to 77% above the pre-war figures. This, in spite of initial Allied restrictions on certain types of industry. The Potsdam Agreement of 1945 had set strict limits for coal and iron production, as well as for sea-going vessels, heavy tractors, machine tools, synthetic fuel and oils and synthetic rubber. In March 1946 industrial production was fixed by the occupying powers at about 50% of the pre-war level. In August 1947 the figure was revised in the British and American zones to 90–95% and wide scope was granted for the expansion of the automobile and chemical industries.

The greatest single step towards financial recovery was, however, the currency reform which was carried out in June 1948. This measure put an end to the black market almost overnight by wiping out all excess funds in private hands. Money had already lost much of its value: the amount in circulation had risen in ten years from 6·4 milliard RM to 72·5 milliard RM. The old Reichsmark was called in and replaced by a new unit, the *Deutsche Mark* (DM), at a general rate of one DM for 10 RM. Thrifty savers, as well as speculators, were the sufferers; but at least the goods re-appeared from their hiding places under the shop counter. The new DM was not linked to the price of gold, and circulation was restricted at first to 10 milliard DM. The responsibility for these decisions was entirely with the Allied governments, but shortly afterwards they began the transfer of political power to the West Germans themselves; the way was now clear for the formation of constructive economic policies.

The transfer of power to a popularly elected Federal Government followed in 1949, and the decision faced Dr Adenauer's cabinet of what sort of economic principles it was to espouse. The choice was that of a 'social market economy', directed by Economics Minister

Ludwig Erhard, in preference to state administration and control. The first steps in such a direction had already been taken by the Economic Council which had decided policies in the combined Western Zones of occupation and whose economic adviser Professor Erhard had been. This was not to be a philosophy of economic *laissez-faire*, for it acknowledged the responsibilities of the state authority in maintaining economic order by means of policies which avoid public indebtedness, maintain social harmony and secure the appropriate conditions for successful trade with advantages to all partners—employer, employee and the state. The constitutional framework for this situation had to be provided by the government, but there was to be complete freedom to operate within these bounds.

A balanced budget was needed as soon as it could be contrived, for only then could the country cease to live on borrowed money. The problem was to raise sufficient funds from a largely impoverished nation, which was in acute need of all manner of relief itself. The policy of borrowing had to continue for some time yet. The largest claim for subsidies came from the refugees and other victims of the war. The currency reform also brought a rise in the unemployment figures in its train. The government of Dr Adenauer immediately embarked on a programme of social relief, which cost 315 million marks; much of this money was devoted to alleviating the problems of the refugees (housing, food and clothes, retraining). In addition, a vast rebuilding programme was started, with the double aim of reducing unemployment and providing much needed housing accommodation. The refugee problem was a continuing one, for between 1948 and 1955 a further 3,700,000 refugees arrived in the Federal Republic from the east.

While the currency reform led to an increase in the purchasing power of the ordinary citizen, the shortage in consumer goods produced a rise in prices which constituted a serious danger to financial stability. The granting of subsidies to keep down the price of imported goods (30 million marks in 1949, rising to 790 million marks in 1950) helped to keep prices stable, and coupled with rising production had stopped the price spiral within six months. An extra load on the exchequer was the Berlin crisis of 1949, when considerable additional funds were needed to sustain the beleaguered city as it struggled against the Russian blockade. A postal surcharge on all mail helped to raise money, but although very considerable sums accrued over the period 1949–54, they were quite inadequate to meet the bill, and Berlin continued to be a constant drain on Federal resources. By the end of 1953, the Federal contribution to Berlin had already reached a total of 3,500,000,000 marks and the figure rose higher each year.

Relief in the other *Länder* was more easily managed by the system of 'horizontal financial adjustment', under which the financially weaker states were subsidized by the more affluent ones. In the year 1949/50 for instance, this 'equalization of burdens' procedure (*Lastenausgleich*) led to the redistribution among the poorer *Länder* of 586 million marks. (By 1968 the figure had risen to 1,579 million DM.)

A fundamental reshaping of financial allocations as between *Bund* and *Land* was one consequence of the adoption of the Basic Law. This had shifted the responsibility for social insurance benefits and the burdens of war from the shoulders of the *Länder* onto those of the Federal Government. To provide the Bonn government with the necessary funds, the Basic Law transferred to it much of the revenue that had hitherto passed to the *Länder*, such as the product of the turnover and transport taxes, customs duties and consumption taxes (excepting that on beer). The *Länder* thus lost the financial sovereignty which they had enjoyed since 1945 and the hand of the Federal authority was greatly strengthened. The *Länder* are also obliged to hand over to the *Bund* a proportion of their income and corporation taxes (see Section I, p. 48).

The government which came into office in September 1949, taking over from the Anglo-American bizonal authority, framed a six-month transitional budget and the financial year 1949/50 ended with a deficit of 250 million DM. Enormous burdens had been shouldered by the incoming government[1], but the economic and financial policies which it followed enabled it to tackle the major problems of investment and work projects to alleviate unemployment, without increasing taxation or embarking on inflationary measures. Indeed, within a short time it was actually able to reduce taxation.

The emphasis was on the encouragement of capital growth, and aimed at the creation of growing tax revenues resulting from an increasing national product, in order to meet the cost of the mounting social burdens. Encouragement was given to new capital formation through undistributed profits; tax exemptions were also provided for investment in industrial replacements and for non-interest-bearing housing loans. By April 1950 the government income from all sources was in excess of budgetary needs and a reduction was made in the very high rates of income tax then in force and also in certain indirect taxation (sugar, beet, cigars) whose

[1] Occupation costs for 1950/51 were 4,645,900,000 DM; post-war social burdens absorbed 5,000,000,000 DM, aid for Berlin another 520,000,000 DM, housing schemes 400,000,000 DM. The total burden was 10,000,000,000 DM.

impact had been a retarding one in sales and production. Production increased, unemployment dropped, and in the next financial year of 1950/51 the total tax revenues were actually higher.

The financial year 1951/52 showed a budget deficit of 1,300 million DM, but the following year, despite rising financial commitments, produced a surplus of 5,800,000 DM. The Federal Government's increased proportion of the tax revenues (marked up to 37%) was mainly responsible for this surplus.

The London Debts Agreement of 1953 made the final arrangements for the repayments of Germany's foreign debts, accumulated since the First World War; they were acknowledged by the Bonn government in a gesture of international goodwill and creditworthiness. The total figure for Germany's public and private debts was assessed at 14,000 million DM, of which the Federal authority accepted resonsibility for 10,500 million DM. Under the repayment scheme, these debts will be finally expunged in 1994, the heaviest period of payment falling within the years 1958–1970.

An increase in the social product in the period 1953/54 made possible a further reduction of income tax and a streamlining of the tax procedure. The year ended with a deficit of 1,500 million DM, arising mainly from the failure to negotiate a proposed loan. However, once the EDC (European Defence Community) treaty came into force the West German economic position improved and, for the first time ever, the financial year 1954/55 witnessed no budgetary increases. Turnover tax produced the biggest yield (40·5%), followed by income and company tax paid over by the *Länder* (20·1%) and the tobacco tax (9·3%). Major items of expenditure were social expenditure, housing and subsidies (41%) and occupation and defence burdens (37·5%). Larger tax reforms became possible in 1955, reducing income and company tax and representing (taken together with the smaller reductions of 1953) a cut of 30% on average. At the same time certain favoured growth-points of the economy could now be deprived of special tax concessions which had earlier been granted to them.

West Germany was now well launched upon her 'miraculous' economic recovery. The consumption of 'fillers-up' such as bread, potatoes and flour shows a steady decrease between 1948 and 1954, while the quantities of meat, fats, butter, milk and eggs that were eaten were all at least doubled, meat consumption being trebled. The pre-war levels of nourishment had been once again achieved. The production figures for non-essential consumer goods (*e.g.* refrigerators, watches, footwear) show a similar increase. By 1952 exports were exceeding imports in value and the favourable gap grew larger from then on, being trebled within twelve months. The proportion of finished goods in the export figures rose steadily, from

65% in 1950 to 75% in 1954, and her share of world trade increased from 4·2% in 1950 (Great Britain 11·6%, France 5·4%) to 5·5% in 1953 (Great Britain 10·9%, France 5·5%). Between the currency reform of 1948 and September 1954 the employment figures show an increase of 3,400,000; in September 1954 the rate of unemployment was 4·7%. Industrial production rose 75% between mid-1950 and the end of 1954, and productivity increased by 35% in the same period. The cost of living index showed the following movements (taking 1938 = 100) :

1949 — 166	1952 — 171
1950 — 156	1953 — 168
1951 — 168	1954 — 169

In this same period of almost complete stability, the levels had risen in Great Britain by fifteen points and in France by twelve. Industrial wages had risen on the other hand from a figure of 110 in 1948 to 210 in 1954 (taking 1938 = 100), though the wages of professional and agricultural workers were still depressed.

A keen sense of priorities had prompted government policies throughout this period. The rebuilding and re-equipment of factories was given precedence over the personal needs of the population, which had increased by one quarter of its previous size. Social injustice may have resulted from the directing of Marshall Plan aid, the capital sums that could be borrowed, the yield of a very high level of income tax and the proceeds of high prices to industrial reconstruction. But as soon as the corner was turned in 1951, the government progressively dropped its special tax concessions on industrial re-investment and sought to ease the tax burden of the ordinary citizen. In the meantime, many more jobs had been created and unemployment levels were steadily falling. The Paris Conventions of 1954, granting full sovereignty to the Federal Republic, also helped matters by removing the last control restrictions on West German industrial production. Her membership of OEEC and the European Payments Union and acceptance of the terms of GATT have drawn her more fully into the pattern of European and world trade, with consequent benefits to her economy. The growing confidence of the West German public in official economic policies is shown by the steady increase in private savings, which rose fivefold between 1949 and 1954, a 50% increase actually being recorded in the course of 1954.

The pattern established by 1955 continued with little change in the ten years that followed. Production continued to rise, exports increased, the Deutsche Mark became a stable and highly regarded currency. It was in this period that the labour movement, which had stayed its hand for so long, began to claim a larger share in the growing prosperity of the country. Increasing shortages in the supply of labour, combined with strikes and threats of strikes, led to considerable improvements in earnings and other benefits, although (as we have shown in Section II) government attitudes to partnership and co-determination showed no liberalization beyond that achieved between 1951 and 1955. Workers' earnings increased more rapidly from now on, and inflationary tendencies began to be noticed.

The storm clouds of an approaching crisis had started to gather well before 1965, and Chancellor Erhard had already set in motion studies to produce new planning which would bring the German economy over the hump. His squeezing-out in 1966 did not prevent the implementation—indeed the enlargement—of this re-planning of the German economy. The troubles which disturbed the economy were inherently in the nature of things. For some time the principle of official non-intervention in the national economy had been proving more and more an unrealizable ideal. The growth of the public sector was increasingly rapid and it soon outstripped the private sector, through the collective income and expenditure of the *Bund, Länder* and *Gemeinden*. Social welfare benefits and public welfare payments (*i.e.* subsidies of various sorts from the state budget) swelled in significance until finally 40% of the gross national product was passing through official public budgets. What was needed was a re-structuring of official fiscal policy and the planning of industrial investments in the light of these changed circumstances. There had been a prevalent fear of 'state intervention' through an Economic Plan, but the necessity was at last recognized for statistical analyses and forward planning. A committee had been set up as early as 1963 for this purpose. The government was called upon to frame a positive economic policy based on the evidence at its disposal, in an annual assessment. Further to this, medium-range five-year programmes were to be announced, which included national budget plans that were to be matched by similar planning at *Land* and *Gemeinde* level. Closer integration at all national levels was thus one of the results which emerged, providing a centralist tendency in economic affairs. In the spring of 1967 the *Bundestag* passed the Stability Act, which provided the government with the powers which it needed for the implementation of those new policies. Since much of the economic crisis of 1966/67 stemmed from overspending by the regions, over which Bonn had no statutory control, the Stability Act provided the Federal Government with powers to restrict the floating of loans by *Land* and *Gemeinde* authorities, and created a uniform capital market policy.

The West German constitution is obviously affected by such economic planning proposals, for they involve a change in the balance of powers between *Bund* and *Land*, with a consequent weakening of the latter's rights. The necessary legislation has therefore been slow to emerge and is often a form of compromise. The vital steps were taken during the summer of 1968, with proposals for a common budgetary policy for *Bund, Land* and *Gemeinde*. This will enable more prompt and universal action to be taken, by fiscal policy, to control excessive fluctuations of the economy. It was in pursuance of these new arrangements that, in March 1969, the Bonn government was able to declare a postponement by six months of the spending of £156 millions, mainly by the ministries of Defence and Transport, and to request the *Land* authorities to take similar steps.

The tendency to greater state control of the economy has grown with an SPD presence in the government, while CDU 'hard-liners' have vigorously resisted any such inclinations. The chief protagonists of these two attitudes have been the SPD Economics Minister, Karl Schiller, and the CSU leader Franz Josef Strauss, who was Finance Minister in the CDU/SPD coalition of 1967/69; the conflict between them had much to do with the breaking up of this coalition in September 1969. A temporary expedient was arrived at in the compromise decision of mid-1969 to allow the Mark to float until it found its own exchange level. After the autumn election which deprived the CDU of power, the decision was taken to up-value the DM by $9 \cdot 3\%$, a move by Schiller which was quickly seen to have been overdue. (It had already been revalued in March 1961, from $4 \cdot 2$ to the dollar, to $4 \cdot 0$ to the dollar.)

Since the advent to office of a predominantly SPD government in 1969 the state has declared its intention of intervening more actively in economic matters. The professed basic aim is to create a more egalitarian society, through the more universal distribution of the social product, an improvement of social welfare measures and a greater capital investment in such sectors as education and housing. The revaluation of the D-Mark is part and parcel of the SPD's social programme, as well as of their anti-inflationary policy. The delay in its implementation increased the threat of inflation against a background of industry producing at full potential and in search of new investment capital, rising interest rates, increasing consumer demand at home, a shortage of labour and steadily growing wage and price levels. The German economy is heavily dependent on a large export surplus, whose long-term continuation cannot be guaranteed; it is accompanied also by considerable investment abroad of industrial earnings and its payment to foreign investors of high interest rates. The purpose of revaluation was partly to divert more effort to the home market, in both sales and investment, and render imports into Germany cheaper, thus easing the severe inflationary pressure of home demand. In the process, the workers would gain from the redistribution of incomes which was to accompany this expansion of the domestic market.

The management of bank rate to help control spending has led to complex results. The bank rate, which had been successfully held down for many years, was raised to a record $7\frac{1}{2}\%$ in March 1970 (equal to Great Britain), in an endeavour to check public spending and mop up surplus money in circulation, as well as to recall foreign investments which had been withdrawn after revaluation. At the same time it increased the level of public and private debt, and threatened to check the growth of savings and investments. It was lowered to 7% in July 1970, $6\frac{1}{2}\%$ in November and 6% in December 1970 partly to discourage borrowing from abroad at cheaper rates, with consequent strains on West German currency reserves, and also to check the flow of 'hot' money into the country.

The West German economy, of course, remains healthy and strong, and she had retained her position as second greatest trading nation in the world, after the United States, until overtaken by Japan's spectacular surge to the fore in 1969. The crisis in the balance of payments in 1966 was quickly surmounted, and a favourable trade balance has obtained ever since. The revaluation of the DM in 1969 was, after all, a manifestation of her economic superiority over her trading partners. By the end of June, 1968, unemployment had dropped to $1\cdot1\%$ from the $1\cdot9\%$ of a year earlier, and there were two-and-a-half jobs waiting for every person unemployed. The gross national product increased by another 30,000 million DM in the course of the year and was $7\cdot2\%$ higher than in the 'plateau' year 1967. In 1969 it rose by another 8%. Unemployment figures fell from 340,000 in 1967 to 170,000 in 1968 and 100,000 in 1969. West Germany was then also employing 1,500,000 foreign workers—rising to 1,850,000 in autumn 1970. Industrial production, having fallen by $2\cdot4\%$ in 1967, increased by $11\cdot8\%$ in 1968 and again by $12\cdot5\%$ in 1969.

The obverse of the coin is also noteworthy. The cost of living, which had risen $1\cdot7\%$ in 1967, rose by another $1\cdot6\%$ in 1968 and $2\cdot7\%$ in 1969, while average earnings increased $2\cdot6\%$ in 1967, $7\cdot6\%$ in 1968 and $9\cdot3\%$ in 1969. The rising scale of wage increases is more than matched by a major increase in tax receipts; whereas *Land* revenues for 1968 showed an advance of $5\cdot1\%$ on 1967, the advance in 1969 was of the order of $18\cdot6\%$. Similarly, *Land* tax receipts for 1968 showed an increase of $8\cdot9\%$, and in 1969 rose by a further $18\cdot4\%$. The *Gemeinden* followed a rise of $5\cdot3\%$ in 1968 with one of $27\cdot2\%$ in 1969. Private consumption rose $5\cdot9\%$ in 1968 and $10\cdot3\%$ in 1969; public consumption by $3\cdot3\%$ in 1968 and $11\cdot4\%$ in 1969. Imports rose by a slightly higher margin than exports, leaving a favourable trade balance of $16\cdot8$ milliard DM in

1967, 18·4 milliard DM in 1968 and 15·6 milliard DM in 1969; while the currency reserves of the Federal Bank, after rising from 33·8 milliard DM in 1967 to 41·4 milliard DM in 1968, fell in 1969 to 27·4 milliard DM. The amount of money in circulation rose steadily, from 33·8 milliard DM in 1967, to 34·9 milliard in 1968 and 37·3 milliard in 1969, but savings showed increases also, from 11·1% of private incomes in 1967 to 12·1% in 1968 and 12·2% in 1969.

The proposition is now heard that West German industrial expansion has reached the limits of its capacity and must turn more of its attention to production for the domestic market, rather than concentrating so intensively on the less dependable export market, leaving foreign producers to make inroads into the home sales field. Industrial plant is reported to be at full stretch, with overfilled orderbooks, and no reserve capacity. The labour force is also fully engaged, with no further reserves to be tapped; even predominantly agricultural regions have been developed industrially, so that farm labour rendered redundant by agricultural re-structuring can be absorbed into industry. The very pressure of demand threatens inflation; the *Handelsbank*, in an economic review in 1969, stated: "Whether measured by the growing volume of unfilled orders, by lengthening periods of delivery or by the disproportion between unfilled vacancies and the small residue of mainly structural unemployment, excess demand again prevails. In these circumstances, exaggerated wage demands are not only asked and granted, but actually offered, because passing them on in prices seems unlikely to cause any difficulty." Wage settlements granting 15% increases were not uncommon in 1969.

The first five-year planning projection, drawn up by the SPD/FDP coalition in January 1970, was rather more sanguine. No misgivings were voiced about the development of the economy, and increases in productivity were looked for as a means of increasing output. The earlier forecast of a 4·6% productivity increase was upgraded to one of 4·9% per annum (estimated at 6% for the year 1970). The projection expected a real growth rate of 4·5% in the gross social product. The expected increase in the gross national product for 1970 was 9–10%. Price rises of 2·2% per annum were forecast, with a 4% increase in costs generally. Gross earnings were expected to rise by 12·5–13·5% in 1970, producing an effective net increase per capita of about 10%. Employment figures were expected to rise a further 1%, and the working day to be shortened by 0·5%. A drop in the export surplus of four or five milliard DM was also anticipated for 1970, mainly as a consequence of revaluation in 1969. Confidence was expressed in the maintenance of stability, continued expansion, financial equilibrium and full employment.

Speaking in June 1970, Economics Minister Schiller proclaimed that the post-war economic miracle had been succeeded by a productivity miracle, and forecast a doubling of productivity in the space of twelve years.

New measures nevertheless proved necessary in July 1970 to meet the still unchecked growth of inflation. Professor Schiller stopped tax concessions on a wide range of industrial investment for a period of seven months, the intention being to delay investment of between £350 million and £450 million (building and aid to West Berlin were exempted). A second measure proposed was a 10% increase in income and corporation tax, to be refunded when the economy had cooled off; workers paying tax of less than 100 DM a month would be exempt. In this way it was expected to mop up about 5,200 million DM of purchasing power. It was hoped that this would come out of consumer spending rather than savings (which would invalidate the exercise).

By the autumn of 1970 it was reported that there was a six months delay in the supply of investment goods (orders having risen by 15% in five months), whose prices had increased 10% between May 1969 and May 1970; that the cost of living rose 3·8% in the same period, and that the cost of building had soared to such heights that many projects had simply been abandoned in mid-course. Observers are now waiting to see which way the balance will tip and the SPD are ready to take further deflationary steps: a 'controlled' inflationary rate of not more than 5% per annum seems to be acceptable to them for the present. Setbacks for the SPD/FDP coalition in the June 1970 provincial elections testified to public disquiet over the whole economic prospect. An improvement in the FDP vote in the Autumn elections was probably a sign of support for the new Eastern policy rather than of reassurance on the economic front.

A division of opinion began to emerge towards the end of 1970, with the bankers expressing fears of a continuing inflation, while the government claimed to have matters under control, actually lowering the bank rate to $6\frac{1}{2}$% in November. The bankers pointed to an earnings increase of well over 12% for the year, compared with a production increase of only 5%, and a rise in producer prices of 6·2%. Certain sectors of industry anticipated falling orders, especially the electrical machinery and steel industries. The number of bankruptcies also increased significantly. Meanwhile, the Federal Government published its budget for 1971, the highest in the country's history, representing an increase of 12% over 1970. Largest consumers of funds were to be education (a 43% increase here), especially higher education, building and transport. Further expansionary budgets were expected to follow. Professor Schiller, in October 1970, advised the trade unions to aim for an 8% increase in gross wages in 1971, which was still very considerable, even if not as great as the nearly 16% achieved in 1970. A price increase of 3% was forecast for 1971, compared with one of 4% for 1970, while unemployment was expected to remain steady at 0·7%.

3. *The Industrial Front*

A certain restructuring of industry took place in the immediate post-war years, partly in order to make good capacity lost to the East German state. Thus the electricity and power industry was substantially rebuilt, and hosiery manufacture was increasingly developed. Entirely new enterprises also grew up, based on post-war technological advances, such as synthetic yarn production and the manufacture and processing of plastics. By the mid-1950s this redevelopment of West German industry, which also involved considerable rationalization, was complete and the production drive moved into top gear. The output levels of 1936 had already been achieved in 1950, though much of this effort had been devoted to reconstruction and replacement. In the following twelve years industrial production was to increase by 163%. However, increased efficiency has always remained a vital consideration, and as recently as 1965 it was announced that investment in modernization and automation exceeded the spending for 1964 by 13%.

The major enterprises of West Germany are processing industries: 89% of production in 1961 derived from these sources. The largest employer of labour is the machinery-making industry, then come coal and iron, electrical goods, textiles, chemicals and food, in that order. The biggest annual turnover is that of the food industry, which is followed by machinery-manufacture and heavy industry. The export of motor vehicles is West Germany's largest single currency-earner, and made up 58% of all exports in 1969. Machinery, standing second, accounted for 20% of the export total.

The main industrial areas of West Germany are the Rhine-Ruhr district, the Rhine-Main region and a concentration in the South-West. The North German coastal belt is also becoming increasingly industrialized, as new smelting works are built beside the great ports into which ores are imported, and where petroleum and natural gas are readily available as replacements for coal. Baden-Württemberg, with 190 per 1,000 of its inhabitants employed in industry, is the *Land* with the highest proportion of industrial workers (mainly in smallish industrial concentrations), but North-Rhine-Westphalia (185 per 1,000) is the chief industrial area, including as it does the Ruhr complex. Then come the Saar (160 per 1,000), Hessen (145 per 1,000), Bavaria (135 per 1,000), Rhineland-Palatinate and Lower Saxony (110 per 1,000 each). The lowest degree of industrialization occurs in Schleswig-Holstein, with 80 per 1,000 employed in industry. Not only have new industries made an appearance since 1945; there have also been radical changes for the established ones. The metal-processing industries for instance achieved an output increase of 282% between 1950 and 1963, and the motor industry one of 580%. From 1963/4 to 1966/7 there was a certain levelling off in these trends, and it was the electrical, optics and instruments industries which went ahead, with increases of 14% and 11% respectively. The chemical industry sustained a steady growth rate and its 1963 output rose 300% above the 1950 level, while plastics output grew by 49% in the years 1963/64–1966/67 alone. The production of consumer goods generally increased by 140% between 1950 and 1963, and by a further 10·5% between 1963/4 and 1966/7. The overall production index of industry increased from 1962 to 1969 by 53%; chemicals increased by 127%, the electro-technical industry by 81%, motor vehicles by 75%, textiles and the mechanical engineering industry (the largest sector of all) by only 31%, and iron production by 55%.

The mining industry has undergone a severe decline on the other hand. Until 1957 output rose steadily, to reach a figure of 26% above that for 1950. Over-production then became a common feature of the European Coal and Steel Authority, and millions of tons of unsold coal were stacked at pit-heads and in miners' gardens, while the industry waited for the market to improve. Between 1957 and 1963 output fell by 4%, between 1963/4 and 1966/7 by 15%. The mining of iron ore presents a similar picture. In 1967 nearly 100,000 people left the Ruhr to seek employment elsewhere. However, a reorganization of the mining industry, plus some renewed demands for coal, have saved the situation. With help from the *Land* Government of North-Rhine-Westphalia, unprofitable pits have been closed, the owners compensated and the miners re-deployed, and the remaining pits concentrated under one company, with an officially guaranteed minimum return on investments. But the output, for 1956, of 133 million metric tons has turned now into one of 90 millions, and may eventually be set as low as 70 millions.

State intervention, here at *Land* level, has helped appreciably in keeping up the pace of industrial development. Generous local government grants and low-interest loans have induced new industries to open up in the Ruhr. In the ten years since its inception in 1960, the *Land* authority has attracted 260 firms to the area, some of them foreign concerns. North-Rhine-Westphalia has followed the lead of the Federal Government in forward planning: its five-year plan for 1971–1975 is an ambitious one and covers economic, industrial and social development. Already a new port is being excavated on the Rhine at Voerde; and Emmerich, about 90 miles upstream from Rotterdam, is building up a container traffic trade with British east coast ports.

Probably the most outstanding achievement in West Germany's post-war recovery has been the growth of her export trade. It was estimated in 1969 that 30% of her total sales was accounted for by foreign trade and operations. The figure for the U.S. was 15% and for the U.K. 25%. Many of the large manufacturing concerns have a higher sales volume abroad than at home: the Volkswagen Corporation and the chemical industry are representative cases. The West German figures have grown steadily more impressive in recent years. From 1950 to 1966 exports increased from 8·36 billion DM to 80·63 billion DM, and in 1967 they grew again to 87·05 billion DM—more than ten times the 1950 figure, the second largest in the whole world. Where West German investment is weak is in subsidiaries abroad and foreign enterprises. This is mostly due to historical causes, for all German subsidiaries in foreign lands were confiscated after both World Wars, and Germany possessed no overseas territories after 1918. Again, she was forced, after 1945, to rebuild her home economy first and there was no surplus capacity available, nor investment capital, for the development of foreign fields. The consequence is that American industry in 1969 derived five times as much return from its foreign trade as did West Germany's and that British industry, with lower export figures than West Germany, still had a larger foreign business return. West Germany is, however, now rapidly catching up on this front by developing her own production plants abroad. The 1966 figures were:

	Industrial Exports	Foreign Subsidiaries	Total foreign business
USA	92 billion DM	350 billion DM	440 billion DM
Britain	52 ,, ,,	60 ,, ,,	110 ,, ,,
West Germany	78 ,, ,,	12 ,, ,,	90 ,, ,,
Holland	20 ,, ,,	35 ,, ,,	55 ,, ,,
Japan	37 ,, ,,	6 ,, ,,	43 ,, ,,

While many foreign firms are establishing subsidiaries in West Germany today, others have acquired partial control of native industrial concerns. By 1966 more than one-sixth of the stock capital of West German corporations was held by foreign companies. Mostly the holdings were in a limited company (GmbH), where they totalled 22·3% of all registered capital, rather than in joint stock corporations (AG), where the holding was only 13·5%.

The largest investors were American firms (holding over half the foreign share capital), Great Britain, Holland and France. Foreign subsidiaries are usually fully owned by the parent company, and if not, the majority control is in its hands: the 1968 figures are 52·2% for the former and 36% for the latter situation. The largest sector of foreign penetration through subsidiary companies is that of oil refining, followed by mechanical engineering and the vehicle industry. The chemical industry, plastics, rubber, asbestos, food and stimulants and electrical engineering are also affected. Early tax concessions, granted to these foreign-owned concerns in the occupation period, have now been abolished, and there is less pressure to develop new openings.

West German investment abroad has grown in recent years. It is most intensive in the neighbouring European countries, but is now also being extended to the so-called developing countries. Belgium, Switzerland, Brazil and France are the principal areas of penetration, followed by the United States. The chemical, electrical and automobile industries are principally concerned here. The latest area to be explored is that of the Soviet bloc, and in several Communist states, Russia included, West German firms are co-ordinating their activities with state corporations in the development of new industrial plants. In the case of West German investment abroad, the parent companies are usually content to enter into a partnership with a native company, rather than having the entire control of their own subsidiary. Their holding usually amounts to 50% of the shares, though minority holdings are also common, leaving their foreign partners the major control of policy.

The control structure of West German industry presents a somewhat different aspect today from its former appearance. The so-called 'lateral' trusts of pre-war days were partially broken up by the occupation authorities after 1945. These firms controlled the majority of a particular sector of industry, such as mining or steel production, and were ordered to sell off some of their assets in the interests of competition, the breaking of price rings and the reduction of their political influence. These measures had only a limited success, however, for in the case of the largest enterprises— Krupps in particular—no one was forthcoming with sufficient funds to purchase the divided empires, and Krupps has today been virtually re-instituted. Anti-monopoly measures (especially in 1957) were also circumvented by the formation of 'vertical' trusts, which control a whole range of production, for example coal, steel and engineering. Such combinations enable a company to supervise the production of a commodity from its initial stages to the finished product and consequently to stand in an economically stronger position. Government statistics of 1959 reveal that half of the coal-mining industry was controlled by the big steel combines, thus undoing most of the Allied post-war legislation on industrial concentration. Coal and chemicals, and chemicals and oil were also closely bound together in large corporations. The electrical power companies controlled 90% of lignite production, the big steel firms exercised control over sections of ship-building, and the coal-mining industry was closely connected with the production of fertilizers. Firms with an annual turnover of more than 25 million DM accounted for over 20% of industrial production. The number of small firms was showing a steady decline. The anti-cartel legislation of 1957 had not forbidden the formation of trusts where exports were to be helped, or production made cheaper, and no new government measures followed the 1959 report. The modern tendency for industry to concentrate into large corporations is today manifest in West Germany, and is indeed a necessary condition for her survival in the context of present-day world trade. Even the trade unions have participated in this trend and now own the fourth largest bank in Germany and operate one of the largest consumers' organizations.

The pattern of West German industrial organization is approximating more and more to the American situation, with large corporations dominating the field: in 1966, among the hundred largest industrial corporations of the world, 68 were American, 13 West German, only seven British (including the Anglo-Dutch ones), four Italian and two French. Siemens, Volkswagen, Krupp and Mannesmann are the largest of the industrial giants, standing in seventh, eighth, ninth and fifteenth place respectively in the world league. In the sphere of retail trade also the American pattern has been copied in recent years and there are many self-service stores, supermarkets and discount houses. State-owned industry scarcely exists. The highly successful Volkswagen works (share value 1,000 million DM), once national trustee property, were sold off to small investors in 1961, in conformity with CDU private ownership principles, after the pilot-scheme selling-off of the Preussag coal and oil company (share value 120 million DM) in March 1959 had proved a success. Several other smaller concerns were similarly sold off to the public in the course of 1959, and in 1965 the government divested itself of the Veba undertaking, its last considerable holding. The state was left in possession of only a few undertakings and a large amount of land, though it also retained minority holdings in the larger concerns which it sold off.

4. *The Statistics of Success*

Almost every aspect of present-day West German life bears witness to the achievement of the 'economic miracle' that took shape from the brave beginnings of 1948. The ordinary citizen has had a certain share in this growing prosperity, even if only in more recent years.

Workers' wages have risen in an ascending pattern. By 1951 industrial earnings had at last reached a level equivalent to the buying power of wages in 1938. By November 1953 they were 24% higher than the 1938 equivalent. By 1967, men's earnings had increased 270% over the 1950 figures, while women's were 302% higher. The following table shows the rate of increase and productivity between 1950 and 1966:

Year	Gross earnings per worker		Productivity per head:	
	1950 = 100	% increase over previous year	1950 = 100	% increase over previous year
1951	116	16·3	108	8·1
1952	125	7·9	116	7·0
1953	133	5·9	122	5·4
1954	140	5·2	128	4·7
1955	151	7·9	138	8·0
1956	163	7·9	144	4·2
1957	171	5·2	149	3·5
1958	183	6·7	153	2·8
1959	193	5·4	162	6·0
1960	210	9·3	173	6·8
1961	232	10·6	180	4·1
1962	253	9·0	186	3·4
1963	268	6·1	192	3·1
1964	292	8·9	204	6·3
1965	319	9·0	212	4·1
1966	342	7·2	218	2·7
1967		2·6		5·0
1968		7·6		6·0
1969		9·3		4·4

Wage increases have thus been generally in advance of productivity increases, but the continued prosperity of the economy is shown by the statistics for the gross national product during these years. The percentage increase was as follows:

1951	=	10·9%	1957	=	5·8%	1963 = 3·5%
1952	=	9·0%	1958	=	3·3%	1964 = 6·6%
1953	=	7·9%	1959	=	6·9%	1965 = 4·8%
1954	=	7·2%	1960	=	8·8%	1966 = 2·7%
1955	=	12·0%	1961	=	5·4%	1967 = 1·2%
1956	=	7·0%	1962	=	4·1%	1968 = 7·2%
						1969 = 8%

Employment figures have also risen steadily. By 1960 West Germany had reached a point of virtual full employment and was faced with a labour shortage. The further three and a half million refugees who had arrived from the East since 1950 (making a total of 12 million since 1945) had all been absorbed into the economy, and the search for labour had to be extended to foreign countries. The following table illustrates the developing trend. (N.B. The international definition of full employment is a rate of less than 3% unemployed.)

Year	No. in Employment	% Unemployed	Year	No. in Employment	% Unemployed
1953	16·9 millions	7·5	1961	20·9 millions	0·9
1954	17·5 ,,	7·0	1962	21·2 ,,	0·7
1955	18·1 ,,	5·2	1963	21·5 ,,	0·9
1956	18·6 ,,	4·1	1964	21·7 ,,	0·8
1957	20·0 ,,	3·8	1965	22·0 ,,	0·7
1958	20·2 ,,	3·9	1966	22·0 ,,	0·7
1959	20·3 ,,	2·7	1967	21·6 ,,	2·1
1960	20·6 ,,	1·3	1968	21·75 ,,	1·5

The economic decline of 1966/67 had produced a growth in unemployment, and for the first time in 7 years there were more people seeking jobs than there were vacancies. There had been a marked improvement already by mid-1968 however, when the unemployment rate fell to 1·5%, with 548,000 vacancies awaiting the 227,000 still out of work. By June 1970, the unemployment figure stood at 94,800 (0·4%) the lowest ever recorded, and there were nine vacancies awaiting each person out of work.

The figures reveal a highly satisfactory state of affairs for the worker, who has benefited also through reduction in the length of his working week. The original arrangement was the 45-hour week, but all workers now have shorter hours than this. By September 1962 72·6% of industrial and office workers were working less than 45 hours a week, 26·6% worked a 45-hour week and only 0·8% put in more than 45 hours. The national average for hours actually worked in 1963 was 40·2 hours (USA 40·5 hours). The longest hours were returned by brewery workers! By 1965 six million workers had negotiated a reduction to a 40-hour week, and many others have followed them since. By 1968 the average basic working week in industry was one of 39 hours. Overtime is, of course, still worked and paid for at an agreed higher rate, but the West German worker generally spends less time at his job than his British counterpart. The working week for the West German, including overtime, amounted to 43·3 hours in 1968, compared with a British average of 45·7 hours. The West German also receives more days off in the course of the year, is better paid and enjoys superior social welfare benefits; he also has a higher productivity record and engages in fewer strikes.

The West German worker is heavily taxed, but the higher salary groups are not so seriously burdened as those in Britain, though more heavily than those in France or the USA. In 1969, a married man with two children below the age of eleven, who earned £2,500 a year, paid £316 in tax, while his British counterpart paid £552; if he earned £5,000 a year, he paid £1,063 in tax, compared with the British worker's £1,401. The disparity increases as the salary figure rises. West German income tax is levied on a sliding scale, and although assessed annually, is payable in quarterly instalments, on March 10th, June 19th, September 10th and December 10th. Payment commences when earnings reach a level of 1,700 DM per annum for a single person, and is levied at a flat rate of 19% up to 8,009 DM per annum. The rate then increases, so that on an income of 24,000 DM roughly 25% is deducted, on an income of 60,000 DM the rate is about 36%, and on an income of 100,000 DM it is about 42%. The maximum rate of contribution is about 50%. Allowances are of course made for married couples and for children, as well as for certain other expenditure, such as interest on debts, payment to insurance funds and building society contributions. Essential business expenses are also allowable. In 1961, half of those in employment were not liable for income tax.

The entrepreneur has also benefited enormously from the economic miracle. The average increase in industrial production to the end of 1961 was 7·1% per annum. The decline in production which marked the close of the Erhard era was followed by a concerted effort to stimulate the economy once more. In January 1967 the Federal Government initiated a series of measures with this purpose in view. Credit terms were made easier for loans from banks, investment allowances were improved and interest rates reduced. The result was a steady, but clearly defined rise in industrial output, leading to an upward swing in the trade figures. By 1968, the following advances on the 1950 production figures were recorded (1962 = 100):

More than 800 points: Plastics, oil refining; oil and gas extraction.
More than 700 points: Construction industry; vehicles production.
More than 600 points: Electro-technical industry; chemicals.
More than 500 points: Musical instruments, sport and jewellery; shipbuilding, electrical power, glass production.

133

More than 400 points: Metal industries; rubber, asbestos, precision instruments; paper industries, clothing.

More than 300 points: Printing, wood processing, leather; machinery manufacture; food.

Only the mining trades showed a decline.

In 1969 there were over 22 million people at work in West Germany (not counting self-employed and ancillary workers), and they received roughly two-thirds of the national income, the employers receiving one-third. In 1950 labour had only taken home 59% of the income, the employers taking 41%. The national income had however increased in the interval from 74·5 billion DM to 361·6 billion DM. In 1957 there were 3,502 millionaires in West Germany (*i.e.* those possessing 1 million DM or more), with a capital of 9·8 billion DM between them. By 1960 there were 9,035 with resources of 28·7 billion DM. (In 1935 there had been 1,967 millionaires in the same territory). By 1966 the number of millionaires had risen to 15,247 and the 34 richest men had incomes in excess of 10 million DM a year. The gap between the affluent and the rest of society had, in fact, widened in the twenty years from 1948 to 1968. The top three million of West Germany's population owned 70% of the money: 450 billion DM represented their financial portion, compared with the 165 billion DM shared by 22 million workers. The social élite is made up of 305,000 families (1·7% of all West German households), who own 35% of all private money and control 70% of the productive capacity of the country. Leading names are those of Flick, Thyssen, Siemens, Bosch, Quandt and Oetker. Their combined resources are four times greater than those of the 13 million workers whom they employ, according to a *Spiegel* survey of July 1969. Their industrial holdings remained intact after 1945, and at a value of 13 billion marks (estimated present value 600 billion DM) were exchanged, in the 1948 currency reform, at a flat rate of 1 RM: 1 DM. Neither were they called upon to contribute fully to the post-war compensation funds, as had been recommended by the Allied experts who devised the 1948 monetary reforms. CDU policies helped them to further affluence, with concessions for industrial investment and savings deposits, between 1949 and 1959.

The Germans are dedicated savers, and the growth in savings and other forms of investment is another index of the increase in West Germany's prosperity. Private savings, at 78 DM per head of the population in 1950, had grown to 1,052 DM per head by the end of 1962. Of the 42 billion DM deposits in public savings banks in 1961, 36·7 billion DM belonged to private savers, of whom salaried employees formed the largest group. Lower-paid workers are less well represented here, and as recently as 1965 only a half of all the 21 million householders of West Germany earned enough money to participate in savings schemes, having a net level of earnings in excess of 700 DM per month.

West German investments abroad totalled 5 billion DM by 1962. Investment at home amounted in 1965 to 28% of the gross social product, an increase of 27% on the 1954 figure, at a total of 91·5 billion DM. The nominal value of share capital at the end of 1962 was 37 billion DM, and dividends amounting to 2·5 million DM were paid out; the average dividend rate was 13·65%. The share index stood at 467 in January 1963 (December 1953 = 100). Again we discover that it is the well-to-do who have benefited most from the radical improvement in West Germany's fortunes. An investor who bought 850 DM worth of shares in the Daimler-Benz company in 1948 could have sold these same shares for 396,300 DM in 1969. The Frankfurt Bundesbank found in 1969 that 86% of industrial shares belonged to the leisured classes, and most of the remainder to the manager-class of the population.

The West German currency is issued by the *Deutsche Bundesbank* (formerly the *Bank deutscher Länder*), in accordance with the Basic Law; it is not subject to parliamentary control. At the end of 1963 the gold and currency reserves stood at 29 billion DM, of which 14·8 billion were in gold. A considerable reserve is, however, essential to West Germany's economic position: the 1964 export surplus of 6 billion DM was just sufficient to meet her foreign currency payments commitments. An exact balance of imports and exports would thus lead to a currency deficit. A considerable part of foreign currency drain arises from the nature of West German industry's capital investment. Only 35% of industrial assets represent share capital and reserves (the British figure is around 70%); the rest of its holdings are loan capital, much of it short-term (hence the collapse of certain business firms in the decline of the mid-1960s). Foreign currency earnings must therefore be immediately transferred to the lending banks—which finance a lot of West German industry—to work off the backlog of borrowing. The export drive therefore must be maintained, and if possible expanded.

The increasing resort to foreign labour (*Gastarbeiter*) is one more consequence of the expansion rate of West German industry. The transfer by these workers of their earnings into their native currencies constitutes another drain on the foreign currency reserves. By 1964 there were already nearly one million foreign workers in West Germany; in 1965 the figure rose to 1·2 million, and in 1966 to 1·5 million. With the temporary recession which then affected the economy, their numbers decreased, but the revival of trade brought them back again, and by 1970 they had reached a total of 1·7 million. They come principally from Italy, Spain, Greece, Holland and Austria, in that order. The agreement is that these foreign nationals must return home as soon as unemployment begins to mount. However, the continuing economic prosperity of West Germany has resulted in many of them becoming permanently established and bringing their families to join them. They thus constitute a not inconsiderable section of West Germany's population, and government committees have been set up to examine the problems connected with their presence, which mirror, on a smaller scale, the problems faced by Britain with her coloured immigrant population. Mostly these people work in the lower-paid and less attractive jobs, and often live in depressing conditions. Their easy dismissability in periods of economic depression is a buffer against serious unemployment among the West German workers.

5. *Agriculture*

West German agriculture is perhaps the one sector of the economy which has not experienced a post-war 'miracle'. In an era when scientific planning, large production units and massive capital investment are the order of the day, it is not surprising that the individual farmer finds himself increasingly unable to compete. The farming industry in Germany has been on the decline ever since early in the nineteenth century. In the year 1800, about three-quarters of all Germany's population was engaged in farming in one way or another; by 1950, the proportion was only 30%, including forestry and market gardening. In 1939, nine million Germans worked on the land and produced four-fifths of the country's food. Two million acres of land went out of cultivation between 1929 and 1939, but the increased use of fertilizers and machinery succeeded in raising production by 15%. Since 1945 the decline in the agricultural acreage and the number of those engaged in farming has continued; and so, to counterbalance these developments, has the rise in productivity. Nevertheless, West Germany is today more heavily dependent on imports to satisfy her food requirements than was ever the case in the past. The average figures for the years 1962–1965 show that food imports (exclusive of coffee and tobacco) made up 21% of the West German import total. The export of foodstuffs on the other hand accounted for only 2·5% of the export trade. Roughly one quarter of her food supplies must be brought into the country.

Despite industrialization and urbanization 86% of West Ger-

many's land area is still devoted to agriculture or forestry (56·7%
and 29% respectively in 1968). Arable land forms the major part
of her agricultural acreage, and the most fertile land is found in a
band running from Thuringia across to Hanover, in Lower Bavaria
and in smaller regions in the valleys of the Rhine, Main and
Neckar. Some of the best land lies today in East Germany. Farms
are usually smallholdings and engage in mixed farming. The
average size is about twenty-five acres. Two-thirds of the cattle
and pigs are kept on farms of less than this size, the owners often
possessing only three of each. Only one in twelve of the farmers
keep sheep, whose numbers had declined by 1969 to 840,000, less
than one half of the 1938 figure. Cattle, pigs and hens all show a
growth in numbers since 1938, and again since 1960: they are
the principal source of farm revenue, especially for the smaller
farmer, and accounted for three-quarters of his financial returns
in 1966. In southern Germany, where the grazing is less good and
cattle are sometimes used for ploughing on the smaller farms, the
milk yield is considerably less than in the well-watered North
German plain. The pig is perhaps the most important animal of
all, supplying two-thirds of the meat consumed in the country.

In the immediate post-war years it was meat production that was
more deficient than that of vegetable or grain. By 1951 the pre-war
level of food production in the West was once more achieved, and
between 1957 and 1962 output was on average 40% above the
pre-war levels. In the financial year 1964/65 production was 16%
higher, and in 1965/66 it was 12% higher than at the end of the
1950s. Meat production had radically improved by now, and represented about 80% of farm output. The increased mechanization
of farming has reduced the necessity for draught-animals and thus
raised the quantities of vegetables which could be grown for the
consumer market instead of for stock-feeding. The 1950s thus saw
an increased flow of produce to the markets. On the other hand,
increased amounts were being spent on the importation of fertilizers
and feeding stuffs.

The fundamental difficulties of West German agriculture lie in
its structure and organization. The great majority of farmers own
and till their holdings as family farms; about one-tenth being
tenant farmers. Mostly the members of the family provide all the
labour that is needed. In 1968 about 89% of farm labour was
provided by the family unit. Much of the work is in fact done by
women, and it has been estimated that three-quarters of the people
engaged in agriculture are women and girls. Often a holding is
too small to support a family and the farmer may also be a crafts-
man in metal or wood, a forester, or even a factory worker. This
is particularly so in the more mountainous regions. The system

of inheritance is a further handicap, in that a farmer's land and possessions (in southern Germany, at least) are normally divided equally between all his sons at his death, resulting in the emergence of even less financially viable units, at a time when larger enterprises are proving to be the only answer to present-day economic conditions. The strip cultivation of fields, so often seen in West Germany, is a reflection of this parcelling out of the land (but see also p. 140).

Many farm buildings are old and badly equipped: more than half are over a hundred years old, and in 1960 only 60% of them had piped water. A survey of 1962 revealed that over half of West Germany's farms are incapable of supporting four or more persons, and that only 32·5% were in fact economically viable. It is this latter one-third which, basically, accounts for the advances shown since 1950. Two-fifths of the independent farmers were, in 1969, deriving less from their farms than the wages of an agricultural labourer. Statistics for 1966 show the following distribution of farmed land, in percentages of the total cultivated area:

Size of Farm (1 hectare = 2·47 acres):

0·5 to 2 hectares	2–5 hectares	5–10 hectares	10–20 hectares	20–50 hectares	50–100 hectares	100 hectares and over
3·2%	8·0%	15·8%	31·9%	30·3%	7·2%	3·6%

We note that 58·9% are smaller than 50 acres in size.

Considerable sums of money have been invested in agriculture by successive West German governments, from the days of Marshall Aid onwards. Credit grants to individual farmers and local authorities under the ERP Programme amounted to 1,100 million DM, for the improvement of production facilities, constructional work, drainage and reclamation and rural education services. The biggest injection of help came with the institution of a *Grüner Plan* ('Green Plan') in 1955. This includes an annual report (*Grüner Bericht*) on West German agriculture, which surveys the achievements and difficulties of the industry and proposes measures to alleviate the problems of farmers, labourers and consumers.

The *Grüner Plan* of 1963 was particularly generous, allocating 2,300 milliard DM in farming subsidies, an increase of 240 million DM on the sums originally proposed. The cost of artificial fertilizers was heavily subsidized and the price of milk was raised, and for the next two years conditions for the farmer improved, only to decline again in subsequent years. The following table shows the net financial yield of agriculture, compared with the rest of industry between the years 1950 and 1966.

Year	Agricultural share of national production	National Index (1950 = 100)	Agricultural Index
1950	10·8%	100	100
1955	7·8%	186	135
1960	6·2%	306	175
1965	4·6%	458	197
1966 (estimated)	4·3%	484	194

Earnings in agriculture are likewise trailing well behind the national industrial average. In 1956/57 they were 36% below the average, in 1960/61 they were 26% below, in 1964/65 they were 22% below. A new system of calculation introduced in 1965 showed them to be 23% below average in 1964/65 and 33% below in 1965/66. The labour force has grown progressively smaller since 1950: the proportion of the population involved in agriculture was 14·1% in 1950, but only 8·1% in 1961, or 4·5 million workers and dependents. They contributed only 3·4% of the national economy. Whereas 3·9 million were fully engaged in agriculture in 1950, only 1·9 million were thus employed in 1966 (exclusive of non-profitmaking smallholdings).

Increased productivity has been the result of greater mechanization and improved cultivation methods. The number of tractors increased three-fold, combine harvesters eight-fold, and automatic milking machines five-fold between 1955 and 1965. Most of these installations were effected by loan capital: in 1948 borrowing amounted to 2·5 billion DM, by 1950/51 the total had grown to 3·7 billion DM, and by the end of the financial year 1965/66 borrowed capital totalled 21·1 billion DM. Between 1960/61 and 1965/66, West German farmers laid out 22·5 billion DM on new machinery and buildings. The production of grain, after increasing somewhat over the pre-war yields, levelled off in the late 1950s and overall has remained almost unchanged since then. There has been a decline in the potato harvest, but a growth in sugar beet production. West Germany is virtually self-supporting in milk, potatoes, sugar, meat, eggs, butter and fat but must import about one third of her needs in grain, vegetables, fresh fruit, half of her fish, poultry and cheese requirements and almost the whole of her vegetable oils and fats.

The greatest present-day challenge to West German agriculture arises from her membership of the European Common Market and the necessity for her to conform to the agreed practices of that organization. On July 30th 1962, common terms came into force for the production and sale of grain, pork, eggs, poultry, fruit, vegetables and wine. Milk, beef and rice were included in the list in the autumn 1964, bringing 85% of West German agricultural produce within the terms of the EEC treaty. The Federal Republic is the chief purchaser of foodstuffs from the Common Market, taking 41% of its food exports in 1965. Biggest exporter was France, with a 32% share of the export total. The only commodity which West Germany does not import at all is milk, so that she is particularly affected by Common Market agreements. Since West Germany is the largest importer of foodstuffs, she automatically contributes most of the funds raised by the levies on food imported from elsewhere, the proceeds passing to EEC farmers, predominantly the French. She contributes twice as much as she receives under this head. In addition farming is organized on a more efficient basis in the other five member states, and the West German farmers find it difficult to sell their own produce at the lower price levels of the imported supplies, while community agreements forbid the imposition of protective tariffs. Direct subsidies to the farmers are against the rules. At the same time, the EEC's guaranteed support payments for agricultural products are often unrealistically high and encourage farmers to produce more supplies than are needed, all paid for by the taxpayer; Professor Schilller estimated that in 1969 the weight of surplus butter produced by the Community was greater than that of the entire population of Austria. The ten million farmers within the EEC states must be reduced to five millions, if a workable food and price policy is to be fashioned. The implications for West Germany are obvious: a contraction of her agricultural industry, cutting out the small-scale, uneconomic or inefficient farmer. It was estimated that, in 1969, West Germany spent more money to support her farmers than was devoted to higher education.

During the permitted transitional period before the full implementation of EEC policies, from 1966 to 1969, determined efforts were made to put West German agriculture on a more competitive footing. The improvement of animal stock and of the land itself was undertaken, farm buildings were improved and new ones erected, social services were more fully developed, agricultural education extended, improved retirement and accident benefits introduced and marketing arrangements more effectively organized. Money was made available for loans at low interest rates, and cheap prices were fixed for diesel oil. The need for larger, more efficient farms is being met by official encouragement of amalgamations, the buying-out of younger members' rights to family farms and the provision of retraining schemes for those willing to leave the land for other occupations. Official estimates speak of reducing the number of farms by half. The *Grüner Plan* cost the West Germans over 19 billion DM between 1956 and 1966, and the regional authorities provided further funds of their own. West German agriculture is nevertheless more efficient than that of East Germany, as the table of comparisons in the appendix shows.

The six member states of EEC finally agreed, in December 1969, on their future financial policy for agriculture. Money was to come from three sources: firstly from import levies on food imported from non-member countries; secondly, from a duty charged on all industrial goods coming from non-member countries; thirdly, a proportion of each member's revenue deriving from value added tax. 1970 was fixed as the base year for the calculation of future proportional payments, which must not rise by more than 1% or fall by more than $1\frac{1}{2}$% of the previous year's amount. West Germany was to be the largest contributor, with $31 \cdot 7$% of the total budget to find; and it was estimated that this would rise, by 1978, to 36% (France dropping from $28 \cdot 2$% to $23 \cdot 7$%). This, however, assumed no change in the composition of the Common Market community. The total charge on West Germany for EEC levies and her own agricultural support payments in 1970 were reported to be seven times greater than her annual investment in mining, mineral oils, air transport, electronic computers and merchant shipping.

6. *West Germany and EEC*

West Germany's membership of the European Common Market has of course implications for all spheres of her national life, and not just for agriculture. She was one of the six founding members in March 1957. Even before this date, she had been preparing herself for closer association with her West European neighbours, and was a member of a number of group organizations, such as the coal and steel authority (*Montanunion*), formed in July 1952, the nucleus from which EEC grew. Membership of the coal and steel union brought with it acceptance of a common policy for prices, subsidies, investments, sales promotion, imports and exports, production and industrial welfare measures. It also abolished import levies between the member states. The EEC was a logical extension of this arrangement.

Although output figures for coal and steel within the Common Market have fallen progressively since about 1962, West Germany has remained its largest overall producer country, with more than half of the anthracite and nearly half of the crude steel output of the community to its credit in 1967. She is, in fact, the dominant industrial power among the Six, and her exports and imports accounted for $38 \cdot 6$% and $32 \cdot 6$% respectively of the Common Market totals in 1968. She is also the most important customer of the other five member states, sending nearly 40% of her exports to them and taking 43% of her imports from them in 1969 (1961 figures were $31 \cdot 7\%$ and $31 \cdot 1\%$ respectively). The largest import item, as we have seen, is agricultural produce, while her chief exports have been industrial finished goods, chemicals and machinery.[2] Between 1963 and 1968 consumer prices rose less in West Germany than in any of the other five member states, while her industrial production showed the fastest rate of increase.

The Federal Republic has, through her membership of EEC, surrendered a certain measure of independence. When, on July 1st 1968, eighteen months earlier than specified in the 1958 Treaty of Rome, the customs union between the member states came into full effect, she accepted a common tariff policy with them for imports from countries outside the union, as well as a common agricultural policy. The free movement of goods, labour and industrial enterprises within the six states was also agreed upon. Far from showing hesitation to commit herself in these ways, she is now pressing for even closer integration at the economic, financial and political levels; and it is France who is showing the principal signs of reluctance, no doubt fearing a European union that would be dominated by German industry and finance. West Germany's membership of the Community gives her one of the six seats on the Council, membership of the coal and steel and Euratom bodies as well as various special committees (especially agriculture, social affairs, development aid and the European investment bank) and 36 seats in the European Parliament (France and Italy 36 each, Belgium and Holland 14 each, Luxemburg 6 seats). The affairs of the Community are subject to the jurisdiction of the European Court of Law, with its seven judges. Community rules already forbid the forming of cartels and price-rings and lay down strict conditions for state subsidization of industry.

General preparation of the country for closer European integration was part of West German policy even before she emerged as a fully sovereign state in 1954. It was one of the dreams of Konrad Adenauer; but it also found practical expression. Many aspects of German commerce, industry and institutions were developed with such an end in view. And it was not just the present relatively small grouping of states that she had in mind, but a much larger community: she was, for example, one of the main supporters of Britain's application for EEC membership.

The West German communication network has been built up

[2] Exports to EFTA countries made up 23% and imports from them 14% of the 1969 totals. The USA and Canada jointly accounted for 11% of her exports and 12% of her imports.

with a regard for her foreign links. The main Autobahnen link her to Denmark and Switzerland (a 600 mile express-way runs from North to South, bypassing more than 160 towns and villages), to Antwerp, Brussels, Rotterdam, Northern France and Austria. Inland waterways join her to all her geographical neighbours, the newest venture being the opening-up of a link, via the River Moselle, with the French canal system at Thionville, near the German, French and Luxemburg border. As a result land-locked Lorraine is now in direct water-communication with Rotterdam and northern Europe, while Luxemburg has access to the sea, via Germany, for the first time ever. Coke from the Ruhr travels to the French steel mills of Lorraine; iron ore from Lorraine can be taken to the Ruhr steel mills; oil from two new Strasbourg refineries can go by ship down the Moselle into Germany, or to Luxemburg or into Lorraine; the Saar's coal and Luxemburg's steel can be transported in similar directions. A system of international pipelines will meanwhile bring oil to West Germany from the Mediterranean and from North Sea ports, especially a Rotterdam-Ruhr link. Her railway wagons have been converted to a common standard which enables them to travel to all parts of the Community without reloading. Even her road traffic measures have been adjusted to fit an inter-community code for loads, widths, vehicle lights and brakes, and even bills-of-lading. Container transportation is particularly well developed.

A common fiscal policy is also envisaged: a generally applied scheme of value-added tax (*Mehrwertsteuer*) is now in force, the West Germans having abandoned their 51-year-old system of a turnover tax on 1st January, 1968. A medium-term programme for economic development has been evolved by the community's council, embodying a common taxation policy, as well as parallel financial, structural and marketing developments for the Six. One of the ultimate aims is a common currency. The more backward areas are to be helped by subsidies from a European investment bank, to which West Germany contributes 34% of the funds. Social policies are also to be brought into line, providing for equal pay between the sexes, and a common basis for annual holidays and leave. Cultural ties have been strengthened, especially between the Federal Republic and France, with provision for school interchanges and the expansion of French teaching in West German schools.

Despite the growing implementation of common policies and practices, the six member states of EEC were still a long way from constituting one economic community at the end of their first ten years of existence together. The organization's information service reported in January 1968 great price differentials for domestic goods between the different members. Generally, the German shopper came off best. Many of the discrepancies arose from different types and levels of indirect taxation, subsidies, and retailers' and wholesalers' profit margins. What is striking is the fact that when the EEC commenced life in 1958 the average earnings of the British worker were 1,689 dollars a year, compared with the Common Market average of 1,450 dollars. By 1967, the position had been reversed, and the Common Market worker earned an average of 2,994 dollars a year, compared with a British figure of 2,716 dollars. Gross wages in Britain rose from a base of 100 in 1958 to 151 in 1967, while in West Germany they rose to 199; consumer prices in Britain rose 29 points within the same period, but only 23 points in West Germany.

B. EAST GERMANY

1. *Natural Resources*

Within a land area of roughly 42,000 square miles, the 17 million East Germans have struggled successfully to create an economically viable unit out of the rump of a state which was handed to them in 1949. Although it is predominantly agricultural in character, and has few natural resources, they have yet managed to maintain, and even expand, the centres of industry left in their possession.

The East German state occupies much of the central area of the North German Plain, and only rises in height along its southern border, where the Mittelgebirge complex forms a natural frontier with Czechoslovakia and then the West German *Länder* of Bavaria and Hesse. To the north it is bounded by the Baltic Sea, with an extensive coastline. The frontier with Poland has been drawn in such a way as to deprive the East Germans of the chief port of Stettin, and they have been forced to make do with the remaining lesser ports of Rostock, Warnemünde, Stralsund and Wismar, but have in recent years developed them into considerable shipbuilding centres. The only significant rivers are the Oder and Elbe, and the DDR has no control of the estuaries of either. The Oder forms the frontier with Poland for a considerable part of its course and empties into the Baltic via Polish territory; while the Elbe, rising in Czechoslovakia, crosses East Germany from Dresden to Magdeburg and then enters West German territory to continue its course via Hamburg to the North Sea. Even road and rail communications with the capital, East Berlin, are considerably hampered by the Federal Republic's enclave of West Berlin.

The physical disadvantages under which East Germany operates

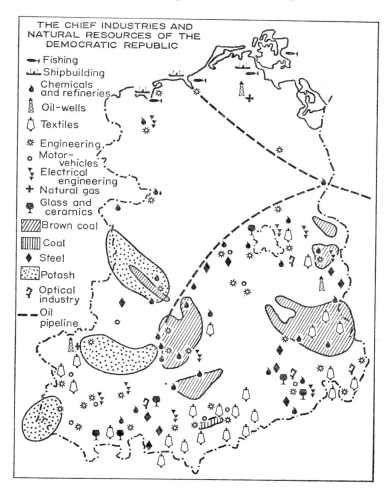

THE CHIEF INDUSTRIES AND
NATURAL RESOURCES OF THE
DEMOCRATIC REPUBLIC

- Fishing
- Shipbuilding
- Chemicals and refineries
- Oil-wells
- Textiles
- Engineering
- Motor-vehicles
- Electrical engineering
- Natural gas
- Glass and ceramics
- Brown coal
- Coal
- Steel
- Potash
- Optical industry
- Oil pipeline

assume greater proportions if we examine her raw material resources. She has virtually no deposits of hard coal (the rich Silesian fields having been transferred to Poland in 1945), small reserves in the area of Zwickau and Oelsnitz in Saxony being intensively exploited; and her supplies of iron ore and non-ferrous metals are of little significance. Her only real assets are vast deposits of lignite (soft coal), in which she leads world production, the mining being normally opencast and concentrated in the areas of Cottbus, Halle and Leipzig, as well as substantial deposits of potash and mineral salts, limestone and raw materials for the glass and ceramic industries.

K

Geological exploration has recently led to the discovery of petroleum deposits in the Rostock and Cottbus regions, while natural
gas is being extracted in the Erfurt district, but these can make only
a marginal contribution to the economy.

East Germany's potash and mineral salt deposits are second only
in importance to her lignite reserves, and in 1966 she extracted two
million tons of pure potash. Her chemical, optical, glass, ceramics
and building industries are helped by the natural reserves of limestone, chalk, gypsum, kaolin, clay, slate, quartz, fluorspar and
barytes, and some of these are also exported.

Not only did the division of East Germany in 1945 leave the
majority of the natural resources in the West; much of the heavy
industry was similarly located. More than two-thirds of the mining,
iron and steel and chemical industries, as well as of the machinery
and motor-vehicle production plants found themselves in the
Federal Republic; while the eastern part of the country contained
most of the glass, ceramics, and electrical industries and the clothing
and yarn-producing centres. East Germany retained 30% of the
former Reich's industrial capacity. West Germany was the loser in
the agricultural field, retaining only 52% of the farming area and
only 45% of the arable land of the former Reich, when about 70%
of the former population was still to be found within her borders in
1960.

Not all of the residue acreage belongs to the DDR, of course,
much of it being now incorporated into Soviet Russia or Poland,
east of the Oder-Neisse line. Of the 107,897 square kilometres of
East German territory, roughly two-thirds are devoted to agriculture, more than two-thirds of this (4·8 million hectares) being arable
land. Another three million hectares are forest. Climatologically,
she is not as favoured as West Germany, experiencing more the
weather conditions of North-East Europe. In addition, stretches of
her northern area are so water-logged or sandy that little can be
grown there. Her sea access, restricted as it is to the Baltic, is again
hardly to be considered a major advantage. Her communications
with the East—the main trade connection—are however based on
relatively easy access routes, across the plains of Poland and Silesia.
Her land and waterway routes to the West are also well developed,
though little used.

2. Official Economic Policy

The conclusion of hostilities in 1945 brought the four-fold
division of Germany into zones of occupation, the largest and most
easterly of them being that administered by the Soviet military

authorities. Russian policy was rigorous in the first post-war years. The wartime losses, in men and materials, had been severe for Russia, and her economy had been gravely undermined by Hitler's all but victorious onslaught that followed the treacherous attack of June 1941. The seeking of compensation was joined by a desire for revenge in the policies which they pursued in their zone of military administration.

Confiscation, expropriation, dismantling and demolition were the main features of economic policy in these early post-war years. Plant, equipment and even livestock that were needed for Russia's recovery and which could easily be transported were despatched eastwards; where industrial or commercial enterprises had their raison d'être in the German context, they were frequently taken over by the Russians and managed for their benefit. More than 200 industrial concerns were turned into Soviet joint stock companies (SAG), and were only returned to East German control in 1953. With the extensive funds which they had confiscated in banknotes and their considerable supply of 'occupation Marks' they bought up many other commodities and supplies for transportation back to Russia. The products of such plant as was left in German hands were also earmarked primarily for Russian consumption. East Germany became virtually a Russian industrial colony, helping to supply the victor's pressing needs. It is still a complaint of East Germany today that she was forced to pay reparations for many years, while West Germany escaped relatively lightly. Many of the goods and supplies that reached Russia as reparations payments were obtained by her at the cost of East German subsidies.

Allied policies at the time of Germany's capitulation in May 1945 were based on the resolve to restrict the German economy to a primarily agricultural role. The Potsdam Agreement of August 1945 concluded by the heads of the American, Russian and British governments granted total power to the occupying authorities, at all levels of government and administration, and refused to contemplate any central German government. At the same time it laid down that Germany was to be regarded as one economic unit for the duration of the occupation. Apart from industrial disarmament measures, it was stressed also that no steps were to be allowed which would help to preserve or strengthen the German economy. The Germans were to be made responsible for their supplies by their own efforts and out of their own resources. Consumption was to be maintained at a minimum figure while the standard of living was not to exceed that of any other European state. Money was to be spent only on the avoidance of famine, disease or civil unrest, and a strict non-fraternization policy was imposed. Severe restrictions were placed on all production which might be used for military purposes and the building of merchant ships was totally prohibited. Reparations-seizures were to be completed within the space of two years.

For a time this policy was rigorously pursued, but its severity was lessened in the Western zones much sooner than in the East. The Russians, partly because of their own domestic needs, maintained their iron grip on the East German economy after the Western powers, sensing the dangers of disaffection and complete loss of civilian morale in their zones, and conscious of their need for allies against Russian ambitions in Europe, decided to turn their captives into friends and embarked on a vast programme of economic assistance under the Marshall Aid scheme. The East Germans experienced no such radical change in their economic circumstances, and had to continue the compulsory delivery of goods to Russia for several years longer. Their ability to do this was reduced by the extent of Russian dismantling of their industry, which is estimated to have accounted for 45% of East German capacity—compared with a figure of 8% for the Western zones.

Another very considerable burden which the East Germans had to bear was that of a vast influx of refugees. It was not West Germany alone which felt the impact of the westward rush of German expellees and fugitives before the advance of the Russian armies, and again, later, following the division of Germany from Slavonic Europe along the Oder-Neisse line. Upwards of four million refugees checked their flight to settle in the territory which is today known as the German Democratic Republic, bringing with them problems every bit as great as those which faced those responsible for West German relief policies. Here, too, they constituted well over 20% of the indigenous population.[3]

The first industrial plan for Germany, worked out in March 1946 by the Allied Control Council, fixed industrial production at between 50% and 55% of the 1938 level. Any production in excess of this was to be seized as reparations or destroyed. Certain branches of industry were completely prohibited (e.g. the production of arms and ammunition, shipbuilding, the manufacture of numerous chemicals, radio equipment, heavy tractors, heavy machine tools, synthetic oil and rubber, and ball bearings). By the end of this same

3 West German figures for the total numbers of refugees are often ambiguously quoted (at times, one suspects, deliberately so). A grand total is frequently quoted, without any indication that many of these settled in East Germany, so that the burden seems to rest on West Germany alone. The numbers are sometimes further increased by including those children who have been born to refugee families since their arrival. In this way it has been possible to refer to as many as 15 million "refugees".

year, American leaders were calling for a policy for Germany's economic development; and following on the failure of the Foreign Ministers' Conference, in April 1947, to agree on terms for a central German government, the Western powers began to draw up an industrial plan for their zones. A German Economic Council for the American-British bi-zone had already been established in the January of 1947. The Marshall Aid Plan for Europe was proclaimed in June 1947, but the Russian Foreign Minister, Molotov, announced the refusal of his country to participate, and the remainder of Communist Europe was forced to withdraw from the scheme. The division of Europe, and of Germany, had become a reality, and East Germany found herself in the Russian camp.

Russian policy in the Soviet zone of occupation was already concentrated on the creation of a thorough-going Communist economic and political system. As early as September 1945, the big agricultural estates had been broken up and nationalized. All farms larger than 100 hectares in extent were confiscated and divided up among small farmers, refugees and other workers. In July 1946 all large-scale industrial undertakings were transferred to state ownership. The power of the upper classes and of big business was thus destroyed and the possibility of directing the economy placed more effectively in government hands. And in May 1946, the first postwar Leipzig trade fair had been held, at which initial contacts with foreign trade partners were made and orders were received which gave the economy its first boost. No other country in the world possesses such a highly developed industry based on such modest local resources. Imports of rolled steel, coal, mineral oil, metallurgical coke, iron ore, non-ferrous metals, cotton, wool, leather are essential to her economy. A corresponding volume of exports must therefore be maintained.

Deprived as she was of natural resources, and with no currency with which to purchase the necessary raw materials from abroad, East Germany struggled to survive, always under the ultimate control of the Soviet military administration. Even the burden of occupation costs, at 2,000 million marks a year, was one-third higher than in the West, for the Russians maintained a greater military presence in their zone than did the Western powers. Gradually, however, the Russians were able to hand over greater discretion to the East German authorities, as the process of communising the political life of the state (outlined in Section I, Part B) was extended and control was seen to reside firmly in the hands of such reliable party men as Pieck, Grotewohl and Ulbricht. The recognition of the East German government in 1949 was a public indication of this new relationship; but economically Russia still retained a dominant voice. A currency reform, similar to that of

West Germany (June 20th, 1948), was carried out from 24th–28th June 1948, thus enabling a fresh start to be made financially.

National economic planning was geared to the Soviet 'Gosplan' programme for the states of the Communist economic bloc, and was adjusted to Soviet needs rather than those of East Germany. Priorities were named and figures fixed for all key areas of production, in particular engineering, machinery, chemicals and electronics. Supplies came from the industrially under-developed countries to be processed and finished by the East Germans, with their superior technical knowledge and expertise, and were then re-exported to the destinations named in the master plan. The development of East German industry was quite intensive after 1946, but little of the benefit went to the East Germans. Domestic economic policies were directed increasingly at state ownership or control of all sectors of production, particularly from 1949 onwards, under the first East German economic plan. The national plans from now on gave favoured treatment to state enterprises with regard to investment credit, the supply of materials and taxation policy, and the contribution of private enterprise to the economy declined progressively over the years.

The Ministry of Foreign and Internal German Trade controlled almost all commercial life and directed the flow of commodities. In the year 1958, 74% of East German trade was with the Communist bloc, almost 60% of it with Russia. Trade with the West was conducted principally for the purpose of obtaining scarce materials. The concentration on heavy industrial production, with long hours of work and high output norms, plus the neglect of the consumer goods industries, led to severe unrest among the workers and culminated in the risings which took place in several parts of East Germany on 17th June, 1953. The danger signal was noted and the planning emphasis was shifted somewhat, to supply more of the needs of the civilian population.

The first economic plan had been a short-term one, to cover the years 1949 and 1950, while more comprehensive schemes were being worked out. It was followed by a succession of five- and seven-year plans, a practice which has been continued to the present day. Within these long-term projections, individual one-year plans are also drawn up. Initially, all sectors of the economy were the subject of the national plan, but the impracticability of the central planning of the minutiae of the economy presently became obvious, and the State Planning Commission now deals only with the essential commodities, such as electric power supplies, soft coal, briquettes, rolled steel, basic chemicals and similar items, whose output figures are fixed by the central planning authority. The planning of production for less important sectors is left to regional authorities, particularly the *Bezirk* and *Kreis* councils. Their detailed plans must nevertheless dovetail with the overall national allocation of resources and production targets laid down in the five-year and annual projections. Each sector of the economy is called upon to draw up its own specific plans for achieving the targets set for it in the national plan, and these plans are formulated at every level of that sector, from individual factory upwards, through *Gemeinde*, *Kreis* and *Bezirk*, to the central authority. Numerous factors must be taken into account, besides the mere quantities produced. There is supervision of the quality of the goods produced, as well as of the social need for their production. A check is kept on matters of quality, pricing, output volume and general standards by means of comparisons made with factories of the same size and operating to a similar programme in the same industry. Supervision of industry is provided by regular statistical reports collected at regional level, and by the Central Office of Statistics. Close analysis of these reports reveals those points in the economy where action needs to be taken, either to ease developing bottlenecks or to control economically or socially undesirable development. Control can be exercised in a number of ways, by the banks and financial institutions, by the factory directors and even by the trade union party within the factory.

The devolution of responsibility onto regional authorities came at a time when similar steps were being taken in Russia, after the fall of Khruschev from the premiership. Similar planning difficulties must be assumed, leading to a common acknowledgement of the need for more authority to be allowed to the regions. The firm hold of the SED party machine at all levels by this time made such a move practicable in East Germany. Economic councils were attached to the *Bezirk* councils to assist the process of planning, and *Kreis* councils were similarly reinforced. Their purpose was basically to ensure the coordinated development of the economy within their areas of competence, to draw up long-term and annual development plans, and also to give advice to the factory managements under their control. It was thus made possible to allow greater rights to local assemblies in planning decisions. A *Bezirk* council receives a monetary target for its industrial output, in which only a few products of particular importance are allocated specific goals, the rest of the detailed planning being left to the regional body. A comprehensive figure is likewise set for the numbers who are to be employed and for the sum to be spent, within the region, on wages and salaries. The total sum to be allocated to capital investment is likewise specified, the only quota that is fixed being that for housing and agriculture.

The directives, overall totals, bloc allocations and priorities are thus identified from above and passed down to the lower levels of control as far as the individual factory. There is a reverse movement to this, as local decisions are reached and communicated upwards through the chain of command. The process begins on the factory floor. Each factory committee is informed of the particular tasks which face the enterprise, and every year a production plan is worked out by workers and management which details the individual targets which the concern will assume and the methods by which it is proposed to achieve them. This plan is then submitted to the local planning commission, to be evaluated and incorporated into its area projections, which are then passed on to the next higher authority. The responsibilities assumed in the factory plan are no light ones, for the factory members are answerable—from works director down to individual worker—for the successful achievement of the goals which they have set themselves. Regional bodies are likewise held responsible for achieving their announced targets. To overbid one's hand, for prestige purposes, is every bit as dangerous as underbidding, which is rapidly identified by the system of comparisons. A tremendous flood of literature concerned with economic planning and industrial management has now filled East Germany's bookshops. There are, of course, expert technical advisers who assist in the drawing up of factory plans; most large concerns also have their own libraries with trained staffs to guide the workers' reading and also to lead discussions.

The transitional Two Year Plan of 1949–1950 having steered the East German economy into the appropriate channels (concentration on mining, electricity production, the engineering, metallurgical, chemical and building industries), the first Five Year Plan was launched in 1951. At the end of December 1946, industrial production had stood at only 42% of the 1936 level for the East German area, but at the end of 1950 it was announced that the economic plan for the year had been exceeded by 9%, an increase of 26% over 1949. The 1936 figures were exceeded by over 50% in the power, chemical and optical industries. There was, however, still an unsatisfactory situation with regard to the metallurgical, building materials and food industries, where production was considerably below pre-war figures. The first of the Five Year Plans having met all its targets by December 1955, thus more than doubling the pre-war gross industrial product, a second Five Year Plan was launched, providing for a 60% increase in industrial products and a 40% increase in consumer goods. This in its turn was to be succeeded by a further economic plan for 1960–65, upgraded on the strength of the previous plan's forecasts having been surpassed. It was intended that by 1965 industrial output should be five times that of 1936. The annual growth rate for industry was now fixed at between 6% and 9%.

Speakers at SED congresses even spoke of East Germany presently overtaking West Germany in per capita consumption of all essential foodstuffs and consumer goods.

These years witnessed what was, however, a crisis period in East German economic planning. The development can be traced back as far as the year 1956, when a general liberalizing of the political atmosphere (with the advent of the Khruschev era) led to more active discussion of planning alternatives and the emergence of a faction which wished to see a greater degree of economic freedom, in the interests of increased efficiency. The de-collectivization of agriculture was even proposed by some. Ulbricht and the older party members, however, were resolute in their determination to follow the new Soviet pattern of decentralization of control, coupled with the extension of state supervision of economic policy; they rejected the plea for a gradual 'withering away' of the state. The state-party won this particular debate and the economic liberalists were discredited. In April 1957, the Economic Council was created as the central body for policy decisions. A conspiracy to remove Ulbricht from the leadership was defeated and his opponents dismissed from office, leaving him stronger than ever to pursue his aim of matching living conditions in East Germany with those in the Federal Republic. At the same time pressure for the diplomatic recognition of the DDR was intensified. But the second Five Year Plan had been interrupted by the debate, and in 1958 a Seven Year Plan was adopted instead.

Early in 1960, in his attempt to bring even more of the East German economy under direct control, Ulbricht announced the nationalization of the 50% of farms that had remained outside the state-owned sector. The measure was rushed through in record time, and led to a spate of refugee flights to West Berlin, which became one of the principal reasons for the building of the Berlin Wall in 1961. These events were followed by a decision to attempt to become fully independent of the West, by producing within the DDR many items which had hitherto been imported through Berlin. The diversion of East German industrial capacity to these purposes was opposed by economic and production experts, but the politicians won the day; the policy was, nevertheless, presently to be abandoned, with the annual growth rate falling from the 8% of the 1950s to $2 \cdot 3\%$ in 1960/62.

The policy debates had, up to now, been won by the politicians and old-style theorists in the DDR: the professional economists and efficiency experts had been repulsed in every confrontation. But from 1963 the influence of the latter grew increasingly strong at all levels of policy-making, and the politicians found their hold progressively undermined. (The developments are outlined by T. A.

Baylis, in the October issue of *Survey*, 1966.) The great slow-down of economic growth in 1962/63, the failure of investment to match up to the planned figures and serious disproportions in the economy led to a rehabilitation of the professional economists and a seeking of their guidance out of the planning dilemma. The outcome was the creation of the New Economic System, or NöSPL (*Das neue ökonomische System der Planung und Leitung der Volkswirtschaft*), devised at the sixth SED party congress in January 1963 and emerging into definitive shape in the following June, after much intensive discussion. Economic principles now became the basis on which production was to be planned, and the profit factor emerged as one of the key elements in the new efficiency drive. At the planning centre stood the National Economic Council (*Volkswirtschaftsrat*) which delegated responsibility for detailed planning to more than 80 group organizations, or VVBs, which represent different sectors of the national economy. This arrangement left the National Economic Council free to deal with the planning of long-term policy and the overseeing of the national economy from a total point of view. The directors of the VVBs consequently become key figures in the nation's economy, though increased responsibility has also been given to the directors of the enterprises themselves. (A recent visitor to East Germany found these individuals to be almost identical with their western counterparts.) Even the party organization of the SED has been modified in such a way that each sector of production is covered by a branch of the party that has been created to specialize in the economics and problems of that sector, and therefore better equipped to understand and advise.

Ulbricht himself embraced the new philosophy and busily propounded it. The catchwords now are technology and science, and their adaptation to the creation of a new society characterized by unprecedented material well-being. It is the East German counter to West Germany's pride in her 'economic miracle'.

The New Economic System suffered a setback in 1965, when Erich Apel, one of its chief architects, committed suicide in November of that year. Opinions vary as to whether his suicide was the result of overwork and strain (the official version) or the result of his unavailing opposition to the government's (*i.e.* Ulbricht's) intention to sign a long-term trade agreement with Russia, which would be economically disadvantageous. No doubt both explanations are valid. The five-year agreement provided for an exchange of commodities, in which Russia would reportedly pay abnormally low prices for East German goods, while East Germany bought Russian materials at excessively high cost. Apel is said to have preferred a transfer of East German trading to the Western powers, who were technologically far ahead of the Russians, with consequent gains for the East Germans. Political considerations won the day, and the struggle between the political party and the economic realists continues still, with Günther Mittag the main proponent of the new economic thinking. Even the formulation of the 1965–70 plan was delayed by this conflict of views. At the eleventh congress of the SED, in December 1965, Ulbricht eventually announced the beginning, in 1966, of the second stage of the New Economic System. The reform of prices, so that they corresponded to actual production costs, was to be completed, and the VVBs were to be made more responsible for finding their investment funds out of their own profits and from borrowed funds. The Council of Ministers was reorganized and four of the ten Deputy Prime Ministers were dropped, to be replaced by economic experts, two of whom (the heads of the Chemicals and Heavy Industry Ministries) had previously been directors of VVBs. At the same time the National Economic Council was abolished as a superfluous producer of paperwork and was replaced by nine new industrial ministries, under the supervision of the Planning Commission. The preponderant number of officials employed in these ministries are trained economists and business experts, and the role of the politicians has been correspondingly reduced in the East German state. The Council of Ministers is dominated by economists, but in the last resort the politicians in the SED Politburo hold the whip hand, with only a sprinkling of professional economist influence, and decisions on fundamental issues like international policies and on Ulbricht's successor[4] will continue to be made here. This uneasy balance of forces seems destined to persist for some time, and the events of 1968 in Czechoslovakia will not have favoured the liberalizers. The directors of the VVBs protested at the high levels set for production in 1970, but were censured for their lack of enterprise and drive. In the end they were proved to have been right—partly because of the lack of organization and rationalization within industry to meet the demands of the planners, who are ruthlessly determined on output increases. Ulbricht was already forced to concede, in 1969, that productivity in the DDR was 20% lower than in West Germany, and the West German Institute for Economic Research put the figure at 30%. Plans for 1970–75 foresee a somewhat slower rate of growth, both in production and household consumption.

East Germany's achievement would have been impossible without the active support of Russia. It has been an even more import-

[4] Ulbricht's resignation, in May 1971, was held by many observers to have been designed by the politicians to replace the 77-year-old leader with a hard-line successor (Erich Honecker, aged 58) before liberal tendencies set in.

ant factor in her post-war recovery than has American support in West Germany's 'economic miracle'. In the first place, East Germany has been very much more dependent on the supply of capital and supplies from her Soviet supporter, and secondly, it has been very much to Russia's advantage, one might almost say vital to her interests, to build up the productive power of the East German state. At first, as we saw, the Russian attitude was very much that of the conqueror who urgently needed to replenish her own diminished resources. Slowly her approach moved from that of exploitation towards one in which East Germany was regarded as a trading partner, and also a shining example of Communist economic planning.

Once the East German economy had been placed on a fully socialist footing, she could be developed as a unit of the East European bloc. Already in the early post-war years Soviet aid in the form of capital loans and raw material supplies had been forthcoming, and in January 1957 an East German mission to Russia achieved a 30% increase in the delivery of Russian goods, plus a credit grant of 340 million roubles. A real rapprochement between the two states took place in 1957, following the dismissal of the Soviet leaders Malenkov, Shepilov and Kaganovitch and the advent to power of Nikita Khruschev. The summer of 1957 witnessed the first official visits to East Germany by leading figures in the Communist movement: firstly by Mr Gomulka, the new Polish leader, whose visit was the occasion for an agreement over Germany's lost eastern territories and East German acceptance of the Oder/Neisse frontier with Poland. Then, in the August of 1957, came Khruschev himself, accompanied significantly by his Trade Minister, Mr Mikoyan. Long talks between Mikoyan and the East German leaders resulted in firmer arrangements for the exchange of Russian raw materials for East German finished products, especially machinery. Russia is reported to have promised to help ease the power shortages in East Germany by sending five million tons of hard coal and a million tons of coke, as well as to increase the basic deliveries of iron ore, pig iron and sheet metal. The East German authorities appear to have undertaken to increase exports of chemicals, heavy machinery and precision instruments (these had previously been seriously in arrears).

All the signs point to a very considerable increase in East German industrial development since the middle of 1957, and in future years it may be possible to look back to this date as the starting point of a new Russian policy for East Germany. Meanwhile, Russian financial support also continues, and a massive loan of 1,300 million marks was made to the East German government in March 1962. A long-term trade agreement of 1959 provided for the delivery to

East Germany of almost all types of raw materials including mineral oil, iron, rolled steel, copper, aluminium, coke, apatite, timber and cellulose for a period of seven years. Oil exports were to be quintupled, until they amounted to 4·8 million tons annually from 1961 onwards. In 1961, Russia declared her readiness to supply all those commodities which West Germany was then supplying, and whose delivery was being threatened.

The Russian share of East German Trade is considerable. 75% of exports from the DDR go to countries in the Communist bloc, 50% of them to Russia herself. Two-thirds of these exports consist of machinery, which is so badly needed by the developing Communist states (four-fifths of the exports to Russia and China are machinery). The value of exports rose by 180% during the first Five Year Plan, and by another 70% in the course of the second one. One third of Russia's total requirements of uranium also comes from East German mines in the Erzgebirge. In December 1965, the controversial long-term trade agreement was signed between East Germany and Russia, which provided for the exchange of 60 milliard marks' worth of goods in the next five years and showed East Germany as a trading equal of Russia and vital supplier of her economy, where only a few years previously Russia had been the economic master. The trade figures for 1968 show that Russian imports from East Germany are greater than from any other individual country, and exceed in value Russian exports to the DDR.

The year 1956 saw the introduction of the principle of long-term co-ordination and integration of the national economic plans of all the Communist-bloc CMEA states (Council for Mutual Economic Aid). Under this scheme comes the development of East Germany's chemical industry, the construction of a long-distance oil pipeline from the Soviet Union to other member states, the development of a collective power industry, as well as increased attention to specialization and co-operation between member states in the field of production. The East Germans have assisted other CMEA states in the development of industries of their own, to aid their economic progress. Between 1966 and 1970 she was to deliver 100 complete chemical plants to the Soviet Union. In the face of this ever greater and ever deeper integration of the East German economy into that of the Soviet bloc, it seems that the prospect of German reunification is receding progressively as time goes by. A friendship treaty between the two states, signed on June 12th, 1964, brought them closer together than ever. The DDR was guaranteed military protection against a Western attack, and she promised similar aid to Russia. This treaty led to the five-year trade agreement of 1965.

Trade with the West plays a much smaller role in the East German economy. This arises not only from the nature of the DDR's close integration with the Communist camp and the seeking to strengthen her relations with the non-aligned nations. It is also the result of the refusal on the part of the West to recognize the East German regime, so that there is no official contact with the government agencies which control East German trade: it also arises from a western embargo on the sale of various strategic commodities to the Communist bloc. Trade with West Germany has nevertheless been fostered and for a time grew steadily: from a figure of 282 million marks in 1952 it rose to 1,000 million marks in 1955 and by 1958 reached the 1,800 million marks level. Intervention by the West German government (which imposed strict limits on iron and steel deliveries, as well as on the engineering and machinery industries, hard coal and electricity plant) then brought a falling-off of exchanges, which only began to pick up again after 1963 and had reached a figure of 2,200 million marks by 1966. This must be compared with a total East German foreign trade turnover of 26,573 million marks in the same year. 72% of this trade was with the socialist states, with Russia as chief customer.

Foreign trade is a state monopoly in East Germany. Trade agencies conduct the import/export transactions for their particular sector of industry, acting as sales organs of the various associations of nationally-owned enterprises (VVBs). In this way, foreign sales have an impact on the economic budgeting and profit and loss account of the individual industries; under an earlier arrangement the close relationship of sales agency to industry was not achieved, and the subordinating of these agencies in the form of branch companies to the VVBs was seen as a means of encouraging the latter's interest in an efficient foreign trade policy. We have here one more reflection of the economic reforms of 1963. These VVBs do their own advertising, marketing, price-fixing and research and development. Some of the larger individual firms are now permitted to deal directly with foreign clients. Zeiss of Jena is a typical example. Overall supervision is exercised by the Ministry of Foreign Trade. An active participation in overseas trade fairs and the regular holding of trade fairs at home is another feature of East Germany's attempt to expand her trade connections. In the year 1966 alone, she took part in 23 international fairs and exhibitions. In addition to these government-promoted ventures, individual enterprises also held exhibitions or conferences in 50 different countries.

A new principle of state participation was introduced in 1956, whereby the government enters into a trading partnership with a private producer or trader, holding 50% of the capital invested in the enterprise and leaving the former owner in charge as manager of the concern's affairs and responsible to the state for the management of his enterprise. This form of indirect control has been applied in particular to commerce and retail trading, where complete state control is a less practicable proposition. Private enterprise had, in consequence, already declined from a 52·7% share of retail trade turnover in 1950, to 30·4% in 1956 and 27% by 1958. State partnerships accounted for 10% of the gross industrial product in 1966, compared with private enterprise's 2·1%. Less than 7% of wholesale turnover is now in private hands. The handicraft trades also have been organized into production co-operatives (PGHs) which give them, among other things, access to wider markets, more sophisticated machinery, cheaper supplies and better research facilities. Whereas in 1955 there were only 85 such handicraft co-operatives, by 1960 the figure had grown to 3,878, and in 1966 stood at 4,235. Their share of total craft production stood at 0·3% in 1955, 28·5% in 1960 and 41·7% in 1966. The years 1956–59 stand out therefore as a crucial period in economic planning.

We are now able to identify three varieties of state control in the East German economic system. There are firstly the nationally owned enterprises, which include those taken over entirely from big business interests and the large landowners (1945–47), supplemented later by the establishment of new plants and industrial enterprises. These form the predominant sector, representing 56·3% of the industrial gross product in 1947, and 87·9% in 1966. National property includes the mineral resources, the greater part of industry, the traffic and banking systems, insurance, postal and telecommunications services, most of the large wholesale firms and a considerable proportion of retail trade shops, as well as the nationally owned farms. Secondly there are the various forms of co-operatives (agricultural, handicrafts, wholesale and retail trade etc.), representing varying degrees of communal ownership and state direction and always with a very small private element. Thirdly, there are the state partnerships, where private capital and state investment are represented on an equal footing. In 1966, nationally owned concerns accounted for 72·6% of the gross social product, co-operatives for 14·2%, state partnerships 6·9% and private enterprise 6·3%.

Of the 7,714,000 people employed in 1968, 5,480,000 worked in state enterprises, 1,041,000 in co-operatives, 420,000 in semi-state enterprises and 773,000 in private concerns. The ten largest industrial employers were textiles (280,000), chemicals (275,000), electrical engineering (230,000), general engineering (205,000), foodstuffs (200,000), mining (190,000), heavy engineering (180,000), vehicle building (145,000), wood and artistic goods (140,000) and metallurgy (110,000).

The banks and finance houses were taken over by the state immediately in 1945, and are a fundamental part of the national system of finance and investment. The principal bank is the *Industrie- und Handelsbank* (Industrial and Commercial Bank) founded in January 1968, which took over the chief functions of the *Deutsche Notenbank,* leaving the latter to operate purely as an issuing bank under the title *Staatsbank der DDR* (DDR State Bank). The banks of East Germany are primarily economic banks, helping in the promotion of the national plan through credits and investments in the business world and the contribution of economic advice to planning councils. Since the VVBs and their subordinate enterprises are largely self-financing, the banks perform a considerable service to them through loans and investment grants, which are carefully vetted for their economic acceptability.

State revenue is derived to a large extent from the profits of the nationally owned enterprises. As greater economic efficiency and rising production bring increased revenues, it is hoped that the proportion of taxation can be reduced. When state budgets are framed, a fixed amount of the profits of state enterprises is reserved to these concerns for investment in expansion and reorganization. The figure for 1965 was 4·4 billion marks. Profits made by local or regional authorities, arising from their efficient operation, may also be retained for their own purposes, as decided by their elected representatives.

3. *The Statistics of Success*

There can be no doubting the successes achieved by the East German economy in recent years. By 1966 she had climbed to the position of fifth largest producing country of Europe (following Russia, West Germany, Britain, and France), and stood level with Italy as a trading nation. By 1970 she was the world's eighth largest industrial power, and had the highest standard of living of all the Eastern bloc nations. Her production figures for 1964 were equal to the pre-war figures of the entire German Reich, of which the DDR constitutes less than one-quarter by size. It had been a long haul, and was not achieved without privations for the East German citizen, who by and large has not derived the personal benefits from the national achievement that his West German cousin now enjoys.

The early years were, as we have seen, beset with all manner of impeding circumstances, but by 1958 industrial output had reached a figure 166% higher than that of 1936, and 141% higher than that for 1951. In 1936, soft coal output in the East German area was 97 million tons; in 1958 the total was 215 million tons—roughly half the world total output. The 1968 figure was 247 million tons and the target for 1970 was 300 millions. In 1966, soft coal still accounted for 80% of all power supplies. To achieve this output new and highly sophisticated excavation plant was designed and built by East German engineers, machinery which is now much sought after by other countries with extensive soft coal reserves. Another considerable handicap was the complete lack of metallurgical coke for smelting (East Germany possessing virtually no hard coal). The problem was overcome by the scientists who devised a process for the production of metallurgical coke from soft coal. It is now being manufactured in large quantities by the newly built Lauchhammer cokery. At Calbe, the world's first metallurgical combine operating with low-shaft furnaces was built, making it possible to use inferior grades of ore found in East Germany. Electricity production has also greatly increased and is extensively used by industry. Present-day capacity is helped by two large power stations, the biggest in the world operating on soft coal, which when ready in 1965 generated more power than Holland and Luxemburg between them. Production in 1960 was 40,300 million kilowatts, and in 1968 63,200 million kilowatts.

The fuel and power industry, taking 1955 = 100, reached a gross output level of 124 in 1960, 153 in 1965 and 172 in 1968. The metallurgical industry achieved a figure of 145 in 1960, 176 in 1965 and 207 in 1968. Industry as a whole (again taking 1955 = 100) rose from a production figure of 42 in 1949 to 155 in 1960, 207 in 1965 and 249 in 1968. The biggest increases are recorded in the electro-technical, machinery, building materials and chemical industries, the first two recording figures of 411 and 309 compared with 1955, while the latter two almost trebled their output. Industrial investment increased, from a base of 100 in 1958, to 131 in 1960, 140 in 1962 and 365 in 1965. Productivity in industry generally increased (taking 1955 as the base) to 141 in 1960, 188 in 1965 and 225 in 1968. Again it was the electro-technical, machinery and vehicles, building materials and chemical industries that led the field, with textiles and light industry close behind.

The chemical industry is maintaining the traditional strong position which it has always occupied in German production and stands in second place, with 15·6% of total production to its credit. Synthetic fibres (*e.g.* Perlon, Lanon, Wolcrylon and Dederon) show particular increases in output. The largest industrial plant in East Germany is the Leuna chemical works at Leipzig: it was a heap of rubble in 1945, but now produces very much more than in 1939, when it was already an industrial giant. Synthetic rubber and fertilizers for much of eastern Europe are produced here. A strong chemical industry broadens the raw materials basis for the processing industries, and in East Germany particular emphasis is being placed on the development of plastics and fully synthetic fibres. A four-fold expansion of the plastics industry was projected in the third Five Year Plan of 1960–65. Chemicals are the leading growth industry of the DDR and have received the largest share of investment funds. The Leuna II Chemical Works, thanks to a high degree of automation, is able to produce with 2,000 what the older Leuna I works produced with 30,000 workers.

The engineering industry, particularly the machinery and vehicle-manufacturing section, is marked out for the next biggest degree of development. Machine tools, precision engineering and optical ware, electrical products, measuring and control systems, textile and printing machinery and packing machines—these are the key sectors of the programme, and in 1960 showed an overall increase of 50% compared with 1955, a rate which was further increased in the subsequent years. This is the largest sector of the East German economy. The accent in recent years has been on the development of calculating and automation-serving machinery. The DDR holds fifth place among the world's exporters of office machines. Some of the new machines designed by East German engineers hold a leading position in the world market (*e.g.* printing and optical apparatus); 70% of her textile machinery output is exported. Engineering products generally accounted for well over half of East Germany's exports in 1968. The steel embargo enforced by the West has compelled the East Germans to develop their own metallurgical industry. Before the war, this part of Germany produced 1,300,000 tons of steel annually, but by 1958 this figure had been increased to over 3,000,000 tons. Pig iron output increased almost five-fold between 1950 and 1957, and local deposits of nickel, zinc and copper were also more intensively developed. Output figures in the metallurgical industry rose to a figure of 122 in 1965, taking 1960 = 100, and to 143 in 1968. Raw steel production in 1968 amounted to 4,374,000 tons, rolled steel to 3,176,000 tons, and pig iron to 2,330,000 tons.

New industries have also come to the fore since 1945. Before the war, there was no shipbuilding worth mention in the present East German ports (N.B. Stettin and Danzig now belong to Poland). Today, however, Rostock, Warnemünde, Stralsund and Wismar are flourishing shipbuilding centres. Output was doubled between 1950 and 1965, largely as a result of the extensive use of automation and prefabrication. The Warnow shipyard at Warnemünde possesses the largest indoor assembly plant in Europe, and by April 1959 had already launched ten 10,000 ton freighters. Most of the ships are built for supply to Russia. Profits, by April 1964, were seven million marks higher than had been estimated.

Oil is now emerging as a competitor to coal, as the raw material basis for the chemical industry. The exploitation of domestic oil deposits is as yet relatively unimportant and most of the oil is imported from Russia. A major supply source is the 4,000 kilometres long pipeline which runs from the Soviet oilfields at Kuibyshev in the Urals, with links to several East European states, and supplies a vast 16-acres refinery and fertilizer plant newly constructed at Schwedt on the river Oder. The Leuna works at Halle, similarly linked, refine supplies for the southern half of the country.

Atomic power stations will soon reinforce oil and coal as producers of electricity. The first atomic station was opened at Rheinsberg in 1966. Gas is also growing in importance as a source of power, and the pressure conversion works at the Schwarze Pumpe (Cottbus) concern now produce a quantity of gas greater than the total output of 200 gas works in the DDR in 1966. The DDR is one of the world's leading producers of power: by 1965 electric energy output amounted to 56·61 billion kilowatt hours (three times the 1950 figure), while gas production totalled 3·4 billion cubic metres (more than twice the 1950 figure). Very large power stations have been built in the middle of the lignite mining area of Cottbus-Senftenberg, and these supply the vast majority of East German needs. The Lübbenau power station, opened in 1964, generates enough electricity to supply Berlin's needs five times over. A long-distance supply network with a capacity of up to 400,000 volts carries power to all parts of the country, and there are links also with the power systems of the East European states. Total production, in 1968, was 3·765 kwh per head of the population, compared with a West German figure of only 3·380. East Germany has a greater dependence on electrical power, however, and still suffers from shortages.

In the textiles field, too, East Germany has achieved a significant technological break-through with the development of the Malimo machine, which combines the sewing and knitting processes into one. At the Malitex cotton mill, 13 such machines now produce 5·6 million square metres of fabrics a year, where previously 225 conventional weaving looms produced 3·5 million square metres. Production of textiles rose from a base of 100 in 1960 to 131 in 1968, and accounted for 7·4% of industrial output.

Between 1950 and 1965, the gross national income of the DDR rose as follows:

	1950	1955	1958	1963	1965
Billion Marks:	30·3	52·6	64·9	76·7	83·5

By 1969 it had reached a figure of 100 billion marks, just over a quarter of the West German figure. Total annual investment increased from 16·8 billion marks in 1963 to 28 billions in 1970, and an increase in productivity of 65% was looked for in the same period.

Both exports and imports have grown apace. East Germany's economy is utterly dependent on imports: 70% of its hard coal requirements, 50% of its iron ore, 100% of its bauxite and petroleum, 50% of its rolled sheet metal and seamless tubes and 70% of its metallurgical coke must be imported, together with certain foodstuffs and much machinery. 95% of her mineral oil, iron ore, grains and butter come from the Soviet Union, likewise 70% of her hard coal, wool and rolled steel and 45% of her meat supplies. To balance this a high level of exports is necessary. The metal processing industries contribute more than 50% to the exports total (more than a half of this from engineering), followed by a 20% contribution from light industry and foodstuffs, 16% from the chemical industry and 7% from the basic materials industries. Deliveries of machinery, or even entire plants, are an important part of this trade. Printing plants, textile factories, glass factories, sugar factories, refrigeration buildings, bakeries, milling, oil extraction and refining plant are all included in the 440 which were exported between 1955 and 1962. More than 500 complete production plants have been installed in 27 different countries, 400 of them in countries of the Communist world, and 93 in developing nation states, and the intention is to expand this type of trade. Foreign trade turnover in 1965 amounted to 24,700 million foreign exchange marks, of which 18,240 was with socialist states and 5,346 millions with the capitalist world. The figures for 1968 were 30,123 millions, 22,938 millions and 5,951 millions respectively. Taking 1960 = 100, the volume of exports and imports followed this pattern :

EXPORTS			IMPORTS	
Year	Total	Exports to Socialist States	Total	Imports from Socialist States
1961	103·6	103·7	102·9	107·3
1963	122	127·9	106·4	110·4
1965	143·1	139·9	130·1	130·9
1967	164·5	161·9	157·8	158·8

The balance of trade has been consistently favourable. In 1960, exports totalled 9,270 million foreign exchange marks, and imports 9,216 millions; in 1965 the figures were 12,892 millions and 11,800 millions respectively, and in 1968 15,893 millions and 14,229 millions respectively.

The home market has not been entirely neglected, though the proportion of private consumption in the social product dropped from 62% in 1960 to 54% in 1969, while the West German figure remained constant. The emphasis has been on price stability, as much as on increasing supplies. Between 1952 and 1957 retail sales prices were actually reduced by 32%. The figures for production of certain consumer goods reveal a steady increase in the DDR's output:

	1960	1965
Refrigerators	138,569	364,805
Motor cars	64,071	102,877
Radio sets and radiograms	809,582	808,008
Television sets	416,490	536,744
Washing machines	132,461	288,908

A comparison with West German figures showed the East Germans still some considerable way behind in these fields however. The picture on the food front is again not as good as in West Germany, but very much better than in 1958, when East Germany became the last country of Europe to abandon food rationing; certain commodities, in particular meat and butter, are still in short supply, and domestic fuel and electricity shortages occurred as recently as the very severe winter of 1969/70. Instead of being officially rationed with scarce foods, householders have had to register at one particular shop, from which alone they could draw their allocation. This ensured price control and an equal share for all. A comparison of prices for a wide range of foodstuffs and consumer goods in 1963 showed them in nearly all cases to be cheaper in West Germany than in the East, but the much greater rate of inflation that has affected West German prices since then has changed this situation considerably.

Wage comparisons are not very meaningful in themselves, but we may note that in 1970 the average West German worker received a net wage of 1,000 DM a month, while in East Germany the comparable figure was 650 DM. Deductions are far higher in the Federal Republic, rising from 15·7% of earnings in 1960 to 20·8% in 1969, whereas East German contributions remained fairly constant around 13·5%. Nevertheless, while gross income has almost doubled since 1960 in West Germany, it has only risen by a third in the DDR. Against this must be set the fact that prices and rents have risen astronomically in recent years in the West, but have remained almost constant in the East. Rents accounted for only 3·4% of domestic expenditure in 1969, compared with 12·5% in the West. Even so, the West German government analysis, drawn up in 1970,[5] claims that the gap in real incomes between the Federal Republic and the DDR grew from about 32% in 1960 to about 45% in 1969.

The basic East German norm is a 40-hour working week; until 1967 it was 45 hours. (A decree of 1961 had fixed a 45-hour week

[5] *Bericht zur Lage der Nation*, presented to the Bundestag on 28th January 1971 (see table p. 249).

for state industry and a 48-hour week for private industry.) The six-day working week is thus now virtually a thing of the past. One difficulty that has arisen here is the shortage of labour: it is estimated that 800,000 more workers are needed for the achievement of the expansion which is now planned. In addition to full male employment, 70% of all women between the ages of 15 and 60 are in part- or full-time employment; they represent 45% of a trade union membership of $6\frac{1}{2}$ millions. Labour supplies are virtually exhausted, and everywhere one encounters advertisements for labour of every conceivable kind. Hence the campaign for greater efficiency and the high rate of investment in automation in recent years. Labour productivity increased generally by 173% between 1950 and 1963, and was planned to increase by a further 65% by 1970, so that the industrial output figure for 1970 would be 60% above that for 1963. In the event there was a slight shortfall, partly the result of two bad winters in 1969 and 1970. (Productivity in fact amounted to only 85% of the comparable West German achievement.)

Annual investment increased by 170% compared with 1963, and the annual industrial income by 130%. Industrial production in 1970 was one-and-a-half times that of the entire German Reich of 1936. The feeding of some of the benefits to the ordinary citizen is now planned; real income is expected to rise 21–23% between 1970 and 1975, working hours are to be further reduced, holidays lengthened and old age pensions increased. This will constitute the third phase of the long-term economic plan.

The Federal Government Report of 1971 nevertheless concluded that the efficiency gap between the two states was widening. Figures for the social product, for economic productivity and for the standard of living were quoted in support of this claim. With 34% of the labour force and 30% of the industrial potential of West Germany, East German industry only produced about 25% of what its Western rival achieved between 1960 and 1968. (Report of 28 January, 1971.)

4. *Agriculture*

Almost two thirds of the total land area of the DDR is devoted to agriculture (6·4 million hectares), of which 4·6 million hectares are arable land. The area of forest takes up another 2·9 million hectares. As we have seen above (p. 108), the vast majority of farms are now organized either into LPGs or VEGs. However, this was not always the case. The original land reform created 745,000 holdings (about twice as many as in Britain). Such units were far too small to work economically or afford the level of mechanization that was called for. The amount of labour which they employed was also excessive and rendered them even less economically viable. They even bought their supplies individually, thus increasing their costs.

Investment in agriculture was clearly relegated to second place in economic planning, leading to shortages in the supply of certain foodstuffs, which the authorities themselves have from time to time acknowledged. The second Five Year Plan, which began on 1st January 1956, foresaw an increase of only 22% in agricultural production by 1960. The problem of low agricultural output was no doubt behind the decision, taken in 1960, to collectivize the private sector of farming. The private ownership of land was thereby virtually abolished. But even three years later, in April 1963, the admission had to be made by Ulbricht himself that the production of foodstuffs—especially eggs, meat and milk—was lagging dangerously. The government voiced its fears that a resort to higher food imports would reduce the level of raw material imports for industrial production—and the consumer had to tighten his belt. Insufficient mechanization and investment, plus low working morale, were at the root of the trouble. Some output figures showed no improvement over the pre-war totals: field crop yields had remained static, while those in West Germany had risen by 20–25%. The dairy industry actually appeared to be going into a decline, and beef production was also showing a downward trend, the production target for 1963 being 10% lower than for 1961.

The advent of the New Economic System, which allowed co-operatives to work on a profit basis, with a greater degree of investment, mechanization and subsidization, together with the right accorded to the members of retaining a small area of land for the growing of private produce (each LPG member may keep up to half a hectare of private land, and a maximum of two cows, two pigs and five sheep, with no limit on poultry), led to a revival in the agricultural industry. The co-operative farms have also received preferential treatment from the state-owned tractor stations, which supply most of the farmers' requirements in machinery and vehicles, including maintenance. Considerable tax concessions have also been used to induce the farmers to become fully collectivized. The reward is 25% less income tax, 50% less property tax and 75% less purchase tax. Low interest rates are charged on long-term credits for development purposes, and interest of only 2% is payable on short-term borrowings for the purchase of seeds, fertilizers and the hire of mechanical assistance. Most of the state farms now have extensive communal and social services at a conveniently close distance, such as laundries, baths and showers, nurseries and kindergartens, clinics, club rooms, sports grounds and youth centres. Some even have their own housing schemes. Improved methods of cultivation, the result of intensive research activity, have also begun to take effect, and collective buying of supplies and marketing of produce have reduced prices. Investment has been intensive in recent years. In 1964 and 1965 some 370 million marks in excess of the annual plan were allocated to agriculture, and yielded an extra 900 million marks. The 1960 investment level of 1,632 million marks had risen to a figure of 2,721 millions in 1966. The industry's share of national investment grew from $11 \cdot 8\%$ in 1960 to $14 \cdot 4\%$ in 1966. Agriculture's contribution to the national income for 1966 was 12%; it then employed $15 \cdot 9\%$ of the labour force. The 1966–70 plan increased the volume of investments by a further 40%.

The mechanization drive resulted in the number of tractors being doubled and combine harvester figures trebled between 1960 and 1968. In 1968, practically the whole of the grain and sugar beet crop was mechanically harvested, and 55% of the potato crop.

The production of many commodities had risen appreciably too. The yield per hectare of grain increased almost two-fold between 1949 and 1969, that of potatoes by 50%, while the sugar beet yield was actually doubled. The number of cattle rose by over a half in the same period, that of pigs was more than doubled; sheep almost doubled their numbers, and laying hens quadrupled their 1949 total. The benefit to the consumer is revealed in the following list of produce for the years 1950–1968 :

| Year | Poultry | Pork | Beef | Milk | Butter | Eggs |
		(1,000 tons weight)				(millions)
1950	—	217·3	158·6	1,739·4	71·2	314·3
1955	3·7	637·0	233·3	3,301·0	143·8	1,031·2
1960	27·0	685·1	377·4	4,878·3	174·6	2,176·3
1965	51·4	880·0	441·8	5,693·6	197·4	2,908·5
1968	73·2	980·6	566·3	6,530·3	221·6	3,060·1

The food situation has also been helped by a considerable growth of activity by the newly built fishing fleet : the total catch of 44,253 tons in 1951, when the East Germans scarcely possessed a fishing fleet, grew to one of 302,104 tons in 1968. By 1967, the East German authorities claimed to have achieved self-sufficiency in meat, milk, eggs, sugar and potatoes, with only a slight deficiency in the butter supply; and 76% of the grain, 84% of the vegetables and 48% of the fruit requirements. Recent reports of shortages in some of

168

those commodities (especially meat and butter) suggest that government and consumer do not see eye to eye on what constitutes an adequate supply. Nevertheless, a significant improvement has undoubtedly taken place since the 1950s.

Section IV

The Welfare State

A. WEST GERMANY

1. *Social Security*

A considerable range of social legislation was already in being[1] when the first West German government assumed the responsibilities of office in 1949, and this has been progressively extended. The biggest single step forward came in 1957, with the programme of social reform which was then introduced. In this year the entire system of pensions insurance was revised, to provide pensions not only significantly higher than had previously been available to sick and retired persons, but also to relate the levels of benefit to earnings and the current social situation.

Today social insurance is compulsory for the vast majority of West Germans. More than 87% are covered by sickness insurance (29 million members with a further 22½ million dependents). The proportion of those belonging to the pensions insurance schemes is scarcely lower, while 34½ millions are covered by compulsory accident insurance. This is far more than the total number of employed persons (22 million) and indicates a considerable degree of voluntary membership by those independent social groups who are not covered by the compulsory provisions of this legislation. In 1960, compulsory pensions insurance was extended to cover all independent craft workers who had not been contributors to a private scheme for at least eighteen years, while in 1957 farmers were provided for in a special retirement pension scheme for self-supporting participants in agriculture. Other groups of independent persons have also organized themselves into regional insurance associations, so that practically the entire West German population is today brought under the terms of the overall plan for social security.

Perhaps the most important field of insurance is that against illness. Contributions to this fund are shared by both worker and employer, in like amounts, at a rate equal to about 10% of earnings, up to a maximum earnings level of 900 DM a month (figure for 1968). This insurance pays for medical treatment, drugs, medicines and hospitalization. From the third day of illness, members receive 90% of their normal pay (the comparable figure for Britain

---

[1] Bismarck had introduced sickness and accident insurance for all workers as early as 1883 and 1884, and death and retirement benefits were added in 1889. Germany was the pioneer of Europe here. Unemployment insurance was introduced in 1927.

in 1963 was 36%); for the first six weeks between 65% and 75% of this amount is paid from insurance funds and the rest by the employer. After this, the sum is met entirely from the insurance. It is basically 75% of the normal basic wage, but with dependents' allowances can rise to 85%. The workers' dependents are also covered by this scheme, which includes maternity payments, family grants and death allowances. Since there is no National Health Service in West Germany, this scheme is vital, and in 1968 was compulsory for all employees who earned less than 900 DM per month. The eligibility levels are regularly revised, to keep them related to current wage movements, the exemption limit being constantly raised.[2]

Maternity payments amount to 150 DM, plus free ante-natal attention, medicines and services, and confinement care in a maternity home; in addition, women in regular employment receive a payment equal to their normal weekly wage for six weeks before confinement and eight weeks afterwards. On the death of an insured person a lump sum is also payable, of at least 100 DM and in some cases 150 DM in value, calculated on the basis of earnings (basically twenty times the daily wage). On the death of any other member of the family, half of this amount is payable.

Accident insurance is also compulsory for all employed persons. It is payable entirely by the employer, and is roughly equal to 2% of his total payroll. Rates of pay and the degree of danger are taken into account in fixing the level of contributions. Benefits include medical treatment for accidents that occur in connection with work, as well as vocational rehabilitation and sick pay for a period of up to 26 weeks. Employers are also responsible for safety measures in their enterprises and for the provision of first aid facilities; both of these are subject to official inspection. Industrial diseases are also included under this insurance. Injured persons receive free medical attention and any artificial aids which are required, in addition to financial relief, including pensions for themselves or their dependents where necessary. There were almost one million beneficiaries of this scheme in 1961, out of 26,350,000 participants.

In the present-day West German boom the question of unemployment could hardly be described as pressing; nevertheless a compulsory system of unemployment insurance is in force. It is payable up to an earnings limit of 1,300 DM per month (1968) and has, since 1957, been borne equally by employer and employee, at a rate which is roughly 2% of the worker's pay. Unemployed persons

[2] From January 1st 1971 payments by employers became obligatory for all employees, in view of the rapidly rising costs in insurance and medical treatment. Employees earning more than the limit of 1425 DM per month may choose between the state scheme and private insurance.

receive for a certain period of time a percentage of their previous weekly earnings, depending on the length of their previous employment. After this time they qualify for government-financed unemployment pay. The extent and level of unemployment relief is under constant review, and a system has been worked out which relates unemployment benefits to the current cost of living index and average earnings in industry. In this way protection is provided against the effects of inflation. The level of benefit is always kept above that of the cost of living, and can compare with any in Europe. These particular provisions were introduced as part of the Social Reform of 1957. A similar anti-inflation safeguard operates in the case of pensions schemes.

Invalidity and retirement pensions are provided out of a separate insurance fund, to which employed persons contribute up to an earnings level of 1,600 DM a month (1968). Membership is compulsory and contributions are paid by both employer and employee, at a rate of about 7% each of a person's monthly earnings. Contributions thus vary according to income and are not a fixed sum, as in Britain. The principle of equality is however stressed in the Social Reform programme. This means that all insured persons receive the same quality of treatment for sickness, and also that a married man with a number of children pays the same contributions as a single employee. These are respects in which the national insurance scheme differs essentially from private insurance.

Pensions insurance covers the financial support and rehabilitation treatment of those incapacitated through illness, the payment of a regular pension (including child allowances) in the event of their unemployability and the provision of old age retirement pensions. In addition pensions are awarded to surviving dependents on the death of an insured person; widows receive six tenths of the total pension rate and orphans one fifth. Money is also allocated from the pension funds for the general improvement of the state of health of all insured persons. A contributory period of five years is required before benefits can be drawn, and old age pensions can only be claimed after a fifteen year contributory period (twenty years for women!). Separate, but similar old age pension schemes exist for retired farmers (since 1957) and for independent craftsmen (since 1960). Men draw their old age pensions at the age of sixty-five, women at the age of sixty. The amount is based on the rate of contributions paid, and is related to the national average earnings level during the three years preceding the pension claim. Pensions are also regularly adjusted to prevailing wage levels, as a guard against rising costs of living. Thus, taking 1957 as the base year (= 100), pensions rose to a figure of 183·8 in 1967. Old age pension rates in 1963, expressed as a percentage of a person's final-year earnings, were 60% (Britain 29%). The Social Reform of 1957 brought about an enormous improvement on the pensions front, raising benefits payments from 6,700 million DM in 1955 to 17,900 million DM in 1961, and well over 25,000 million DM in 1966.

Employers are also taxed another one per cent of the total payroll to provide funds for the payment of children's allowances. These allowances are paid for the second child of a family whose earnings are below the level of 7,800 DM a year, and for the third and successive children of all families, up to the end of their eighteenth year of age or the completion of their full-time education (maximum age 25 years).[3] For the second child a monthly sum of 25 DM is paid, for the third child 50 DM, for the fourth 60 DM, and for the fifth and all subsequent children the monthly allowance is 70 DM (figures for 1968). This provision was introduced in 1961, replacing an earlier and less generous scheme of 1955.

Payment of family allowances is the responsibility of the Federal authorities, under the general supervision of the Ministry of Family and Youth Affairs. The other insurance schemes are managed and administered by autonomous bodies, normally at regional and even local level. The rates of contribution to health insurance are actually determined by the local bodies. The organizations vary in character. Industrial workers are covered by a different pensions scheme from the salaried employees (*Angestellten*), while the miners have an insurance scheme entirely their own (*Knappschafts-versicherung*) which is the oldest in the country. The three principle branches of social insurance are differently organized, but de-centralization is the rule in each case. Sickness insurance is supervised by about two thousand agencies (*Kassen*) throughout the Federal territory, at various levels of social organization; each is self-administering and has a committee and representative body of its own, usually made up in equal numbers by employers' and employees' representatives. Associations of these agencies exist at *Land* and *Bund* level. Accident insurance is administered by 97 separate offices; while pensions insurance is the concern of eighteen *Land* organizations, as well as one for railway employees, one for seamen and one for miners. A similar representation of interests is found here as in the case of sickness insurance.

A certain amount of state subsidization of pension funds is proving to be necessary, though the other categories of insurance are self-supporting. The state has also had to find the funds to finance relief to refugees, war victims and expellees, though this is

[3] Since July 1970, 300,000 pupils in the higher classes of secondary schools have been eligible for state subsidies, estimated to total 500 million DM in 1971. The individual grant is 150 DM per month for *Gymnasium* study and 290 DM for other types of secondary school.

now, of course, a reducing charge on the budget (*Bund, Länder* and *Gemeinden* provided 7,000 million DM under these heads in 1966). Both individual and state seem to have reached the limit of what can reasonably be expected in contributions to social insurance. The working man contributes about 30% of his gross earnings (if we include the portion paid by his employer) for these purposes. The Federal authorities insist that higher contributions than this are only permissible under private schemes of insurance and are a matter of personal decision. State support for certain sectors of insurance has proved necessary at times, and in 1966 the *Bund, Land* and *Gemeinde* authorities contributed 116 million DM to the total of 18,460 millions for sickness insurance payments, while their contribution to retirement pensions amounted to 6,718 million DM (1970: 11,000 million DM) out of a total sum of 34,388 millions. Two major threats have emerged to the stability of the social insurance system. The number of retired persons is growing faster than that of the number of those at work, thereby making heavier demands on a diminishing source of funds; this is partly corrected by the steady growth in industrial earnings. This rise in the size of West German wage packets has produced the second danger, however, as it is carrying a steadily increasing number of people over the statutory contribution levels, so that the supply of funds is again diminished; hence the frequent upward revision of these contribution limits.

Social security, we see, has been a vital concern of successive West German governments. The proportion of the Gross National Product spent on such measures in 1963 was 20% (France and Italy 18%, Great Britain 12%). By the year 1967 social security accounted for 21·6% of the net social product (1950: 16·3%) or 90,300 million DM, more than half of which was spent on pensions. The number of persons in receipt of pensions in 1966 exceeded eight millions, while those contributing numbered twenty-two millions. Two-thirds of the pensions payments were to people who had not yet reached the official retirement age, but were suffering from some disability—notably heart and circulatory ailments.

Industrial firms frequently assume added responsibilities in the furtherance of the workers' welfare. Up to 2% of the total wages bill is often invested in the provision of such facilities as factory medical staff, convalescent homes, canteens, housing programmes, sport facilities, kindergartens and extra holiday pay. Many firms also provide retirement pensions for their employees, which are additional to the official retirement pension. Length of service is an important factor here, and some workers are actually able on retirement to draw benefits which exceed the level of their former wages, when state and employer's pension are combined. Here is one means by which, in a tight labour market, employers attempt to discourage workers from leaving their employment to work in another undertaking.

2. Housing

Social conditions have undergone a radical improvement since the dark days of 1945/48, and the transformation has perhaps been nowhere so marked as on the domestic front. There was an acute housing shortage for many years as a result of the wartime devastations, and the problem was further aggravated by the arrival of millions of refugees. The building programme has been one of the first priorities of each administration since 1949 and still receives massive governmental support.

At the end of hostilities in 1945 the number of homes that had been completely destroyed in the territory of the Federal Republic amounted to 20% (Great Britain 2%). By 1962 new building had created 6,800,000 homes for something like 22 million people. By 1970 the total built had reached the 11 million mark. Since 1953 a house a minute has been built, giving West Germany the lead among all West European nations. Between 1960 and 1965 the proportion of the Gross National Product devoted to housebuilding rose from 5½% to 6% (Great Britain 3%). The fact that many of these dwellings are actually flats diminishes the achievement a little but it remains nevertheless an impressive one. The financing of this massive building programme was partly the responsibility of the Federal exchequer (29% of costs), partly the product of capital loans (46%) and partly the responsibility of the private builder. Since 1959, the capital market has supplied more than 50% of the necessary funds. 3,600,000 of these homes are occupied by people whose rents and other burdens are carefully held down by low interest rates on local authority loans, or long term borrowing facilities. Especial attention has been paid more recently to home ownership by less well-paid sections of the community, and much official help has been channelled in this direction, in particular a high interest-bearing investment scheme with building societies at an annual premium of 624 DM introduced in 1970 (the *624 DM-Gesetz*). A 'property-owning democracy' is the aim of such policies. Close restrictions were placed initially on the size of homes built, with a general limit of four rooms (including the kitchen) per family, but since 1961 71% of the new homes built have had four or more rooms. In the immediate post-war situation, the allocation was one room to each member of a household, kitchen included, and families possessing more accommodation than this were compelled to take in those without a home, until their quota was filled.

The clearing and rebuilding of derelict and slum areas has added to the size of the housing problem. It was estimated in 1961 that of the 15,600,000 homes in West Germany, 900,000 were ripe for demolition, 3,500,000 were in need of basic repair, and 3,400,000 of modernization. The cost of building rose by 117% between 1950 and 1961, but this was accounted for partly by the vastly improved quality of houses then being constructed; their ground-area was considerably larger, and 96% of all homes built in 1961 had a bath, compared with 79% in 1954, and only 50% in the 1920's. A big slum clearance programme is at present under way and is one of the first priorities of SPD/FDP social policy. At the end of 1969 there was still a deficiency of half a million dwellings; and the population growth necessitated an annual increase of a further quarter of a million homes.

This need could scarcely have arisen at a more inopportune moment, for the increasing rate of inflation has led to soaring costs in all sectors of the building industry. Scarcity of land, combined with land speculation, led to an increase in the price of building land of the order of 40% between 1968 and 1969: in one Hamburg surburb land prices increased eight-fold between 1956 and 1969. In addition, building wages increased by 19·5% in the course of 1969 and many workers also earned massive bonuses on top of their basic wage.[4] Earnings of up to 2,800 DM a month were achieved by specialist workers. House prices have been known to treble in the space of fourteen years, and rents have even increased fourfold. Building society interest on mortgages has risen in many cases to 9% and local authorities have had to subsidize many families (over one million people in 1969) whose wages were not high enough to meet increased rent charges; the general increase in rents in the period 1968/70 was three times that of the rise in workers' earnings. All married workers with a wage of less than 12,000 DM a year now receive rent subsidies; an extra amount is allowed for those with children. In a situation where building costs rose from a base of 100 in 1950 to 230 in 1969 (against a cost of living index increase to 160), the extent of building operations has inevitably contracted. Whereas 204,000 dwellings were constructed in 1968, with the assistance of considerable public loans, the figure for 1969 dropped to 165,000.

In many West German homes, particularly in apartments and

---

[4] We must note, however, that wages of workers in the chemical industry increased by 24·5%, and coal miners received 28% more pay in this same period.

flats, the shortage of space is met by combining two functions within one room (kitchen and dining room; lounge and bedroom), with appropriately adaptable furniture. Attics and basements are also fully exploited, the former as lumber rooms, workshops or clothes-drying areas, and the latter, considered an essential feature of a house, serve as wash-houses, boiler rooms and fuel stores. Central heating is regarded as a necessity rather than a luxury, and double glazing of windows is also common.

The national census of 1956 revealed the existence of almost 16 million households, contained within 12,730,000 dwellings; the number of households had increased to $20\frac{1}{2}$ millions by 1968. About one third of occupants own the house or flat in which they live, 50% are tenants and the remainder are sub-tenants.

In a survey of 1960 it was found that about a third of all families live in a private house; another third shared a house with one or two other households; and the remaining third lived in large blocks of flats. Home ownership is growing, and by 1961 had reached a figure of 39% of all householders, but only 2% of flat dwellers.

Home ownership is commonest in rural areas, where almost two-thirds of the people have a house of their own; in cities of more than half a million inhabitants, the proportion is only 11%. There is a growing tendency today for people to live outside town and travel into the city to work; of 17 million households in 1960, 4·2 millions were already in this category of commuters, and every tenth worker spent more than an hour over his journey to work. This desire to live 'outside' has led to an astronomical rise in the cost of building land since 1960.

Rents, which had been subject to official controls ever since the days of the acute post-war housing shortage, were set free in 1965, when it was argued that the housing shortage had been virtually met. No increases above 1936 levels had been permitted up to 1955, when a 10% rise was authorized, with a figure of 15–20% in exceptional cases. Rents have risen more steeply since the end of restrictions in 1965, for there still exists a shortage of living accommodation. In 1970 a worker earning 1400 DM per month probably spent one fifth of this on the rent of quite a small flat.

Obtaining a mortgage for the purchase of a house is facilitated in a number of ways. The purchaser, having produced 25% of the price, can obtain up to 60% more from a mortgage bank, savings bank or insurance company, at market rates of interest. The balance can be raised at a much lower rate through a second mortgage, either with a building society or a public organization. Savings banks are a chief source of mortgages, and many West Germans invest in them with a view to a subsequent request for mortgage facilities. One in every thirty members of the public had a mortgage with a savings bank in 1963, representing a sum of 1,500 million DM; they belonged mainly to the well-to-do class of society. West German building societies are co-operative in character: money for mortgages is provided by investors, who hope subsequently to become house owners themselves. They must therefore contribute for a minimum period of four to five years, before they can qualify for a building loan. The repayment period is usually eleven years, and interest is paid at a fixed rate throughout, being about 5% in 1965. In 1963, out of the total of £2,040 million that was spent on new housing, £380 million was produced by the promoters themselves, £450 million came from public funds, and £1,210 million was lent by financial organizations, of which £440 million, or 36%, was contributed by the building societies. Money for building schemes provided from public funds is in the form of loans, which are interest free or at very low rates, and are repayable over periods of up to 100 years. Both private and public building organizations may borrow on these terms, the only restriction being that dwellings to be built must be occupied by lower paid workers; they must also conform to prescribed limits of size and cost. Such policies aim at keeping down the levels of rent that must be charged.

3. *Social and Family Life*

West Germany is today a nation of urban dwellers: whereas in 1871 64% of her population still lived in the country, by 1961 almost 78% of West Germans lived in townships of more than 2,000 inhabitants. Of a total present-day population of roughly 60 millions, 29 millions are engaged in some kind of gainful occupation; 78% of these are employees of a firm or institution and 18% are civil servants or salaried officials. The purchasing power per head of this population increased from 2,411 DM in 1954 to 4,675 DM in 1963 and 6,689 DM in 1968. Whereas forty to fifty years ago the leading figures in society were the officials and civil servants, it is now the industrial managers, the free professions and technological experts who enjoy most social prestige and generally earn the largest salaries.

The average employee has appreciably improved his position since the 1930s. The number of motor cars owned by workers rose from 9,800 in 1952 to 1,346,000 in 1961, when every fourth car belonged to a worker. Around the year 1900 civil servants earned on average ten times as much as unskilled workers; today they earn only three times as much. A skilled worker will often take home more pay than a professional employee with a university education.

In many workers' families, several members of the household will probably be contributing to the domestic budget. There were, for instance, 5½ million married women in employment in 1963. Salaried employees and industrial workers spent almost equivalent sums on the basic necessities of life, but the former tend to spend a larger proportion on rents and the latter on food.

The size of the family has declined significantly since the days of the *Reich*. The 1871 average of 4·6 persons had fallen, by 1956, to three persons per family and the trend is still a downwards one. The tradition is that of the two-child family, but the average is brought down by the considerable number of one-person households (18·2% of the total in 1956). Wartime losses, resulting in orphaned children and a large surplus of unmarried women, are the main immediate cause of these lower figures; in 1967 there were three million more women than men in West Germany, almost entirely above the forty-year-old level. The imbalance of the sexes is slowly being corrected by the post-war birthrate (6% more male than female births) and men will, it is calculated, eventually outnumber the women. In 1967 there were 9,900,000 unmarried women above the age of fifteen, of whom 4,200,000 were widows and 650,000 divorcees. On current showing (1967 figures) 7·8% of marriages are childless, 21% produce one child, 35% two children, 19% three children, 8·5% four and 7·6% five or more children. The birth rate is low, compared with that of many countries, standing at 18·3 per thousand in 1961 (cf. 37 per thousand in China!). Illegitimate births, now less frequent, account for only 4·6% of the total. The death rate is even lower than the birth rate with a figure of 12 per thousand in 1968 (birth rate 16 per thousand), so that West Germany's population is steadily increasing in size. The surplus of births over deaths in 1961 was 398,000, but fell to 236,000 in 1968. Since the average expectation of life has risen from 37 years in 1870 to 69 years in 1960, the age structure of the population has also undergone a radical alteration, the older generation now constituting a significant social force—and creating many problems of medical care, financial support and accommodation. The average marrying age has, on the other hand, fallen significantly. In 1960, it stood at 28 years for men and 25 for women, but in 1968 half of the men and two-thirds of the women were already married at the age of 25. Marriages are also more stable than they were twenty years ago: the divorce rate was 33·8 per 10,000 marriages in 1961, but has shown a tendency to rise again since.

The pattern and incidence of illness has changed considerably in recent times throughout the western world, and West German statistics reflect this situation. Heart and circulatory diseases today head the list, with 40% of all deaths attributable to them, while cancer, with a figure of 18%, comes second. Infectious diseases, on the other hand, are on the decline.

The West Germans have no National Health Service, but the state has intervened in a number of ways to ensure efficient care of the sick and injured. In addition to the compulsory insurance schemes, the authorities are responsible for the provision of many medical services. More than a half of the hospitals and clinics are supported by funds deriving from *Bund, Land* and *Gemeinde* and from social insurance sources, but more than a third are maintained privately, by churches and independent charitable organizations, which dispose of nearly a half of all hospital beds. There are 3,600 institutions in all, with 670,000 beds available. About two-thirds of the doctors practise privately, being consulted by patients at the expense of the health insurance fund. Many of them specialize in a particular field of medicine, and patients visit a doctor who is skilled in the particular treatment which they require, rather than visiting the same doctor for all their complaints. Only private patients, who are not contributors to the state insurance scheme, pay independently for their treatment. The same principle applies in the case of hospitalization.

The hospitals are however faced with a serious crisis today, arising from a shortage of both capital and staff. Between 1950 and 1963 the percentage of those who required treatment rose from 4·03% of the population to 6·24%; yet in this same period the cost of treatment increased fivefold. Only 4% of the gross national product has hitherto been spent on West Germany's hospitals, considerably less than what was spent by most of her neighbours. Many hospitals are antiquated and lack modern equipment. Junior doctors are in short supply because of low pay, poor promotion prospects and long hours of overtime. The same is true of the nursing staff. Some wards have had to be closed, and many nurses have been recruited from abroad, from the Philippines, from India, Turkey, Finland and Jugoslavia. In 1970 hospitals were operating at an overall annual loss of two billion marks, and the Brandt government formulated emergency proposals. Basic decisions taken in December 1970 were that capital for the reinstatement of the hospitals was to come from the *Bund* (one-third) and the *Länder* (two-thirds), and that the full costs of a patient's treatment should be borne either by the patient or his insurance fund. These measures are expected to produce more than 600 million marks a year, plus further contributions from the *Länder*. A considerable increase in health insurance contributions seems to be one likely consequence. To eliminate the considerable disproportion between private and 'standard' treatment of patients, SPD members have further proposed the building of 'one-class' hospitals, where no distinction would be made between the rich and the less wealthy. A further improvement could be achieved if the hospitals merely released their patients sooner: the average length of stay in a West German hospital is nineteen days, compared with fourteen in Sweden, Belgium and Russia, ten in Finland and Canada and eight in the USA. A reduction of only one day would liberate 21,000 beds. Since health matters are primarily the affair of the *Land,* and most of the smaller clinics are in private hands, the process of reform is likely to be uneven and protracted.

The geographical distribution of the West German population shows a fairly even pattern. There are fifty-two *Großstädte,* that is cities containing more than 100,000 inhabitants, and in them live 16·6 million people, representing 30·8% of the 1963 population. A further 24·9 million live in townships of between 2,000 and 100,000 residents (46·1% of the population) and 12·5 million live in smaller communities (23·1% of the population). There are three cities with more than one million inhabitants: West Berlin (2·2 millions), Hamburg (1·8 millions) and Munich (1·1 millions). The even spread of large urban centres throughout West Germany ensures the continuation of a lively regional tradition and is a safeguard against excessive centralization. It has resulted in the establishment of a widely developed communications network and an even spread of business and industrial enterprises.

In October of each year a mini-census of the West German population takes place. The survey of 1968 showed that for the 26,665,000 persons gainfully employed, there were 33,520,000 nonworking persons. Men accounted for 64% of those at work, women for 36%. 14% of the population lived on pensions or allowances and a further 41% were dependent relatives (wives, children, non-employed relations). Of the 26,665,000 actively engaged, three millions were operating independently, nearly one-third of them being farmers. Of the working population, 47·9% were classified as wage-earners, 28% as salaried staff (*Angestellten*) and 5·3% as officials. The remainder were self-employed (11%) or unpaid ancillaries (7·8%).

Families on low and medium-range incomes find little chance of saving any of their money, and even the middle-management employee only succeeded in saving about 5% of his earnings in 1970, which is the same proportion as in 1960, despite the considerable rise in income levels in recent years. In the *Land* of Hessen in 1969, only 42,156 citizens were eligible for wealth tax; more than five millions did not incur liability. Consumption of many goods is steadily rising and has now reached a level generally comparable to that in Great Britain. Spending on potatoes, flour and peas, beans etc. has declined progressively since 1950, while that on meat, fruit, eggs and fats has increased, together with coffee and tobacco (See also pp. 214–215 for tables of comparison). We may also note in passing that 60% of the population now invest in either football pools (*Toto*) or lotteries (*Lotto*).

Spending habits are also changing. As incomes rise, less money is devoted proportionately to food. In 1953, 50% of income was spent on food; in 1965 the proportion was only 34%, and a figure of 27% was expected for 1970. By 1975, it is also reckoned, the population of West Germany will have increased to over 64 millions, and a shift in demand will follow, as the number of consumers under the age of 15 will grow by 34% and that of elderly consumers by as much as 60%. Spending on food is expected to rise by 66% in the ten years 1965–75, but that on non-foodstuffs by as much as 133%. One of the most significant recent developments has been the growth of frozen food sales, which up to 1965 lagged behind the figures for Britain, Scandinavia and the United States.

The rate of inflation up to 1969 was slower in West Germany than in most other countries of Europe: between 1950 and 1962 consumer prices rose 28%, while the figure for Britain was 60%, for France 88% and for Italy 46%. While this price rise of 28% was taking place, the average West German worker's wages rose by the amount of 119%. Although the inflationary process has intensified since 1962, it has generally been more controlled in West Germany than elsewhere, so that the cost of a refrigerator, vacuum cleaner or television set has remained comparatively lower than in other countries. It was reported in 1965 that money-values had declined by 25% since 1950, an annual depreciation rate of 3%.

The West German middle-income group comprises about half of the social spectrum and is the solid, tradition-bound, conservative element in the population. Correct behaviour, the maintenance of standards, punctuality, diligence at work, team loyalty, orderliness and dependability are the ideals of this broad social group. They are ready to sacrifice material comforts for some future goal and lay particular emphasis on good education. Although representing only about 45% of society, they supply the universities with 95% of their students. Civil servants in particular, who constitute only 6% of the total working force, produce more than one-third of the university population.

In the present-day affluent society of West Germany, leisure time activities assume ever greater significance. Here the tendency is to operate in fairly close social groupings, carefully avoiding one's social inferiors and superiors. Much time is spent in the home, in particular watching television, and the living room has developed into a centre for the comfortable pursuit of all manner of hobbies. The cinema is patronized mainly by the young, seeking to escape parental supervision: 70% of cinema audiences are between the ages of 16 and 24. Membership of clubs is, however, popular and 40% of the adult population belong to a sports, cultural or hobbies club. Holidays are generous in length : Federal legislation guarantees to all employees a minimum of fifteen days' annual leave after six months' regular employment. After the age of 35 this minimum is increased to eighteen days. Many workers receive more than these minimum amounts of leave, and there is an enormous exodus of West Germans into the other countries of Europe, especially Italy and Spain, during the summer months. Others flock to the North Sea and Baltic coast resorts, or go camping at the many mountain and forest sites which have been established by the authorities. German tourists abroad spend considerably more money than do foreign tourists in Germany. From a negative disparity of 500 million DM in 1959, spending by German tourists abroad produced a deficit of 4,600 million DM in 1962, as compared with foreign spending in the Federal Republic. The gap declined to 2,700 millions in 1969.

A factor making for higher prices is the Value Added Tax (*Mehrwertsteuer*) which is charged on all sales of goods and services, and is fixed at a level of 11%. It was introduced in January 1968, in accordance with agreed EEC policy, replacing an earlier Turnover Tax which had produced 14% of Federal revenues in 1967. Food and agricultural products carry a tax load of only 5·5% under the VAT system. Other taxes include those on property, company and death taxes, and certain special taxes on tobacco, coffee, tea, sugar, beer and a range of other commodities, as well as gaming, land purchase, insurance and exchange transactions. In addition, taxes are collected by the local authorities on entertainments, land and land purchase, profits, and certain licence dues (*e.g.* from dog owners).

When we speak of the West German worker, we must bear in mind the large number of women who are included within this term. The proportion of single women in employment is now roughly two-thirds, and of the married women, one-third are in regular employment. Female employment today accounts for just over one-third of the total labour force. Yet West Germany remains a man-dominated society. Although there were 3¼ million more women electors than men, only 247 of the 2,563 candidates in the 1961 Federal elections were women; only 43 were elected, to constitute 8·3% of the Bundestag's membership. In September 1969 they won only 34 seats out of 518. Women have had the vote since 1919 in Germany, but there have been only three female cabinet ministers in Bonn since 1949—two of them at the Ministry of Health.

Although granted full legal equality and the right to equal pay in 1958, true equality has still not been achieved by West German women. In 1970 they were still earning between 20% and 30% less than men, and promotion even to posts in the middle management range is very rarely achieved. Only 3% of judges and 4% of university teachers are women, and only 54,751 of the total of 230,500 university students in 1963 were female. The blame is laid partly on the continuing German patriarchal tradition and inferior level of female education, but also on the attitudes of the women themselves. Opinion polls have revealed that the vast majority of West Germany's women still regard their main role to be that of looking after the home, their children and their husbands and have no higher ambitions. (We may recall here that women are the main supporters of the CDU). They appear, however, to have a large voice in the disposition of the family income.

Many West German women therefore spend their day running the home—often in a surprisingly inadequately equipped kitchen—and helping the children with their schooling to compensate for a frequently unsatisfactory level of primary school instruction. Husbands have tended in the past to regard domestic chores as something beneath their dignity, resolutely refusing to help prepare a meal or do the washing up, but these attitudes are now changing to a concept of marriage as a partnership of equals (legally, a wife is entitled to one-half of her married partner's earnings), especially in an era where so many wives also go out to work. Some of those who work do so out of economic necessity, but others seek jobs out of sheer boredom in the home, dislike of domestic work and the lack of cultural interests which might otherwise reveal ways of using their leisure hours profitably—and they consequently find their unchallenging jobs equally boring. It is to be hoped that improvements will come from the changing pattern of West German education.

The children of working mothers can frequently be cared for in a variety of kindergarten-type institutions, which receive children between the ages of three and six (primary school begins at six). There are places for roughly one million children here. These kindergartens or play schools are run by a number of organizations, ranging from the local authority or church to voluntary groups and, of course, industry itself. Some are entirely free, while others charge a nominal fee. It is unusual for any formal education to be attempted here; we shall find a marked difference of policy in East Germany in this respect.

185

4. *Education*

When we come to the field of education in West Germany, we encounter one further example of a well-established tradition that is no longer proving adequate for present-day needs, and is currently undergoing a process of change and reform. We may conveniently divide the formal education pattern into the three sectors of elementary, secondary and higher education; allied fields are those of adult education and vocational training.

Compulsory school attendance commences, as we saw, at the age of six. The Basic Law lays down that education must be available to all citizens, irrespective of means, race, creed, or political persuasion; and all the *Länder* have laws which require full-time education of children for a minimum period of nine years. Education, we must remember, is a *Land* responsibility, and each state frames its own policies, though a Standing Committee of the Ministers of Education for each *Land* has striven—if not entirely successfully—to keep educational planning and practice in step throughout the Federal Republic. The financing of education is shared by *Land* and *Gemeinde*, the former paying all salaries and the latter providing the buildings and equipment. Only one-eighth of the burden is shouldered directly by the *Bund*.

Children enter school at the beginning of the school year (August 1st) following their sixth birthday, the operative date being June 30th. A child who reaches the age of six in the first quarter of the school year may also be admitted, if his mental and physical development are considered to be sufficiently advanced. On the other hand backward children (examined by a school physician) may be kept away for a further year or even longer.

West German schools are really only half-day schools, for at most of them the pupils attend in the mornings only (usually from 8 am to 1.0 pm), the afternoons being left free for private activities, for sport, for homework and extra subjects being voluntarily studied. There is no school meals service, as the children go home for lunch. The school week is one of six days, extending from Monday to Saturday. During the early post-war years, as a result of the acute shortage of classrooms, many schools operated on a two-shift basis each day. Almost two-thirds of the teachers are men, though women predominate in the primary schools. Boys' schools have men teachers and men are often found teaching in girls' schools too, though the head teacher here will always be a woman. All the primary schools are co-educational, but in the higher types of school the sexes are frequently segregated.

The Volksschule. The elementary school is the basic feature of the school system in every *Land*. Many pupils attend no other school; in the 1950s the ratio was as high as 80% of the school population; by 1969 it had dropped to 66%. A *Volksschule* normally has nine grades, leading to the ending of compulsory schooling at the age of fifteen. The first four years are known as *Grundschule* ('basic school'), though Bremen and West Berlin have a six-year *Grundschule*. Beyond this basic level, the grades are known as *Hauptschule* ('main school'). All children must attend the *Grundschule*, and the satisfactory completion of this stage is necessary before any child can advance to a further stage of his education. On successfully reaching the fifth year of school, the large majority of West German children enter the upper school, or *Hauptschule*, where they receive the remainder of their education. This usually consists of religion, German, mathematics, geography and history, nature study, drawing, singing and physical education. One foreign language is also commenced, and this will usually be English. The aim of the *Volksschule* is stated to be the harmonious development of the child's faculties, so that he or she will be successful either in practical affairs or in catching up and rejoining those brighter pupils who transferred at the age of eleven to higher schools. Few indeed follow the second course.

After completing their studies at the *Volksschule* young people are still subject to compulsory education requirements. Those who do not enter into full-time vocational training must attend a part-time vocational training school until reaching the age of eighteen. About 95% of those leaving *Volksschule* therefore attend, for between six and twelve hours a week, a centre for further education and training. Germany was, in fact, the first country in the world to institute compulsory post-school education up to the age of eighteen, in legislation of 1919, which created the *Berufsschule* (vocational school). Public expenditure on education in 1962 was 7% of all public spending (increasing to 11·8% in 1968), and of this sum nearly 12% went to the *Berufsschulen*. These institutions are intended to add to the general education of the young, and also to supplement the practical experience gained in the place of work by supplying fundamental theoretical information (*e.g.* knowledge of materials), and in particular to give instruction in certain skills necessary in their trades, such as technical drawing. At the end of their three years of study in the *Berufsschule*, young people take an examination, the nature of which is determined by the type of vocational school which they have been attending—industrial, domestic, commercial, agricultural and so on. Much attention is being given to the improvement of these vocational schools. In the cities they are usually large and diversified enough to meet the demands of a wide range of interests; but in smaller localities there are shortcomings and considerable expansion is needed.

Of the 5% who continue in full-time education after leaving the *Volksschule* almost all attend a *Berufsfachschule*, or trade school. These are mostly commercial colleges, domestic science institutes or technical colleges, and are financed either by the local authorities, by vocational organizations or by private persons. Courses of study here last from one to three years, according to type, and can even be a substitute for apprenticeship, leading to acceptance as a *Geselle*, or journeyman. Twice as many girls as boys attend these colleges, for in addition to training in the domestic sciences they also provide courses in stenography, typing and secretarial work.

Advanced vocational training is provided in the *Fachschule*, where full-time courses are provided for students, normally from the age of 18, who have already acquired some practical experience in industry or a trade. These colleges offer courses of varying duration (up to four years) and lead either to the examination for a master's diploma or else to qualifications of a university pass-degree standard. Students successfully graduating from a *Fachschule* are eligible for university entrance.

For the much smaller proportion of children who do not receive all their education in the *Volksschule* there are various prospects after completion of the basic four years of *Grundschule*. The fundamental division is into education up to the age of sixteen, and attendance up to the age of nineteen. Full time education up to sixteen is provided in the **Mittelschule,** or Intermediate School. This, as its name suggests, is a half-way house between the *Volksschule* and the grammar-school type *Gymnasium*, and in some ways follows the pattern of the English secondary modern school. It is also known as the *Realschule*, and is a post-war development. In 1953 only 5% of the children attended these schools; by 1962 the proportion had risen to 11% and by 1970 to 17%. It is thus the principal growth point of West German education, the aim being to reduce progressively the numbers of those attending only a *Volksschule*. Many primary schools are in fact extending their advanced classes to cater for entry into the *Mittelschule*. The main emphasis in the *Mittelschule* is on social studies, mathematics and the sciences. One foreign language is started immediately on entry, and a second one may be added in the seventh grade (*i.e.* at age 12–13). Optional subjects include shorthand, typing and book-keeping. Pupils from the ages of ten to sixteen study here, and on completing the curriculum are eligible to sit the examination for *mittlere Reife* ('intermediate maturity'). This education prepares children for entry into the intermediate grades of commerce, technology and administration. West Berlin, Bremen and Hamburg have a four-year type of *Mittelschule*, following on the six-year *Grundstufe*.

The other type of secondary school is the more academic **Gym-**

nasium (roughly equal to the English grammar school, or Scottish academy), also referred to as the *höhere Schule* or *Oberschule* (high school). About 19% of West German children attend this type of school, nearly 50% more boys than girls, for the higher education of boys is considered by parents to be much more important. The expansion of this sector of education was planned to bring roughly one million children into *Gymnasium*-type schools by the end of 1970.

The *Gymnasium* is the oldest type of senior school in Germany; during the nineteenth century it enjoyed an immense reputation abroad, and is still highly esteemed. Its purpose was to mould the minds of a selected group of pupils, by means of a rigorous course of studies, centred around Latin and Greek, with some mathematics, history, German, one modern language and a little science and PT. The mental discipline instilled by such studies was considered to be at least as important as their factual content. Today, this 'classical' (*altsprachliches*) *Gymnasium* has been to a large extent superseded by the 'modern language' (*neusprachlich*) and 'natural science' (*naturwissenschaftlich*) forms which have developed rapidly since 1945. The modern language *Gymnasium* is the form most frequently encountered, and the stress here is on the study of German and two modern European languages, plus Latin. More attention is also given to mathematics and the sciences than in the classical *Gymnasium*. The natural science *Gymnasium* also teaches two modern foreign languages, but lays its main emphasis on the sciences and mathematics; this type is already more numerous than the classical *Gymnasium*.

The course of studies in all these versions of the *Gymnasium* lasts for nine years (*i.e.* ages 10–19) and leads up to the *Abitur* or *Reifezeugnis* ('certificate of maturity') which gives automatic entry to university or openings into managerial and administrative posts in industry and the civil service. The course lasts six years in West Berlin, Hamburg and Bremen, that is from age thirteen to nineteen, the children transferring at a later age from the *Volksschule*. The pace is inevitably hard and intense and there is a high rate of leaving, especially at the age of sixteen, with the acquisition of the intermediate maturity certificate. Only 50% of pupils in fact stayed on at the *Gymnasium* to take their *Abitur* examination in 1965.

The *Abitur* examination is based partly on continuous assessment of pupils and partly on written papers. Less important subjects are dropped a year or two before the final examination, being awarded an assessed grading; but the candidate is still likely to study from six to eight subjects for the *Abitur* examination paper. If a pupil achieves in the written examination the grade which was forecast by his teachers, this becomes his effective mark. Should he however fall below or significantly exceed the expected grade, an oral examination is also held in order to clinch matters. Marks run from grade 1 to grade 6, and numbers 5 and 6 are fail-marks. The final grading for the whole examination is obtained by taking the average for *all* subjects examined. The *Abitur* is an internal examination conducted by the school itself; this makes for more flexible syllabuses and examinations (there is some official supervision, of course) but has some disadvantages also: comparability with other schools, and even worse with other regions, is a constant problem. In the school year 1966–67, 53,372 pupils gained their *Abitur*; this was 7·4% of the national age group, and represented an increase of 6% over the previous year. Their average age was 20·3 years, and 36·5% of them were girls.

The question of selection for secondary education is a troubled one, and the West Germans are still exploring the possible answers, in an attempt to achieve fair educational opportunities for all. The main selection occurs, as we have seen, on the completion of the *Grundstufe* of the *Volksschule*. Parental wishes are one factor that is taken into account, but the criteria are primarily of an educational nature. Entrance tests are still very widely used, but are usually supplemented by intelligence testing, as well as by consultation of school records and teachers' assessments of a pupil's suitability for the proposed type of study. In addition, children may attend at the new institution for a trial period of one or two weeks, being closely observed by both elementary and secondary school teachers. The first term, and even the first year in some cases, is also regarded as a probationary period.

Transfer at a later age is also possible. In most *Länder* parallel courses are conducted in grades five and six (*i.e.* ages eleven and twelve) of *Volksschule* and *Mittelschule*, so that late developers can transfer at the age of thirteen. In addition, there is the so-called *Aufbaugymnasium*, which receives able pupils from the *Volksschule* at the age of thirteen and from the *Mittelschule* at the age of sixteen, and continues their education up to *Abitur* level at the age of nineteen or twenty.

Nevertheless, an analysis of the social origins of *Gymnasium* pupils in 1965 suggests a failure so far to achieve the desired goal of educational equality. One third of these children were found to belong to the families of salaried employees (*Angestellten*). Children of self-employed or independent professional parents accounted for roughly 30% of the total. Children of working-class parents made up only 10% of the sixteen-year-olds, and as little as 6·4% of the eighteen-year-olds. The distribution of the sexes is also uneven. More girls than boys attended the *Mittelschule* in 1966, but only 41·8% of the *Gymnasium* pupils were girls; this proportion sank to 37.9% by the final year of studies, and only 35.5% of those taking the *Abitur* examination were girls. In this same year, 5·7% of the female age group, but 9% of the male age group in the population obtained their certificate of maturity. There are even serious discrepancies from *Land* to *Land*. The proportion of schoolgirls studying at *Mittelschule* in 1966 was 24·6% for Schleswig-Holstein but only 7·7% for the Rhineland-Palatinate; those studying at a *Gymnasium* represented 13·2% of the schoolgirl population in West Berlin, but 20·6% in Hamburg. Girls passing the *Abitur* in Bavaria represented 4·1% of the schoolgirl population, whereas in Bremen the figure was doubled, standing at 8·2%.

The earliest post-war attempt to reform the traditional pattern of education was the introduction of the *Einheitsschule* ('unitary school') in regions controlled by the Social Democrats. This type of school has a common lower level (*Grundschule*) of six years, and a differentiated upper level which caters for the varying educational needs of young people up to the age of nineteen. Pupils of the same age group are kept together whenever possible, so that they engage in certain common activities, such as music, civics, and physical training. For the more academic subjects pupils are organized, not on an age-basis, but according to ability and achievement, so that clever children are not held back by their slower brethren. Further to this, pupils may specialize in particular options, related to their future intentions (*e.g.* foreign languages, technical or scientific courses). The problems of transfer, late development and faulty assessment can more easily be dealt with when the different curricula are thus assembled under one roof. The Hamburg *Einheitsschule* even includes the part- and full-time vocational school courses in its programme. This serious attempt at a solution of educational problems became suspect because of its introduction by a particular party; it was soon the centre of political wrangling and was seldom assessed in an objective way. It finds no mention in the (CDU/FDP) government's report on education in 1963!

The British comprehensive school has also excited interest in West Germany's educational circles, and at the instigation of the committee of *Land* Ministers of Education a number of experimental *Gesamtschulen* have been built and are now coming into operation. They are encountering stiff opposition from the *Gymnasium* world, which sees its traditional prestige position, and indeed its very existence, threatened by the new educational concepts.

Private education plays a very small part in West Germany. At the elementary level this is particularly the case, constituting less than 1% of the total attendance figure. At secondary level the provision is greater and caters for 12% of the children at *Mittelschule* and *Gymnasium* type institutions. Private schools are permitted to operate, as long as they meet the requirements of the authorities with regard to the qualifications and payment of teaching staff and the adequacy of their courses. They are regularly inspected. Many of them are boarding schools, and some conduct valuable educational experiments which are not possible in the state schools. The state also provides special schools (*Hilfsschulen*) for children who are blind, deaf or otherwise handicapped; here remedial treatment, as well as education, can be provided, often on a boarding school basis.

Considerable use is also starting to be made of radio and television for both adult and school education purposes: in 1969 one million children in the Rhineland area watched complete television courses on six separate subjects, mainly at *Mittelschule* level, while Bavaria and other *Länder* have also offered much educational material for schools on television. The Hesse broadcasting service has, since 1966, run a 'university of the air' service, with lectures by professors from Frankfurt University. Those following the course do written work and attend weekend seminars. If they pass an examination after two terms' work, they are eligible for university entrance. Most of those participating live in small communities, or in the country, and are often of working class families.

In the meantime the educational crisis has grown more acute, as a post-war bulge in the birthrate has worked its way along the educational pipeline. The number of children in full-time education reached the eleven million mark in 1970, necessitating a further increase in teachers and school buildings. 18·6% of the total population was then at school, compared with 15·4% in 1961. With the extension of compulsory schooling to a 5–16 year-old basis, it is estimated that there would be twelve and a half million schoolchildren in 1980. To meet this situation, two Federal Committees (one for schools, one for universities) were in 1968 charged by *Bund* and *Land* authorities to draw up proposals for a complete reform of the structure of education. The Schools Committee reported in April 1970. Already, in 1964, the Committee of *Land* Education Ministers had called for a raising of the school leaving age to sixteen, and a greater degree of specialization. But the April 1970 report of the Federal Educational Council (*Bildungsrat*) constituted an all-embracing plan for the ten years 1970–80. The recently created Federal Ministry of Education will perhaps be more effective in developing the drive to implement such reforms than would the separate *Land* authorities; much of their financing will also be the responsibility of the *Bund*. But only 'framework' legislation can be passed by the Federal Government, and the degree and speed of reform will depend on the individual *Länder* and their political allegiances.

The 1970 plan covers the whole range of the school system, from kindergarten to further education. Essential features include the expansion of the kindergartens and nursery schools, to provide pre-school training for all children between the age of three and five. An additional 800,000 kindergarten places will consequently have to be provided by 1980. The age for the commencement of full-time schooling is to be lowered from six to five. Since it is not expected that provision for all of the five-year-old group will be possible by 1980, it is proposed that one quarter of them remains in the kindergarten and commences school one year later. Compulsory education is furthermore to be extended to the age of sixteen, instead of the present fifteen; and a basic division of the school into Primary Stage and Secondary Stage I is proposed. The Primary Stage is further sub-divided into three phases: for five- and six-year-olds the Introductory Stage (*Eingangsstufe*), followed by another two-year division, the Basic Stage (*Grundstufe*) and then a so-called two-year Orientation Stage (*Orientierungsstufe*), which is a preparation period for the Secondary Stage I, and can be integrated into either the lower or upper of the two main stages. The Secondary Stage I would take pupils to the age of sixteen and the completion of compulsory schooling. A revision of the present examination system is also recommended, dividing the *Abitur* into two levels, the first of them *Abitur I*, to be taken after four years in the upper school. A child who commenced school at the age of five would thus take his Abitur I after ten years, at the age of fifteen; he would still, however, have one more year of compulsory schooling to complete—something of a loose end in this present plan for the *Sekundarschule*.

For those staying on at school for a longer period there would be an *Abitur II*. A greater diversity and a much more liberal scheme of secondary education are called for. Courses of different lengths and with differing emphasis of subjects are envisaged. In addition to the existing classical, modern language and scientific forms of the *Gymnasium*, economics, technical and musical forms would be equally strongly developed, and a new Senior Trade School (*Fachoberschule*) would also have a final three-year stage of *Gymnasium*-type studies. At all of these institutions it would be possible to take the *Abitur II* examination; and students in the vocational training years of the *Sekundarschule* would have similar opportunities.

The abolition of a rigid grouping into classes, and its replacement by compulsory and voluntary courses would make it possible for gifted children to take their *Abitur II* sooner than the slower ones.

N

and one year earlier than at present: in fact, after only two years. (One suspects considerable influence here of the English O and A Level examination structure.)

A further radical change is contained in the proposal to introduce whole-day schooling in place of the present half-day system. A better ratio of teachers to children (one teacher to 20–25 children is proposed generally, rising to 1 : 15 at *Gymnasium* level), the provision of more ancillary staff and the broadening of all curricula are further proposals in the report, which calls in particular for greater attention to primary education, with smaller groupings of children and more individual attention to their needs, from an increased number of teachers.

The cost of such a programme would clearly be immense, but the Federal Government has accepted the plan and hopes to implement it. Spending on education has been inadequate in the past; as recently as 1965 only 10% of total public expenditure was devoted to it, whereas in the USA, Russia, Sweden and Britain the figure lay between 20% and 22%. In 1969, exactly 11% of the spending by *Bund*, *Land* and *Gemeinde* went to education, while 19·5% was allocated to social security and 11·2% to defence. In 1968, total spending on schools amounted to 12,900 million marks; the figure for 1980 is estimated in the *Bildungsrat*'s plan at between 35,000 million and 45,000 million marks. In addition, the development of the kindergarten sector would cost a further 7,500 million to 9,000 million marks. A similar enormous increase in spending on the universities is also envisaged. The total sum represented by current planning would thus add up to between 50 and 60 thousand million marks a year. To raise this sum, it is estimated that, on current economic trends, it would be necessary to allocate at least 20% of public expenditure—or double the present rate—to education. It can only be achieved by an increase in taxation or substantial reductions in other sectors of the economy.

Universities. The report of the second committee, the *Wissenschaftsrat*[5] dealing with university education, was presented on June 8th 1970 and was incorporated in the overall plan for education announced by the Federal Government on June 12th of that year. It is hoped that by 1980 about one-half of all West German children will sit the *Abitur II* examination and that one half of these will proceed to studies at a newly conceived 'comprehensive university' (*Gesamthochschule*). A total of one million students is

5 The *Wissenschaftsrat* (Council for Education and Science) was formed in 1957, and is made up of academics and figures from public life who are interested in the furtherance of learning in West Germany.

envisaged by 1980, studying the vast range of advanced courses which these institutions will offer. This suggestion is little short of revolutionary in the present-day West German context.

A distinction is still made today between full universities (*i.e.* those where all faculties are represented), technical universities (lacking the *philosophische Fakultät*, or arts faculty), and university level colleges of technology, education, music, theology, forestry, economics and so on. In 1970 there were upwards of 30 full universities and 12 technical universities and colleges in operation; an intensive programme of new foundations in the second half of the 1960's has made it difficult to keep an exact tally. At least ten further universities had been planned or were under construction by the end of 1970. The West German university is generally larger than its British counterpart, averaging about 10,000 students, Munich being the biggest with 25,000 students in 1969. Altogether there were 290,000 students in the universities and university-type institutions in 1969, and places had been planned for a further 100,000 by 1975. The proportion of women was constant at 24%. The favoured subjects were arts (26·6%), natural sciences (16·1%), economics (14·6%), medicine (11%) and law (10%). The total number of students in institutions of higher education in 1970 was 440,000.

The West German student, as we saw, gains automatic entry to a university (average age 20/21) by passing his *Abitur* examination. The only restriction on his freedom to study wherever and whatever he wishes is the 'numerus clausus', a restricted entry figure which some university departments have had to impose because of their lack of teaching staff and accommodation. In theory all students also continue to enjoy the traditional freedom to move from university to university in the course of their studies, in order to be taught by the eminent names in their subject throughout the land, but the imposition of the 'numerus clausus' and the acute shortage of student lodgings have greatly reduced this practice. The old liberal academic tradition is beset with a great number of defects for the student. There are no prescribed courses of study to follow, no intermediate examinations or regular written work to assess his progress, not even a fixed length of study before graduation. There is little guidance of any kind for the newly arrived freshman, who must discover for himself which lectures and seminars he would be wise to attend; in the overcrowded lecture halls he will find students in their first and final years attending the same lecture; and if he wishes to consult his overworked professor, he must make an appointment well in advance and be prepared for a long wait in the queue. Staff-student ratios in 1963 were 4·8:100 in West Germany and 11·4:100 in Great Britain. Life is likely to be materially tough, too, for student grants and loans are not easily obtained. It was not until 1955 that a system of government support for students was inaugurated: the so-called *Honnefer Modell* (it was negotiated at Bad Honef) introduced grants of 150 DM a month for students in their first three terms of study (exclusive of vacations!), rising to 200 DM for their subsequent terms (inclusive of vacations). These grants are, however, subject to a parental means test, and the increased amount of 400 DM a month (= about £45) granted in 1970 is only paid to students whose parents' income does not exceed 850 marks a month (*i.e.* less than £25 per week). The cost of living for a student was estimated in 1970 to be considerably in excess of even the maximum 400 DM, the figure of 520 DM a month being quoted. Only about one half of West German students receive a grant of any kind, and few of these receive the full amount. Private sources and research institutions provide a proportion of these grants. The consequence of this financial situation is that most students must be supported by their parents, and the majority of university students are of middle or upper class origins. Less than 5% are from working class families. Many students take up part- and even full-time jobs to help finance their studies; consequently they are often in their late twenties by the time of their graduation. There are a small number of scholarships from private and industrial sources which can be awarded to students of particular promise, and students who produce good work can be excused the payment of certain of their fees.

The West German university year is divided into two equal terms (*Semester*), extending from November to February and from April to July, and a student's attendance is counted in semesters rather than years. Students take their final examination when they feel they are sufficiently prepared, and may do so in any semester after their seventh. The average length of study works out, however, at twelve semesters (6 years), for the going is hard and standards high. The student must have attended certain lectures and seminars (detailed study groups) before he can proceed to his graduation. He may graduate in either of two ways; sometimes he chooses both. There are, in other words, two types of examination, the *Staatsexamen* and the *Doktorprüfung*. The former consists essentially of an extended written examination in two subjects, and is obligatory for all intending secondary school teachers and lawyers. This written examination is followed by an exhaustive oral examination, conducted by a university professor and a civil servant from the appropriate Ministry—for this is a state-supervised examination, as its name implies. For the other form of graduation, the doctor's examination, the essential matter is the writing of a dissertation, which must be approved by the examiners before the written part of the examination can be proceeded to, to be followed by a long private oral examination between professor and candidate—the subject of much criticism and misgiving among the student body. Whereas only legal or school subjects can be studied for the *Staatsexamen*, the student writing his doctorate has a considerably wider choice of themes, which must of course first be approved by the supervising professor.

The existing system is far from efficient. The number of student failures and drop-outs is significantly high (often in excess of 20%) and although there are always more students actually in attendance at West German universities than in Britain, the numbers of those graduating annually are higher in British universities.[6] Reforms have long been toyed with in West Germany, but they became imperative after the student demonstrations and direct action which brought many institutions to a halt in the period 1967 to 1969. The most frequently heard plans from the authorities' side were for fixed-length courses (basically four years), better integrated teaching programmes and less demanding examinations for the less brilliant student; greater efficiency and reduced costs were the main criteria here. From the student side demands were voiced for full participation in all decision-making, for improved staff/student ratios, better study guidance and counselling, and for the study of many subjects from the aspect of contemporary politics and ideologies, especially the Marxist and Maoist approaches; the aim here was essentially a complete transformation of the concept of a university. It was like the meeting of two different worlds, each determined not to yield, and it nearly destroyed the West German universities. Changes must come quickly if further damage is to be prevented.

The reforms announced in the Federal Government's policy statement of June 1970 include the setting up of comprehensive universities, establishing a new pattern of higher education. The plan anticipates the presence of one million students in institutes of higher education in the year 1980, and calls for the building of thirty new comprehensive universities. The estimated cost, about 30,000 million marks, is five times greater than the figure spent in 1969 on the universities, and will represent 8% of the gross social product calculated for 1980. The *Bund* has undertaken to help the *Länder* (who finance their local universities) by increasing its contribution from one eighth to one third of the total costs, and has

---

[6] Many comparisons of student numbers in the two countries overlook this important fact. The German student, on average, spends almost twice as long over his studies as his British counterpart.

given them a year in which to draw up their plans for expansion. Behind the carrot, the big stick is flourished: if the *Länder* fail to respond, Education Minister Leussink has threatened to seek an increase in the powers of the Federal Government over the *Länder* in educational matters.

Other parts of the reform plan include a radical improvement in the staff/student ratio by doubling the present number of teaching posts to 100,000; a complete review of the present curricula and examinations system (to be conducted by the academics, but with advice from trade unions, industry and professional organizations); a demolition of the old hierarchy, with equal participation by professors, lecturers and students in decision-making, and a closer attention to the alignment of study courses to society's requirements. The present system of student grants would be discontinued and students would instead receive an allocation, independent of their family's means, which would enable them all to receive the appropriate training for graduation in their subject. The status of commercial, technological and similar applied studies would be considerably enhanced under this programme. Its execution undoubtedly depends on the continuation in office of the present political parties, and the lasting quality of West Germany's current economic prosperity.

Adult education has been a significant part of the German educational scene since the second half of the nineteenth century, when it was an industrial, rather than an academic or cultural venture. Today adult education facilities exist in more than 6,000 centres, in city, town and village, and some 7,400,000 people attended classes in 1967. They are organized mainly by local authorities and communities and offer a wide range of subjects, some of them studied in seminar-type classes. Meetings are weekly, but residential sessions are also held at special centres for intensive study. At least half of the class members are preparing for some kind of examination.

One sector of further education which has met with considerable adverse criticism of late is that of apprentice training. The criticism has been of the employer rather than the courses of study, though the latter are also found to be wanting. It is complained that little or no instruction is given at the place of work, the apprentices being regarded primarily as a source of cheap labour, and that they have no right to strike or even to participate in the election of delegates to factory committees if they are below the age of 18. Their pay is also inadequate, usually amounting to only one third of the rate for unskilled labour, though they comprise a very considerable part of industrial manpower (one apprentice per two trained workers in the motor industry, and a 50/50 proportion in the radio industries) and must often work overtime—sometimes without pay. In 1970 there were 1·4 million apprentices in the Federal Republic. An apprentice then received 140 DM per month in the first year, 170 DM in the second year and 205 DM in the final year of his apprenticeship.

The basic scheme of apprentice training is a well-conceived one. About two thirds of young people leaving school enter into apprenticeships, nearly $1\frac{1}{2}$ million per annum. They are the responsibility of 25,000 training instructors, all of whom have passed their master's examination, and the period of training takes, on average, three to three and a half years. Training courses and examinations are supervised by the 81 Chambers of Industry and Commerce, and 45 Craftwork Chambers, membership of which is compulsory for all firms. As many as 367 industrial careers and 37 careers in commerce can be studied under this scheme. Many West German businessmen have obtained a diploma (*Diplom*) in this way; almost half a million youngsters are currently undergoing management training, the girls outnumbering the boys. Since part-time vocational education is compulsory up to the age of 18, the apprenticeship schemes fit well into this pattern: training in the workshop is supplemented by one day a week spent at a vocational school. For industry, the qualification obtained is the 'skilled worker's certificate' (*Facharbeiterbrief*), for commerce the 'commercial certificate (*Kaufmannsgehilfenbrief*), and for craft work, the journeyman's ticket (*Gesellenbrief*). Critics of the system point out, however, that all the instructors are appointed by and answerable to the employers, and have no say in the devising of the courses of instruction or the examinations, which often contain much that is antiquated and have even at times remained unchanged for over a hundred years. Very moderate reform proposals for the courses, drawn up by the *Bildungsrat* (Education Council) in March 1969 were rejected out of hand by the employers' organizations, and in 1970 there were widespread demonstrations by the apprentices against the inadequacy of their training. A survey of that year revealed that nine-tenths of all apprentices were employed by small or medium sized firms which had no proper instructors or equipment with which to supply the necessary training. It was further established that half of the apprentices received less than the statutory hours of instruction, while there was a 40% shortage of vocational teachers in the *Bund* as a whole. Future education plans will have to take these factors into account.

5. *Provision for Leisure*

The quality of life in any society depends to a considerable extent on the provision which is made in the field of the arts and of leisure-time pursuits. The responsibilities of government in these matters are readily accepted in the Federal Republic, at *Bund, Land* and *Gemeinde* level. Spending in the *Länder* on cultural affairs increased from a figure of 11 billion marks in 1962 to $18\frac{1}{2}$ billions in 1967 and 20 billions in 1970. Considerable funds are also provided by private organizations.

The visitor to Germany is always struck by the universal accessibility of music and drama. All large towns and cities have their own theatre, usually supported by the municipality; opera houses and concert halls are also well represented. A count made in 1963 revealed twenty state theatres, eighty civic theatres, eighteen provincial theatres and about fifty-five private theatres. One hundred and thirty-five of these theatres were subsidized in some way. Seventy of them were the direct descendants of court theatres maintained by German princes and dukes in centuries previous to our own. Such a richness of theatrical life can only be preserved by means of heavy subsidization, but the West German public willingly pays the price. Aid from *Land* and *Gemeinde* amounted to 450 million marks a year in 1963 (forty times the British contribution to the theatre!), the equivalent of 4·50 DM per theatre ticket. Many theatres are visited by groups of workers from factories and offices, who can purchase their tickets at reduced prices through their membership of a theatre club; best known is the *Volksbühne*, with nearly half a million members in over a hundred different area organizations. Of particular renown are the productions of the theatres in Hamburg, Düsseldorf, Munich, Göttingen and Bochum, while West Berlin is a special chapter in itself: there are seventeen permanent theatres operating in this outpost of the Federal Republic.

In the sphere of music, we find sixty regular opera companies, again maintained largely out of public funds, while every town of any size has it own orchestra. In addition to the civic orchestras, there are also those maintained by the nine broadcasting companies, which often have a considerable reputation both inside and outside Germany. They mostly also possess their own choir—for Germany has a strong tradition of choral singing which has lost none of its fervour in modern times.

Broadcasting is the concern of nine self-governing corporations, some representing one particular *Land*, others a group of *Länder*. They control both sound and television services and provide a fair range of programme choice. They are supported largely by the yield of radio and television licences, the rest of their revenue deriving from the limited amount of commercial broadcasting in which they engage. In 1970 holders of television licences totalled more than sixteen millions; there were about nineteen million radio licences. The radio programmes are devoted principally to music and light entertainment, only about 20% of their material being of a serious or instructional character (including news). The nine broadcasting corporations combine to produce a daily television programme (Programme I), the major contributions deriving from the West German, North German and Bavarian stations, which produce about two-thirds of the items, on the 625 line system. Each station also transmits a certain amount of local material every day. There are three national television programmes. The Third Programme, separately inaugurated by several of the stations in 1964 and 1965, is a cultural and educational service, operating in the evenings only, and in some instances carrying adult education courses. (A Third Programme on local radio discharges a similar function.) A considerable amount of live reporting and political commentary is carried by the other two television channels, and criticism is unrestrained and in general devoid of party political commitment. Films, plays, operas, serials, discussion and topical programmes and sport take up much of the remaining time. The Second Programme, inaugurated in April 1963, is a completely separate organization from the other two, being controlled by a public corporation of all the *Länder,* and draws 70% of its revenue from commercial advertising. Colour television was introduced in August 1967, receiving only four hours a week initially on its two national transmitters, but these hours have been rapidly extended. It was estimated that by the end of 1970 there were over $1\frac{1}{2}$ million colour television sets in West German homes.

The West German public is not as addicted to newspaper reading as the American or British: the daily sale of copies is 31·5% of the population, compared with 35% for the USA and 57·3% for Britain. And many of these are local papers, containing mainly local news, and filled with advertisements of every conceivable type. Something like 1,300 daily papers are printed in West Germany, and only the Springer Press's *Bildzeitung* achieves a circulation of significantly more than half a million.[7] Its average daily sales amount to four million copies, and are estimated to be read by 14·5 million people, from all walks of life and all levels of education. Its title refers to its preference for presenting news through pictures rather than through words.

[7] Its closest rival, in 1968, was the *Westdeutsche Allgemeine* of Essen, with a circulation of 526,000 copies daily.

In 1968, the Springer publishing house controlled 92·7% of the national daily and Sunday newspapers of the Federal Republic, and 37% of all newspapers, local and national. In addition, it sold 57·3% of the publications containing the details of radio and television programmes. Axel Cäsar Springer is Europe's largest publisher. He produces the largest national daily in West Germany (*Bildzeitung*), the largest evening paper (*Hamburger Abendblatt*) the two largest Sunday newspapers and the largest television and radio magazine.

Another combine, Gruner und Jahr GmbH, controls the majority of the illustrated and women's magazine market. Formed in July 1965 from three separate magazine publishing firms, its produces such widely selling periodicals as *Stern, Constanze, Brigitte* and *Die Zeit*. There is an unwritten understanding between this group and the Springer concern: the former will publish no daily or Sunday newspaper, if the latter stays out of the women's and illustrated magazine market. These two giants between them leave little room for other major concerns.

There are, however, a number of independent publications, while certain dailies represent the views of particular political parties. *Der Spiegel* is probably the best known of the independent journals. It is published by the firm of Rudolf Augstein, and had increased its circulation from 15,000 in its initiation year, 1947, to pass the million mark by 1971. Modelled in the style of the American *Time* magazine, it inspects all facets of German and international affairs, concentrates on uncovering scandals, injustice, and inadequacies at governmental, institutional or personal levels, and delights in political gossip and speculation.

Another independent publication is the much respected *Frankfurter Allgemeine Zeitung*, produced by a public corporation, though this daily tends to follow the CDU line. The CDU has a number of newspapers specifically committed to the support of its policies, produced by the Verein Union-Presse, founded in 1947. They are economically independent and have no organizational links with the political party, and include such regional papers as the *Aachener Volkszeitung,* the *Kölnische Rundschau* and the *Rheinische Post*. The total local and regional publications of this Verein Union-Presse group represent a circulation of one million copies per day. Other newspapers, without being specifically committed to the CDU's policies, nevertheless give it their general support, even when claiming to be independent and non-party. The CSU in Bavaria has its own weekly, the *Bayernkurier,* which under the control of Franz Josef Strauss unashamedly proclaims the policies of that party and has risen to considerable prominence as a barometer of right-wing CDU/CSU thinking.

The SPD has the support of a group of presses similar to that supporting the CDU. The organization into which they are joined is known as *Konzentration*, and it comprises twenty-six daily and weekly newspapers, with a combined circulation of 1·4 million. Their editors meet periodically to co-ordinate policies, though each is free to follow its own course and there is no control by the SPD itself. Employees are not required to be SPD members. The *Hannoversche Presse* and the Berlin *Telegraf* are two of the better known and long-established representatives of this SPD grouping.

Little need be said of the West German cinema. The loss of the film studios in Berlin to the East Zone in 1945, plus the film's aesthetic decline under Nazism, have never really been surmounted.

The longer-established tradition of the museum and art gallery, on the other hand, remains strongly entrenched. 326 museums are maintained by the local authorities, and are being utilized increasingly for school and educational course requirements. Of especial interest and a particularly German phenomenon are the local history museums (*Heimatmuseen*), of which there are 112, and which contain all conceivable types of objects and records from their surrounding area. The cost of maintaining these various museums is borne almost entirely by *Land*, *Gemeinde* and local associations. The art galleries must, of course, be included in this list, for they are numerous and contain some splendid collections of paintings and other works of art. The most famous are probably those in Munich (the *Pinakothek*), Düsseldorf (20th century collection), Cologne, Essen, Hanover and Frankfurt.

The younger generation necessarily receives its due in the various authorities' social policies. Chief provider here is the Federal Government, which spent 65 million marks in 1968 on its *Bundesjugendplan* (Federal Youth Plan); the figure had been greater in earlier years. The largest individual item was political education (including international contacts, discussions and Berlin visits), but an almost equally large portion was devoted to help in the form of vocational training assistance, the building of hostels, educational centres and youth clubs, re-settlement hostels for young refugees and the general furtherance of youth associations' activities. A sum of nearly fourteen million marks was also allocated to the promotion of the various youth organizations (*Jugendverbände*), fourteen of which are organized into the German Youth Ring, with a membership of six millions. Largest of these is the sports association (*Deutsche Sportjugend*), with nearly 2½ million members. A Protestant and a Catholic youth movement each have a membership of one million, while the trade union youth organization has 750,000 members. The scout and guide movement has 150,000 followers. Other independent groups also exist, some of them with a primarily political purpose. At local level there are many clubs which represent the interest of film, jazz and photography enthusiasts, as well as literary, artistic and discussion groups. The seven hundred youth hostels of West Germany also receive a considerable subsidy from the state, enabling them to provide for eight million overnight visits annually, more than half a million of these by foreigners.

Sport, being little provided for in the schools, is one more sphere where the state shows its helping hand. The most popular sport of all is football, but gymnastics follows as a close second. Athletics are also very popular. There are about 32,000 sport clubs, with $5\frac{1}{2}$ million members, one fifth of whom are women. Nearly 67,000 football teams play matches on behalf of 15,000 clubs; while $1\frac{1}{2}$ million gymnasts belong to the 7,600 groups of the *Deutscher Turnerbund*.

In an attempt to counteract the record of declining physical fitness in the Federal Republic, the authorities have set themselves the goal of providing sporting facilities in the ratio of four square metres per head of the population, but are still far short of its achievement. Medical statistics show that almost one child in two enters school already afflicted with some form of infirmity, that the proportion of young people in commerce who require medical treatment rose from $17 \cdot 8\%$ to $31 \cdot 2\%$ in five years alone, and that the affluent society is characterized by a statistic of 70% of all employees retiring, on average, ten years before the statutory retirement age. Children in the *Volksschule* receive only two hours' physical education in the course of the week's lessons, those in secondary schools only three. The hoped for introduction of full-day schooling should make possible an improvement on this front, with consequential benefits to the nation's health.

B. EAST GERMANY

1. *Social Security*

Commitment to social policies is an article of faith for socialist states, and we discover, in the case of East Germany, widespread provision for all sections of the community. The welfare system has developed and improved as conditions within the country have themselves improved and a greater degree of social relief has proved possible.

Social insurance in the East German state is controlled and administered by the Trade Union Federation. Every factory or workshop has its own elected social insurance officers, who not only deal with cases of sickness or injury, but also matters like massage treatment, the provision of spectacles and so on. The social insurance scheme is comprehensive: it includes not only the sickness fund but also pensions and accident insurance. The scheme is a compulsory one; every insured person pays a contribution equal to 10% of his gross wage, but never more than sixty marks per month. Another 10% is contributed by the employer (20% in the case of miners). All scholars and students are automatically included in the scheme, being freed from the obligation to contribute. The employing firm also pays a contribution for each employee into an accident insurance fund, calculated on the basis of risk estimated for that particular enterprise.

During the first six weeks of illness, a payment is made equal to 90% of normal earnings (50% from the social insurance fund and 40% from the employee's firm); after this period, the figure is reduced to a rate of 50%, with a ceiling of 600 marks a month, in the case of people without dependents, and 80% otherwise. Clinical and hospital treatment is entirely free. Extra allowances are payable to victims of Nazi persecution and to workers in the mining industry.

A person in need of medical attention has the choice of either going to a doctor in an individual practice or attending a *Polyklinik*—a communal medical centre. There is no charge in either instance, for all doctors are organized into the state health service. The polyclinics are often located in the factory itself or are attached to hospitals, and can provide a comprehensive range of services which the individual doctor could not himself supply. There were 423 such clinics in operation in 1967. They normally have at least five separate departments, each under the charge of a specialist, providing treatment for internal diseases, surgery, women's diseases and maternity care, children's diseases and dental care. They are therefore being developed on an increasing scale, especially in rural areas, where there is a lack of individual doctors' practices. Travelling clinics provide some of the needs of those areas; they numbered 367 in 1967.

In addition to free hospital treatment, the East German citizen also receives free medicine with a doctor's prescription (he may buy other medicines if he wishes from the chemist's shop), as well as all orthopaedic aids, artificial limbs, spectacles, false teeth and so forth. There were in 1968 1·7 registered pharmacists for every 10,000 inhabitants, and special medicament supply centres have been established in rural areas where prescriptions can be collected. East Germany produces nearly all her own requirements in the medical field, from antibiotics like penicillin and streptomycin to highly sophisticated instruments and machinery. Courses of treatment at spas and other health resorts are also free, and on the recommendation of a doctor a patient usually spends four weeks undergoing such treatment, though longer visits are also possible if the case merits it. The number of people attending such courses in 1967 amounted to almost one third of a million.

There were 721 hospitals in service in 1966, with 202,000 beds at their disposal, giving a ratio of 119 hospital beds to 10,000 inhabitants. For every 10,000 citizens in 1968 there were 14·4 doctors, 3·9 dentists and 1·7 pharmacists, and particular stress was being laid on increasing the number of practising doctors. Immunization against certain diseases is compulsory, leading to the virtual elimination of poliomyelitis by 1963. Annual chest X-rays are also compulsory for adults, as are tuberculosis innoculations. The tuberculosis rate for 1965 was only one sixth of the 1950 figure, standing at 1·5% of the population. Much attention is paid to preventive medicine, as well as to convalescence and after-care, and these services are normally organized alongside those for curative medicine, so that a continuity of treatment is facilitated. In most places of work the employees receive a medical check-up when they commence employment and their subsequent state of health is periodically checked. A big drive to improve safety measures in the factories resulted in a drop in the accident figures from 57 per thousand workers in 1952 to 43 per thousand in 1966.

A system of family allowances is also in operation in East Germany. On the whole its terms are more generous than those offered to West German citizens, or indeed, those of the UK. On the birth of her first child, a mother receives a maternity grant of 500 marks; the amount of this grant increases with each succeeding child, to reach a total of 1,000 marks for the fifth and each succeeding child. Then, for each child in the family, a monthly allowance is paid by the state up to the age of fifteen. For the first, second and third children the amount is 20 marks each, but the fourth child receives a grant of 60 marks a month and all subsequent children receive 70 marks. Women in regular employment are entitled to fourteen weeks' leave both before and after the birth of a child, and their jobs are kept open for them for a period of up to one year.

In addition to the above benefits, employed persons are also eligible for retirement pensions. These are calculated on the basis of length of service. There is a basic payment of 150 marks a month for all retired persons, and to this is added an increment of 0·50 marks a month for every year of insurance in excess of a basic ten year period. A working life of forty years would thus entitle the retiring person to the basic pension of 150 marks a month (in 1968) plus 15 marks increase for thirty years' service over and above the initial ten years, giving a pension of 165 marks a month. The East German authorities have experienced difficulty in building up this pension fund; a reserve of 500 million marks had first to be achieved, in 1964, before a pensions level even more modest than the present restricted one could be introduced. As a result of the last war's manpower losses and the flight of many of the younger workers to the West prior to 1961, there are today something like 32 pensioners to every 100 people of working age.

Retirement is normally at the age of 65 for men and 60 for women, but an earlier retirement is permitted in special cases, as for instance, victims of Nazi persecution or workers in unhygienic occupations. People who wish to continue working after reaching the retirement age are free to do so, if found to be medically fit, and they sacrifice none of their pension, which they draw in full, in addition to their wages. They also no longer need to pay social insurance contributions. There is a certain amount of residential provision for the aged and infirm, and many community groups also make it one of their concerns to attend to the needs of the elderly. A scheme of public assistance is also in operation for the benefit of the needy and the down-and-out, who have not been contributors to the pensions scheme; allowances are paid in accordance with the specific needs of the individual, according to fixed scales which are regularly reviewed.

Freelance and independent workers, professional men and the self-employed are also included in the social insurance scheme. Their contributions are graded according to the level of their earnings. There is complete parity of treatment for all participants in the insurance scheme. Additional insurance may be taken out with the Insurance Institution, to obtain increased sickness, retirement and accident benefits. Every second citizen was estimated to have entered into some such insurance scheme in 1967. State schemes also exist for the insurance of the person and of personal and communal property against accident, damage and other risks. Life and house insurances are frequently taken out by East German citizens, and all owners of motor vehicles are compulsorily insured. There is only one insurance organization, and this a state-owned institution.

An increased indebtedness in the social insurance fund has led to a growing need for state subsidization. Insurance revenue in 1957 totalled 6,067 million marks, expenditure 6,680 million marks, necessitating a state subsidy of 613 millions; by 1965 the subsidy had to be increased to the level of 2,532 million marks, revenues then totalling 7,015 millions and expenditure 9,547 millions. In all, the state had to find an extra 11,500 million marks in 1965 to support the various forms of social insurance payments and benefits. Total state spending on health and the social services in 1965 came to 16,700 million marks.

The employees of large concerns receive numerous additional benefits, such as the provision of hot or cold meals and certain durable goods. There were 9,000 works kitchens in operation in 1967, which in addition to supplying their own factory, also provided meals for smaller enterprises in the neighbourhood. State subsidies help keep the price of meals at a low level, ranging between 0·70 and 2 marks. State enterprises must also assist their employees in finding housing accommodation and obtaining repairs, and by looking after the children of those mothers who are at work. There was nursery provision for nearly a quarter of a million children below the age of three in 1968; that is almost one quarter of those eligible.

2. *Housing*

The destruction of residential property in East Germany as a consequence of war was just as severe as in the West. Probably the most destructive single attack of all was the British/American bombing raid on the city of Dresden on 13th February 1945, when 135,000 human beings perished—more than in the first atom bomb raid on Hiroshima in Japan. The general shortage of housing in the immediate post-war years was greatly aggravated by the arrival of millions of refugees from lands further to the east, whose numbers presently accounted for almost one quarter of the total East German population.

The beginning of reconstruction was slow, for materials and finance were scarce, and the first priority was given to industrial building. The pace has quickened in more recent times, and between 1950 and 1966 an increase of 271% was recorded in the building industry's production; between 1964 and 1966 the increase amounted to 12%, the value of building construction in the latter year totalling 9,000 million marks. By 1968 it had reached a figure of 11,000 millions, and 16·5% of this was allocated to the construction of residential accommodation. An equal sum was devoted to demolition, repair and alterations. (Nevertheless, the West Germans built three times as many homes per head of the population between 1950 and 1968).

The number of dwellings (houses and flats) in existence in 1967 almost reached the six million level, providing for a population of just over seventeen millions, with a total floor area of 314,530,000 sq. metres. 76,000 new units came into use in 1968, though the peak figures were for the years 1959–62 (1961: 92,000 new homes). The figure fell in 1970, and only 73,000 units were planned for 1971. Increasing use is made of prefabrication, especially in the building of blocks of flats, with a consequent speeding up of the building process; more than two thirds of housing construction is now carried out by this process. Frequently, entire room units are installed in this way, and parts arrive for assembly with windows already inserted and the walls with their outer coat of plaster already applied. There has also been a considerable degree of mechanization in the building industry and work study has been devoted to the establishing of the most efficient ways of performing jobs, sometimes with the use of a computer. Roughly three quarters of house building is in the hands of state-managed enterprises.

The face of a number of East German cities is changing radically as post-war reconstruction proceeds. Some, like Dresden, have had their former beauties restored, while others, East Berlin in particular, have been transformed by the building of tall blocks of flats, impressive boulevards and soaring structures like the Television Tower, second highest in Europe (it discreetly concedes a foot or two to its peer in Moscow). The drab Russian-style housing blocks, reminiscent of the Stalin era, are now giving way to more varied, open designs, with contrasts often achieved by the alternation of external colours, mural patterns, porches, lighting and ornamentation. Instead of massive groups of identical type, the tendency nowadays is to design neighbourhood areas, which in addition to dwelling accommodation also include shops, schools and open spaces for play and recreation. It is often possible to exclude motor traffic from such areas.

While vast sums of money are being expended on the reinstatement of aristocratic palaces and castles from the past, as in Dresden (the baroque *Zwinger*) and Potsdam (Frederick the Great's chateau of Sanssouci), to help develop tourism, entire new townships are also springing up as fresh industries are developed whose employees need homes to live in. Halle-Neustadt is one example, a monumental undertaking designed to house 80,000 people connected with the Leuna chemical works. Other similar townships are Hoyerswerda and Eisenhüttenstadt (for lignite and metallurgical plants respectively). Such developments tend, however, to stand in splendid isolation, with few local amenities, almost frightening in their stark splendour, on which the East Germans themselves comment. (Similar things can happen in the West of course: the planners of one new residential suburb in Brunswick forgot to include shops in their scheme.)

The private ownership of residential property is permitted, and owners who wish to renovate their buildings receive tax reductions and loans at favourable rates. Most people, however, live in rented accommodation, and in the towns this usually means a flat. 857,000 flats were either built or reconstructed between 1950 and

o

1966, which meant one flat every eight minutes in 1965. The new flats mostly incorporate features commonly associated with modern building design: $42 \cdot 1\%$ of those built in 1965 had central heating, $77 \cdot 3\%$ had running hot water and $85 \cdot 2\%$ had built-in kitchens. Older flats often leave much to be desired and little money is available for their improvement. Lower rents are, however, charged for all accommodation built before 1966, in which year the average expenditure by all employees on rents amounted to no more than $3 \cdot 8\%$ of their spending. In small towns and rural areas, rents ranged between $0 \cdot 6$ and $0 \cdot 8$ marks per square metre, in the cities between $0 \cdot 8$ and one mark, and in Berlin between $0 \cdot 9$ and $1 \cdot 2$ marks. Extra rates are charged for central heating and running hot water. These levels of rent were found to be inadequate to cover the increased costs of modern building and supply of services, and in 1966 the decision was taken to raise the level of rents on all post-1965 building so that they covered building and maintenance costs. A two-room flat in East Berlin in 1969 cost 45 marks a month without bath and central heating, and 90 marks if it included these facilities. The average West German household in 1968, with an income of 1,300 DM, spent 163 DM ($12 \cdot 5\%$) of this on rent; the corresponding East German income was 948 marks, with 37 marks ($3 \cdot 9\%$) spent on rent.

The obtaining of accommodation is no straightforward matter, and social or industrial need must first be proved. Housing offices of the local state organs normally allocate such accommodation, the housing commission (consisting of three to five domestic planning experts) being also a party to the consultations. Recommendations are made on the basis of the urgency of the case and the applicant's contribution to society. Families with many children and disabled persons receive priority.

A considerable number of flats are built by Workers' Housing Construction Co-operatives (AWGs). These may be formed by any group of workers, who combine to build flats at lower cost and therefore capable of being let at a lower rent. They receive from the state free land on which to build, in addition to interest-free loans of up to 85% of the building costs. The rest of the finance is raised by the members themselves, who buy shares in the enterprise, at a rate of 300 marks per share. These shares remain their personal property. A one-room flat costs, on average, 1,200 marks and each additional room 300 marks. Contributions of equipment, labour and additional funds from various voluntary sources also help to defray costs. The allocation of these flats is carried out on the basis of social need: a single person receives one room; a 2–3

person family receives a two-room flat, a 3–4 person family a two-
or three-room flat, and so on. Kitchens, bathrooms and halls are
not counted as rooms. These co-operatives only came into existence
in 1955, but by 1968 they were providing one quarter of all dwellings
built.

Many landlords of old properties, finding themselves restricted
to the official level of rents fixed for older accommodation, discover
the unprofitability of their assets and are increasingly ready to turn
them over to the state. They can then often be renovated and re-let
at economic rents by the local authorities; but much sub-standard
housing still exists, since the cost of repairs would be prohibitive
for private owners. The five-year plan for 1971–75 looks forward
to the provision of 500,000 new flats, compared with the total of
365,000 for the preceding quinquennium.

3. *Social and Family Life*

The population of East Germany has experienced a slight but
consistent decline in numbers ever since 1945. The total for 1949
was 17,285,902: in 1968 it stood at 17,084,000. The principal
reason for this fall is the flight of people to the West: another
factor is the low birth rate. After hovering between 16 and 17 per
thousand from 1950 to 1955, the birth rate fell slightly in the three
succeeding years and then rose to a peak of 17·6 per thousand in
1963, since when it has fallen progressively; in 1968 it stood at 14·3
per thousand (West Germany 17·7). The number of marriages has
also shown an overall decline, from 11·7 per thousand of the population in 1950 to 7 per thousand in 1968. The one positive factor
has been the decline in infant deaths and still births which have
been reduced by two thirds since 1950. We must also note that the
birth rate has always exceeded the death rate, though they did just
draw level in 1968.

The population structure shows a similar imbalance of the sexes
to that in West Germany. In 1968 there were 7,834,000 men to
9,249,000 women. In the working age group, women outnumbered
men with a total of 5,060,000, compared with a male total of
4,819,000. This group's proportion of the population stood at
57·8%. The statistics for children, however, showed the same corrective process at work that we encountered in the case of the West
Germans: boys outnumbered girls by 2,017,000 to 1,918,000. Together they comprised 23% of the population, leaving retired persons to account for 19·1%. The principal surplus in the female

population occurs as we should expect in the fifty to eighty years old age group, at least half of the women above the age of seventy being widows. Men are most scarce in the fifty to fifty-five years age group.

The favourite age for marriage among men in 1967 lay between twenty-two and twenty-six; for women between eighteen (the minimum age) and twenty-one. Marriages are also proving to be more stable than was the case in the early post-war years: the divorce rate in 1968 stood at 1·63 per thousand of the population. A divorced woman is only granted alimony from her husband if she is incapable of earning her own living. On the other hand there has been an increase in the number of illegitimate births, the total rising to 10% in 1968. The number of deaths from infectious diseases has declined dramatically to reach a level of 0·8 per 10,000 of the population in 1967; tuberculosis has shown an even steeper decline, from 7·8 in 1950 to 1·2 per 10,000 in 1967. On the other hand, deaths from heart and circulatory trouble (44·1 per 10,000) and from malignant growths (24·2 per 10,000) had increased steadily up to 1967.

The basic working week in East Germany is, since 1967, one of five days, so that there is now greater opportunity for leisure pursuits. In many families the wife is also at work, so that such free time as exists for her is likely to be devoted to domestic tasks. More than 70% of women between the age of sixteen and sixty are in some form of employment, and the majority of them remain at work after the birth of their children. Factories and offices make as many concessions as is practicable to facilitate this situation, granting women not only the statutory maternity leave, but also paid leave of absence when children are ill (up to four weeks) and one free day per month in any case. Works and school canteens help solve the meals problem for the family, and there are now available in the shops ready-prepared and frozen foods for quick cooking. Where women work with machinery, steps are usually taken to ensure that it is adapted to their requirements, and if possible provision is made for them to be seated whilst working. An interesting reflection of the emancipation of women is the arrangement whereby a couple, on marriage, may assume the woman's maiden name, instead of the man's.

Holidays are another matter fixed by state decree, and the relevant figures have been quoted (see p. 103). Extra paid leave is granted in certain deserving cases, and where husband and wife are entitled to different lengths of holiday, extra unpaid leave is granted to the less privileged one, so that they may share the full holiday. Urgent family matters can also be the basis for the granting of paid leave for one or two days. The holiday needs of the worker are catered for in a number of ways. The trade unions maintain holiday homes in many parts of the country, both by the sea and in the mountains. One million such holidays were booked in 1965. The average length of stay was twelve days; the cost is calculated according to family income. A family with two children, staying full board and enjoying all the facilities offered, would pay only 172·5 marks in the high season for a twelve-day holiday, assuming the parents' joint earnings to be 1,200 marks a month. Non-trade union members pay higher rates. The state railways also grant a 33⅓% fare reduction for such trips.

Holidays abroad can also be arranged through the trade union organization but these can only be taken, of course, in countries of the Communist bloc, for travel to the West is banned. Cruises on the two holiday ships belonging to the trade union organization are popular, and some factories run holiday homes of their own. There is in addition a state travel bureau, through which holidays at home and abroad can be privately booked. In 1966 some 650,000 people took foreign holidays in this way, many of them being of the package tour variety. The number of these doubled in the period 1963–1966. Favourite destination in 1968 was Czechoslovakia, with Poland, Russia and Bulgaria as poor seconds. Some East Germans have solved the problem of keeping contact with West German relatives by arranging to take their holidays together on the sands of Black Sea resorts! Camping holidays are also popular, especially with the younger generation; charges are only 10 to 30 Pfennig a day, and it is also possible to hire various camping requisites on the spot. Youth hostels are also available for the use of the young: there were 251 of them in 1967, in addition to other overnight accommodation and camps for young people. The charge at a youth hostel is 25 Pfennig a night. Special cheap walking and sports holidays are also organized for students and apprentices.

A determined attempt is made by the state authorities to keep prices stable, and during the past few years it has been largely successful. While wages have doubled since 1950, many prices have actually been reduced, those for food and consumer goods by as much as one half (taking 1960 as a base). The purchasing power of the mark in 1967 was still 99·7% of its 1960 value, according to the official statistical report of 1969.

The following table gives price comparisons of certain foodstuffs and consumer goods in East and West Germany for the years 1962 and 1969:

	1962		1969	
	W. Marks	*E. Marks*	*W. Marks*	*E. Marks*
Potatoes (5 kg.)	1·74	0·85	1·90	0·85
Wheat flour (1 kg.)	1·04	1·32	1·04	1·32
White bread (1 kg.)	1·24	1·0	1·56	1·0
Stewing steak (1 kg.)	7·62	9·80	9·74	9·80
Pork chops (1 kg.)	7·06	8·0	7·88	8·0
Mettwurst (1 kg.)	6·03	6·80	6·97	6·80
Drinking milk (½ litre)	0·29	0·36	0·37	0·36
Butter (1 kg.)	7·21	10·0	7·72	10·0
Margarine, best quality (1 kg.)	2·20	4·0	2·52	4·0
Eggs (each)	0·20	0·37	0·20	0·36
Filter cigarettes (ten)	0·83	1·60	0·91	1·60
Beer (1 litre)	1·24	1·50	1·24	1·50
Coffee (1 kg.)	17·19	70·0	15·56	70·0
Tea (50 gr.)	1·20	1·20	1·32	1·20
Electricity (23 kwh.)	5·68	3·84	6·69	3·84
2nd class rail fare (50 km.)	4·0	4·0	4·25	4·0
Local phone call (one unit)	0·20	0·20	0·20	0·20
Cinema seat (2nd cheapest)	1·72	1·0	2·89	1·06
Men's leather shoes (one pair)	30·75	42·25	35·10	41·75
Man's two-piece suit	129·0	188·0	139·0	188·0
Girl's woollen dress	13·20	13·80	13·90	13·80
Man's shirt (nylon)	22·80	75·0	22·0	75·0
Woman's stockings (20 denier)	2·65	11·60	2·50	7·47
Bed sheet	10·18	17·40	11·23	17·40
China plate (24 cm.)	1·24	1·40	1·46	1·40
Electric light bulb (24 watts)	1·0	1·0	1·20	1·0
Electric iron with regulator	28·25	33·60	24·60	35·50
Electric cooker (3 plates)	340·0	630·0	295·0	642·0
Television set 23 in.	780·0	2,050·0	564·0	1,760·0
Refrigerator	380·0	1,350·0	301·0	1,250·0
Man's bicycle	154·0	242·0	159·0	242·0

(Source: *Bericht zur Lage der Nation*, Bundesministerium für innerdeutsche Beziehungen, 1971.)

In 1969 47% of all West German households possessed a car, 73% a television set, 91% a radio, 84% a refrigerator, and 61% an electric washing machine; the figures for East Germany were 14% for cars, 66% for television sets, 92% for radios and 48% for both refrigerators and washing machines.

The average East German household of four persons had 78·6% of its income disposable after taxation and other deductions in 1967, and spent 30·7% on food, 8·9% on consumer goods, 10·2% on clothing and textiles, and a further 15% on industrial goods. Very small amounts needed to be spent on transport (1·8%), rents (3·4%), gas and electricity (1·4%), while culture and recreation accounted for 2·2%. Most of these latter items are state-subsidized.

The following is a comparative list of per capita annual consumption levels in both states for 1960 and 1968:

	1960		1968	
	West	*East*	*West*	*East*
Beef (kgs.)	19·5	17·5	23	18·4
Pork (kgs.)	30·9	33·3	37·7	39·0
Poultry (kgs.)	3·9	3·7	7·1	4·6
Eggs	228	197	254	220
Milk (litres)	112·7	94·5	104·1	99·2
Butter (kgs.)	6·4	10·4	7·1	10·8
Margarine (kgs.)	8·4	8·2	7·4	8·8
Potatoes (kgs.)	133	173·9	110	150
Vegetables (fresh) (kgs.)	45·8	48	62·9	56·7
Flour and cereals (kgs.)	81·7	99·2	68·9	95
Coffee (kgs.)	2·9	1·1	4·1	2
Beer (litres)	94·9	79·5	129·4	86·3
Cigarettes	1,282	1,069	1,753	1,201
Shoes (pairs)	3	3	3·8	3·4
T.V. and radio sets (per 1,000 people)	85·2	72·8	92·8	68·1
Motor cars (per 1,000 people)	18·4	3·4	22·8	6·2

There is considerably less variety in the shops than one finds in the West, and the more extreme fashions in dress and furnishings are absent, but there is a fair selection of modern design in most things—including the mini-skirt. Young people enjoy modern pop music and appear in public places carrying transistor radios which play the latest hits. Most cafés, bars and places of entertainment, however, refuse to admit 'rowdies' and display notices calling for decent dress and behaviour.

The home is more the centre of leisure activities and constitutes the place of relaxation to a greater extent than in the West. It is difficult, out of doors, to escape the party presence, for so much of the provision there is the effort of state and party organizations; pictures of Walther Ulbricht confront one at every turn, and even the public buildings and factories are likely to be hung with placards which proclaim such messages as: *Aus der Geschichte lernen heißt die Zukunft meistern* ('To learn from history is to master the future') and *Was des Volkes Hände schaffen, das ist des Volkes eigen* ('That which the people's hands have created belongs to the people'). The East Germans are family-centred and move house infrequently (cf. the removal rate of 18% per annum, compared with 48% in the Federal Republic). Their static habits arise largely from the great difficulty of obtaining accommodation elsewhere, because of the housing shortage; even when they marry they hesitate to leave the family home, for official regulations demand that the rooms they vacate must be made available to persons on the housing list, who would thus become invaders of the family circle (for the same reason other relatives are often found to share the accommodation of the resident family). We might also note that East German life is much more that of a small-town society, and therefore less sophisticated. There are only eleven cities with more than 100,000 inhabitants, and only six with more than 250,000. One person in five lived in a *Großstadt* in 1970, compared with West Germany's one in three.

Traditional family occasions are being invaded by the state at another level also. The ceremonies of baptism, confirmation, marriage and even burial, traditionally associated with the sphere of the Church, now find socialist equivalents established alongside them. East German citizens may make their vows to the state, rather than to the Church, at a socialist wedding, and are actively encouraged to do so. Principal target of these policies is the young generation, who are encouraged to undergo the ceremony of Youth Dedication to the State (*Jugendweihe*), in place of the customary confirmation by the Church. Nearly all children in the upper classes of schools receive preparatory lessons for this dedication ceremony, taken at the age of fifteen, which confers on them the status of adult citizens of the Workers' and Farmers' Republic, with the right to be addressed as *Sie* instead of the junior's *du*. Even the names of the traditional events in the Christian calendar are being secularized: Easter, for instance, has been renamed Spring Festival (*Frühlingsfest*), and dates are given in terms of 'before our time' (*vor unserer Zeit*) and 'after our time' (*nach unserer Zeit*) instead of the conventional Christian formulation of BC and AD. The Church is hard pressed to maintain itself, even though not actively harassed by the state authorities. Theological training colleges and their students are still supported from official funds, and the clergy are permitted to carry out their proper ecclesiastical duties. No religion is, however, taught in the schools, and this must therefore be the responsibility of the Church itself; Sunday-schools exist, but may teach only religion, and church societies may not discuss anything outside the field of religion at their meetings. The clergy are also severed from their Western brethren by the authorities' refusal to permit their Western bishops to visit them, or to allow their travel to the West, even to attend church congresses in West Berlin. The Church in East Germany is self-supporting and still has a considerable following, though its adherents are to be found in the older generation rather than the young. The policy of the Ulbricht government towards non-violent opponents of the regime seems to be one of distant tolerance; the opposition is dismissed as insignificant or simply ignored, while the important job of building the new East German Democratic Republic is enthusiastically publicized.

"We hope to persuade, not to compel" is the official approach. In this way martyrs are avoided and alien causes become lost ones.

4. *Education*

(a) Schools

The basic feature of the East German educational system is the **Ten-Year Polytechnical School**, introduced in 1959, and compulsory for all East German children. It replaced the old, Weimar-type school system, and became legally compulsory in 1965. It was hoped that it would be in universal operation by the end of 1970. No private schools are permitted, and education commences at the same basic level for all. Compulsory education covers a period of twelve years, of which ten are spent in full-time education and the final two years in part-time vocational training.

The school system is unified, from the nursery school right through to the university. Education of a very rudimentary kind is even attempted in the crèches (*Kinderkrippen*) where mothers leave their babies while they go to work (they are mostly open for 24 hours of the day). Here babies are encouraged to perform exercises and do simple tasks which will help to develop the co-ordination of mind and body. At the nursery school, attended voluntarily between the ages of three and six, a more deliberate effort is made at instilling mental and physical disciplines. 50% of the children go to nursery schools, whose syllabus—like that of all subsequent education—is laid down by the Ministry of Education. Whether in nursery, collective, factory or school, the type and manner of instruction given will be nationally integrated and synchronized—as in Napoleon's France. The educational programme is indeed part of the Five Year Plan!

The nursery, or kindergarten, schools are organized either by the local authority or by an industrial enterprise, and are intended to prepare children for the start of full-time schooling at the age of six. Music, singing and poetry are used as a means of encouraging linguistic ability, and developing the memory and the imagination. Painting and drawing are also featured, but free expression is not encouraged, realistic representation being preferred. A certain amount of physical training is also included. More ambitious and questionable are some of the attempts at character training, stress being laid on self-discipline, adventure, self-advancement and respect for parents and working people. Certain duties connected with the running of the kindergarten are also assumed by the children, so that they learn a sense of co-operation and responsibility. For those children who do not attend these preparatory classes, there are many organized play groups available.

Full-time schooling commences at the age of six. The ten-year curriculum is divided into a lower and a higher stage of studies: the lower stage, constituting the first six years, is again divided into two three-year phases, the *Unterstufe* ('lower level') and the *Mittelstufe* ('intermediate level'). Then, from the age of twelve to sixteen, comes the four-year *Oberstufe* ('upper level').

In the *Unterstufe* classes the basic subjects are taught, and with the same strict attention to individual performance that characterizes the West German system. The only essential difference, in East Germany, is that already the social and political implications of the pupils' studies are stressed. These aspects are underlined with increasing emphasis as the child progresses up the educational ladder, culminating in the compulsory study of Marxism/Leninism and economic planning at the stage of higher education.

In the three years of the *Mittelstufe* (ages 10–12), new subjects are added to the course of studies. The first foreign language, normally Russian, is commenced now, the brightest pupils making a start immediately, and the others at the latest by the age of twelve. Other languages which can then be started include English, French, Spanish, Swedish, Polish and Czech, in that order of priority. Factual learning is still the main aim in all subjects, and their practical application is constantly kept in mind. The children learn basic mathematical and industrial skills, with an eye to their future employment: they learn to weigh and measure, to handle tools and perform simple mechanical operations. We begin to see the sense of the term 'polytechnical education'. A considerable amount of sport is also included in the timetable; here stress is laid on the improvement of one's performance, by concentration on technique. Pupils at this stage also receive their first guidance on the choice of a career, so that they may prepare themselves in good time; talks and advice are given to both pupils and parents on the prospects ahead, and national economic needs are naturally stressed.

The upper school, or *Oberstufe*, comprises, as we saw, the last four years of compulsory schooling. A second foreign language is added here, and basically all the pupils study all the subjects in the curriculum. All therefore learn technical drawing and the handling of simple machinery. Practical instruction is an essential feature of the course, each school possessing its own workshop where articles are produced for use; the stress is on making something *to be used*. All the basic practical skills are covered, including the planning, drawing and costing side of the operation, and some of the articles produced by the upper classes are actually supplied to local industries for use (screws, small components, simple tools). On one day of each week the entire class works in a factory or collective, learning how a production line is run, machinery maintained, or farming processes carried out. By the end of a course, the class is sometimes able to take over an entire production line. Some concern has been expressed that the children might become too specialized in a particular process, rather than acquiring a general, basic knowledge of industrial processes. In class, the children are taught to concentrate on facts and systems, and the learning process is predominantly mechanical and the instruction direct; there is no encouragement of imaginative freedom, and the ideal of the objective search for truth is rejected as "a remnant of the bourgeois way of thinking". Nevertheless, the level of knowledge and ability attained by East German children is generally found to be superior, at the age of sixteen, to that of West German children, according to recent studies of refugees arriving from the East German state.

All pupils follow the full school curriculum up to the age of sixteen, when compulsory attendance finishes. There are, however, higher classes for those more able children who wish to stay at school to the age of eighteen. It is at this level that specialization really begins, leading to the *Abitur* examination at the age of eighteen or nineteen (generally one year earlier than in West Germany). In this *erweiterte Oberstufe* ('extended upper level'), in addition to continuing with the study of their basic subjects, pupils select a group of subjects for more intensive study, such as mathematics and science, modern languages, or—more rarely these days—classical studies. The study of some less important subjects may be dropped, in order to provide more time for intensive specialization.

It is now that guidance in the choice of studies becomes more significant. The national interest and the need to supply manpower shortages are guiding factors in the directing of pupils to particular areas of study, and this policy becomes even more pronounced at university level, where freedom to study a subject of one's own choosing is considerably restricted by the requirements of the national economy and official social policies. The education plan is, again, a constituent part of the national Five Year Plan.

Special educational facilities are, however, provided for unusually gifted children, who may attend language, sport, music, art, mathematics or technology institutions. In addition, there are special schools which provide for the needs of children with severe physical and mental deficiencies, roughly $2 \cdot 8\%$ of the school population. About $93 \cdot 4\%$ of all pupils attend the basic ten-year course of the polytechnic secondary school, only $3 \cdot 8\%$ remaining at school for the extended course leading to the *Abitur*.

Children who leave school at the end of the tenth year must still fulfil compulsory educational requirements in the field of vocational training, as in West Germany. Many of them will already have embarked on apprenticeships during their final years at school. The nature of this training will depend in part on the range of provision supplied by local industry, and is usually carried out in the workshop or industrial plant. The Five Year Plan for 1966–70 envisaged a total of one million young people in receipt of vocational education. The period of vocational education was double that provided in the Federal Republic in 1970; and whereas 58·4% of East German schools were vocational, the West German figure was a mere 1·3%. The proportion of advanced vocational schools was more than twice that in the Federal Republic. The instruction is given, essentially, at 1,145 vocational schools (*Berufsschulen*), where they attend for 14–21 hours instruction, on two days of the week. It is also possible to complete an apprenticeship during the final three years of the 'extended' polytechnical school. At the end of their period of vocational training, young people take an examination for the award of a 'skilled worker's certificate', and a good performance here can be followed by further studies, particularly in a *Fachschule* (technical college) and can lead to the master's examination, and also to entrance to the university, via the *Abitur*. The ratio of time spent on theoretical training to that allocated to industrial practice is roughly 1 : 2 (in West Germany it is 1 : 5).

Apprenticeships are normally concluded with a particular industry or firm, often while children are still at school. The apprentices are paid an allowance by their sponsors, amounting to 40 marks a month in the ninth class, 50 marks in the tenth class, then 60 marks and 70 marks a month in the two ensuing years. By commencing their apprenticeships while still at school, young people are able to complete them more quickly under the vocational training schemes. In 1965, 108,284 people obtained skilled workers' certificates through apprenticeship schemes, and a further 89,472 without apprenticeship contracts, mainly at local vocational training centres. This system of registration with a particular enterprise also renders possible the control of the flow of recruits to specific sectors of the economy, once more assisting the planning of industrial output. It also provides a means of channelling recruits away from undesirable utilization; apprentices may only be taken on in the private sector of industry when the requirements of the public sector have been met.

Much attention is now being directed to the improvement of educational facilities in rural areas, and most of the small, one-teacher type of schools have been replaced by central schools, established at communications centres in rural areas, to which children can be brought by bus or where they board during the week. These are ten-class polytechnic schools of the normal pattern, usually attended by children who have spent their first five years at a local school. The vocational training here is mostly devoted to agricultural matters.

Teachers at the different levels of education in East Germany receive different types of training, but all of them must undergo the nationally prescribed 'foundation' courses in Marxism-Leninism, pedagogics and psychology. Success in their teaching activities is rewarded in a number of ways: the 12th June of each year is the Day of the Teacher, when those with outstanding achievements to their credit are rewarded with titles and medals. (Salary increases are attached to these awards!) After a probationary period of two years, teachers are permanently established and eligible for additional old age pensions (60% of the terminal year's earnings) and their widows to one half of this sum. Pupils who achieve very good results at school are rewarded with free holidays at Youth Pioneer camps, and even with holiday visits to other socialist states.

There is constant association between the schools and the state. The declared aim of East German education is unambiguous: "The basis of socialist education is the knowledge of the objective general laws of the development of nature, society and of thought", says a government pronouncement of 1960, and continues: "This can only be achieved with the help of the only scientific philosophy, dialectical materialism". The preparation of nearly all children for the youth initiation ceremony during their eighth school year is one token of this link, as is also the close relationship of school and Free German Youth; each school possesses a Young Pioneer organization, whose committee includes the headmaster, several teachers, parents and Young Pioneer leaders. Parents' associations also exist, their councils elected for a two-year period, whose task is to bring forward criticisms, enlighten the parents on schools policy, and generally to assist in the running of the school. Teachers must hold regular sessions at which they may be consulted by parents; in return they have the right to visit and question parents about their children's education. Each class has its parents' committee. The school as a whole is also guided and advised by local industry and technical experts on the conduct of its courses, as well as by the Free German Youth organizations.

(b) Higher Education

In 1970, seventeen out of every thousand inhabitants of East Germany were attending a university, college or technical school (in West Germany the figure was only fourteen in every thousand). There were 44 universities and colleges, with 110,000 students (less than a third of them women), and 189 technical schools, with 120,000 students (one third of them women). The number of full universities was, however, only seven—Berlin (the Humboldt University), Rostock, Greifswald, Jena, Dresden, Halle and Leipzig, all with long traditions of learning.

The social origins of the various categories of students, in 1967, were as follows:

Social Origin	In Colleges & Universities	In Technical Schools
Workers & office staff	61·7%	72·5%
Production Co-operative Members	7·8%	11·7%
Intelligentsia	20·4%	8·9%
Others	10·1%	6·9%

Almost 85% of those engaged in full-time study at a university or college receive state grants for the period of their studies. In addition, many modern hostels have been built, in which students can live at the extremely low rent of 10 marks a month, inclusive of heating and lighting. About 25% of the students are accommodated in this way. It was estimated that each student at a college or university in 1967 cost the state the sum of 6,500 marks annually. Student's grants are calculated on the basis of need, the highest amount paid being 190 marks a month, and depend also on the level of parental income (other children in the family being also taken into account). A student not eligible for a grant receives a monthly assistance allowance of 80 marks. Students producing work of high quality can also be awarded extra grants of 40 or 80 marks a month, as well as certain special scholarships and prizes.

Entrance to higher studies depends first of all on the possession of the *Abitur* certificate, but it is customary for universities and colleges to hold an entrance examination in the subject which it is desired to study. Finally, the applicant must appear before a selection committee, made up of teaching staff, students and the trade unions. Here the would-be student's past history and social attitudes are scrutinized, as well as his examination achievements. Preference is given to those who have served their time in industry or completed their military service. In 1958 a decree was promulgated which introduced a period of one year's 'social service' work for all young people, between leaving school and entering on a degree course. The intrusion of state policies into higher education is again illustrated in the official statement of 1960: "Dialectical materialism, the only scientific philosophy, is the basic philosophy at institutes of higher learning. Its study, during the whole course, including post-graduate courses, forms the basis of scientific work". Failure in these particular studies leads to failure of one's entire course. There are three topics to be studied for examination: the historical study of Marxism, the philosophy of dialectical material-ism and the social statistics of the East German state.

At these universities and colleges the students follow curricula which are much more typical of British than of West German pro-cedures. They must attend prescribed courses and engage in set work, and they are closely supervised in their studies. Each term has its pattern of obligatory main lecture courses and planned classes. The academic year has been legally fixed at ten months' duration, the programme being laid down by the Ministry of Edu-cation. There are yearly examinations for the students, but these at least result in 30% of students obtaining the 40 marks per month bonus for good work, and a further 10% the 80 marks for very good work. Length of study varies from three to five years, accord-ing to subject, but failure in the annual examinations leads to the loss of one's grant. The final examination is normally the *Staats-examen*, but a few students take the doctor's examination (D.Phil.). First year students in technology faculties spend alternate weeks in study and industrial employment, so that their studies retain a practical basis. Between 1962 and 1967 the proportion of technical graduates rose from 14·9% to 20·4%, whereas in West Germany it sank from 10·5% to 9·3%.

A succession of reform programmes has been implemented by the state Ministry of Education in its effort to gear university education to the national effort. The first reform, of September 1951, brought universities and colleges onto a common basis in their relationship to the state and provided more direct control over their affairs. The system of fixed-length studies was introduced, with prescribed courses of lectures, the compulsory study of Russian and special stress on social studies. The second reform, of 1955, brought much internal change, breaking down the age-old structure of the disciplines, reducing the power of the professors and heads of departments and introducing much greater flexibility in planning, teaching and organization.[8] Arts subjects were considerably restric-ted and greater emphasis placed on the sciences. The third reform programme was probably the most fundamental of all, for it aligned courses of study to the specific needs of the society which these institutions serve. A lot of dead wood was cut out in the process; but so were many liberal studies. The theme was that of "education for the polytechnical society". All courses of study must be proved to be socially useful. It was this last reform, of 1968, which divided

---

[8] A consequence of these measures was an increase in the flight of academics to the West, reaching its peak in 1958. In this year, it is esti-mated that 410 academics left East Germany, including 51 professors and 52 university lecturers.

up higher studies into four distinct stages: those of basic study, subject study, specialization and research. The first two stages take four years, giving the student a thorough grounding in his subject, so that he can later follow up any aspect of it at the specialist level. Stage three, that of specialization, leads to graduation. National economic needs often play a part in the process of choice here. The fourth stage, research, is embarked upon only by a few select students.

Study for a degree is also possible by correspondence courses, and many workers in industry graduate through this arrangement. 25% of university students studied in this way in 1970, while the proportion of technical college students was as high as 39·3%. The curricula for these external students are the same as for students in full-time attendance at a university or college, and special concessions are made to assist them through their studies. Free days are granted to enable them to attend special lectures, and additional holidays allow them to participate in study courses and to take examinations. The six months preceding the final degree examinations are usually a period of leave on full pay, so that they can prepare themselves adequately. The total length of study is usually one to two years longer than that for full-time students. The subject of the course is normally closely related to the student's work in industry, so that practical experience is constantly available; and industry itself is the beneficiary, through the improved knowledge which the graduate subsequently brings to his job. In 1965 there were 30,610 students taking such correspondence courses at university institutions, and 66,800 at technical schools.

Students enjoy the right to participate in the government of their university or college, being represented by the Free German Youth organization on all decision-making bodies, where they have a consultative vote. Most students belong to the FDJ, and attend conferences and discussions which it organizes with the university staff to consider such matters as teaching, research and the structure of courses. Social policy generally is also submitted to the consideration of the student body.

Accommodation, equipment and teaching facilities have improved enormously in recent years, with obvious benefits to the student. The growth of East German industry has made possible a much greater degree of practical experience for students of science and technology (specialization is often related to the nature of neighbouring industrial activity), while recent western innovations, like the modern languages laboratory, also feature in the teaching programme of East German universities and colleges.

(c) Adult Education

Adult education is the concern mainly of the local 'academies' and evening schools ('People's Colleges'). The instruction here is wholly serious, mainly of an academic character, and has no element of the 'hobbies' classes that frequently feature in British evening class programmes. The People's Colleges run courses based on the curricula of the upper level of the polytechnical schools, preparing the participants for examinations which will admit them to studies at a college or technical school. They thus constitute another avenue of approach to higher education. In addition, there are courses in individual subjects, such as foreign languages, shorthand and typing, and art. Many of these People's Colleges are attached to the factories or collectives, making it easier for working people to study. The cost is borne almost entirely by the state, a two-hour lesson costing the student as little as 30 Pfennig, and sometimes even less. Special technical skills can, of course, also be acquired through study at these colleges, and particularly at an academy attached to a particular factory.

In rural areas, it is the 'village academies' that carry out this educational function, and here the principal stress is on agriculture and rural science. Lessons are assisted by the support of the national television service. These village academies, which also provide scope for the arts and cultural and discussion groups, have been increasingly developed in recent years. Their 1961 attendance figure of 34,000 students had grown to over 100,000 by 1967. Attendance at the People's Colleges amounted to 320,000 in 1966.

Research in East Germany is also planned on a national scale, with the *economic and technological* interests of the state in the foreground. A Research Council was established in August 1957, now composed of eighty members, nearly all of them leading specialists in science, industry, technology and teaching, and drawn from the national industries, from universities, institutes and industrial scientific establishments. This Research Council helps to fix priorities, and advises the government on the formulation of the annual national economic plan. It also advises on the setting up of new industries and research establishments and gives general guidance in the state planning of research. Nuclear research comes under its jurisdiction.

5. *Culture and the Arts*

The flourishing of the arts which we recorded in the case of West Germany is also a feature of the East German state, though

P

once again we encounter the phenomenon of state intervention at most levels of activity. There are 95 regular theatres in operation, presenting a representative selection of the world's drama from ancient times to the present day. Although works of a progressive or Marxist character receive preferential treatment, most Western drama of recent centuries can be seen on these stages. The quality of the productions is generally high, though provincial theatres suffer somewhat from the tendency of East Berlin to draw the leading talents into its orbit. There are thirteen theatres in East Berlin. A visit to the theatre or opera is regarded (as in West Germany) as an important social occasion, and the audience dresses up accordingly in its 'Sunday best'. Plentiful literature about the productions is supplied, both in the theatre programme and in general information sheets; this aims at educating the audience to a fuller appreciation of the particular play and of the contribution made by the various members of the production team. The temptation is not often avoided here of stressing political points, and many plays are seen in terms of the proletarian struggle. Thus Schiller's *Wilhelm Tell* is presented as his greatest play, on the strength of the fight against tyranny which forms part of its content. Theatre clubs for workers and schoolchildren exist, which not only entitle their members to price reductions, but also provide for discussion of the productions to be visited, members of the theatre company itself often participating. Sometimes the choice of plays for a theatre season will illustrate a particular era of theatre history.

In 1962 East Germany spent almost ten times as much as Britain on subsidies to drama, opera and ballet, in the form of grants from the state or the municipalities: this was the equivalent of 62p per head of the population in East Germany, and 2½p per head in Great Britain! Much amateur theatrical activity is also encouraged, especially in the 120 workers' and farmers' theatres, which gave 1,925 performances in 1966. Prizes and medals are awarded for the best performances at the annual Workers' Festival.

Public library facilities are well developed. There are 20,688 lending libraries with a total of 23 million volumes, some of them general public libraries, and others organized by trade unions (7,700 in 1965). The museums, to which entry is usually free, number 582 and contain some excellent collections, particularly those in East Berlin. Perhaps the most popular of all, however, is the State Art Collection in Dresden, which is visited by more than 2¼ million people annually; it is a superb collection from the past of both German and European painting, which only survived the 1945 blitz on Dresden because it had been carefully stored away in local quarries and vaults.

The cities have good opera companies, especially East Berlin,

Leipzig and Dresden, and there are eight state symphony orchestras, two radio symphony orchestras and about seventy others. The choir of the Thomas Church in Leipzig (the *Thomanerchor*) and the *Kreuzchor* of Dresden are also internationally famous.

For those who prefer to spend their leisure at home there are radio and television services. East German television programmes were first transmitted in December 1952, and a regular service instituted in 1956. By 1968 there were about 3,900,000 television licence holders, or 56% of all households. There is only the one television service, at Berlin-Adlershof, which devotes much of its time to news items and documentary programmes, but also devotes a fair proportion of its attention to sport, entertainment and cultural programmes. It also receives some of its programmes from other Communist countries, through the Intervision network. For those viewers who seek a wider range of choice there is also the possibility of watching West German television, though this is officially frowned upon. Many East Germans nevertheless do so, finding it one means of keeping in touch with 'the other side'; their number was estimated at 70% of viewers in 1969.

Radio programmes are more numerous. They are controlled by a state radio committee and number six in all, though only three of them (*Deutschlandsender, Berliner Rundfunk* and *Radio DDRI*) are major programmes. Mostly they disseminate information and carry propaganda against West Germany, though a certain amount of cultural and educational matter is also featured and there is some popular musical entertainment. Radio Berlin International broadcasts foreign language programmes for overseas consumption. Local radio programmes are also broadcast from the fourteen regional capitals during the major part of the day.

In 1968, 6½ million newspapers were printed daily in East Germany, but only half a million were produced by the 'bourgeois' parties. Each group in the National Front produces its own papers, the SED's *Neues Deutschland* taking pride of place. There is only one national news agency, the ADN, or *Allgemeiner Deutscher Nachrichtendienst*, and the guidelines for the presentation and selection of news items are laid down by the government Ministry for Agitation and Propaganda, for the central committee of the SED. Methods of approach and the type of argumentation to be applied are officially prescribed, leading to a noticeable similarity in the headlines, editorials and commentaries of the principal newspapers. Political propaganda campaigns are mounted on a long-term basis, the planning extending over a period of weeks and sometimes even months.

Although the East Germans produce a very handy little car in their Trabant (in addition to the much-exported larger models in the Wartburg range), they are expensive and there is a long waiting list for them, too. The roads are therefore less busy than in many European countries. On the motorways, which are good, there is a speed limit of 100 kph for cars and 60 kph for lorries and buses. These motorways often have pleasant lay-bys, with painted tables and benches for picnics. Drivers are not permitted to drink alcohol during daylight hours. For East German drivers the petrol stations sell only 88-octane fuel, and their engines have to be adapted to these circumstances, but foreign motorists can buy 98-octane petrol at special Inter-Tank stations—at much dearer prices, of course (unless paid for in foreign currency). Minor roads are less well maintained, and can be a severe test of a car's stamina.

For the more robust, there is a wide range of sports facilities. Most popular sports in 1967 were football, gymnastics, angling, bowls and handball, but there are 26 different varieties of sport listed in the official report for 1969. There were more than 7,250 sports associations, with a membership of two millions in 1968, there being almost four times as many male as female members. Junior members numbered half a million. Sport also plays an important part in the curriculum of East German schools. The achievements of East German sport in recent Olympic Games have been impressive: five gold, thirteen silver and five bronze medals were gained in 1964. They have won many European competitions and set up a considerable number of world records, substantially outshining the West Germans in this field.

Membership of the sports associations is very cheap, and members also pay no charge for the use of most of the facilities. Subsidies come from the government (74,433,000 marks in 1965), from trade union committees and from the cultural funds of factories and other enterprises. There are no full-time professionals in East German sport, but athletes and team members are allowed time off for training and competitions, without loss of pay. Many of the international competitors are students.

Most young people are also members of the Free German Youth (FDJ) or its junior branch, the Young Pioneers (*Ernst Thälmann Jungpioniere*), for those below the age of 14. This is the only youth organization permitted in East Germany, and it provides varied leisure time activities for the young generation, ranging from club meetings and discussion groups on social themes, to games, camping or even holidays abroad. Many hobbies are pursued at its club houses, but here also political education is carried out, the children learning the essentials of the Marxist philosophy and studying the history of the German workers' movement. Here, too, the younger members are prepared for their Youth Dedication ceremony.

The question might well be asked here of the position of the artist in a controlled society, and of the possibilities for freelance activities. State promotion of the arts certainly exists, normally in the form of commissions extended to artists and writers by local or national organizations. There are also prizes to be won in state-sponsored competitions, and decorations are awarded to successful creators, usually with a monetary reward attached. Each year the highest honour, the National Prize, is awarded to outstanding artists and writers: the first class prize is worth 100,000 marks, a second class prize 50,000 marks and a third-class prize 25,000 marks. In addition to these National Prizes, there are a large number of other awards in the fields of art and literature, such as the Arthur Nikisch prize for music, the Heinrich Greif prize for film art and the Heinrich Mann prize for literature.

Fundamentally, artists and writers must earn their living by accepting commissions, either from the state or from cultural institutions. A Central Commissions Board, composed of representatives of the state and the Artists' Association, gives commissions to artists for work on central projects (*e.g.* large building schemes). For local commissions, there are *Bezirk* boards with their own funds. In the case of musicians, the distribution of commissions is controlled by the German Composers' Association, and in the case of the theatre, by the Union of Theatre Workers. In the same way writers of literary works can receive commissions from the Writers' Union and from publishers. The artist, or author, is free to create within a prescribed context. The official formulation runs as follows: "This does not mean a limitation of artistic freedom, because the artist and all people who work are building Socialism together. There is a basic unity between the interests of the State and of the artist. As the artists are materially secure, they are in a position to develop their talents to the full".[9]

Significant writing has certainly been produced in East Germany, but one suspects that it has been in spite of, rather than because of, these circumstances. The authoress, Anna Seghers, after producing work of high quality in the early post-war years, has sunk to the trivial and banal in her attempt to remain loyal to the official line. Other writers, finding the constraint too great, have fled to the West. Yet others, like Wolf Biermann, have continued to write in their own chosen way, and have found that since 1965 their work remains unpublished—except in the West. Many intellectuals have turned from an unappealing reality to an escape world of the mind, in the study of old languages, abstract science and even more

[9] This last statement, of course, begs the whole question of the nature of artistic inspiration and the artist's motives for self-expression.

229

eccentric hobbies.[10] There has nevertheless been some good writing produced within the terms of the SED credo, such names as Christa Wolf, Peter Hacks, Hermann Kant, Johannes Bobrowski and Franz Fühmann being noteworthy.

Even the form of the East German language is being modified by the new political reality. Influences of Russian speech styles and vocabulary have been noticed, and a whole range of official jargon has crept into everyday use; one of the main disseminators of the new speech styles has been the official daily newspaper, *Neues Deutschland*. One constantly encounters expressions like *Pionier*, *Neuerer* ('innovator'), *Schrittmacher* ('pace-setter'), *Spitzenleistung* ('peak performance'); workers are credited with *aktiver Einsatz* ('active application'), and words like *technisch* ('technological'), *wissenschaftlich* ('scientific') and above all *sozialistisch* are worked to death; *volkseigen* ('state-owned') and *genossenschaftlich* ('co-operative') confront the visitor at every turn. When we take into account the equivalent influence on West German usage of western idiom—and particularly that of English—we realize that here, too, the division of the two halves of Germany is growing steadily wider. This division will be the subject of our concluding survey.

[10] The term *innere Emigration* ('emigration into oneself'), formerly applied to the days of the Hitler regime, is now frequently applied to this present-day 'switching off' from external events.

Section V

Taking Stock

The visitor to East Germany is struck by the many resemblances which he finds to West Germany, and is reminded constantly of the previous entity that is now parted. The division of Germany into two separate national states is indeed a piece of nonsense, socially, geographically and economically. Her territory is of major importance to Europe's transport network: many of the lines of communication between East and West cross German soil, utilizing the broad North German Plain which joins the western European seaboard to Slavonic Europe. Many lines between northern and southern Europe likewise pass through her territory. Her largest rivers bring traffic from the North Sea and the Black Sea to countries as far spread as France, Switzerland, Czechoslovakia and the Balkans. The frontier itself which divides Germany is but an arbitrary line on a map, without any essential geographical *raison d'être*, cutting at times through the centre of villages and even of farmsteads. That the two separated halves complemented each other economically and industrially has been shown in our foregoing analysis, where the problems of an isolated East Germany have been particularly clear. In human terms, too, the division has meant hardship and anguish for families now permanently sundered by a political act.

The division is nevertheless a reality, a *fait accompli* brought about by political exigencies. Yet, with the passage of time, it has assumed consequences of economic, social and indeed human significance which tend towards its consolidation and perpetuation. The West German Federal Republic and the East German Democratic Republic are today fully established political realities, and cannot realistically be thought of in any other terms. Our preceding analysis has demonstrated their almost totally different approach in such fields as political philosophy and institutions, administration, economic principles, education, social legislation, industrial organization and the role of the worker and the citizen. Their economic systems are closely integrated with those of rival economic camps, and their military commitment is to mutually opposed power blocs. The striving of the East German régime has been for general diplomatic recognition and political legitimation as a separate, sovereign state; the striving of West German governments in the 1950s and early 1960s was to frustrate such attempts. Alienation rather than rapprochement was then the order of the day.

To trace out the sequence of relationships between East and West German authorities is to record a consistent refusal to compromise or even to listen to the other side—at least until the late 1960s. The initial wartime decision of the Allied powers to divide Germany into zones of occupation resulted in Russian control of the East German zone; but this was no more an act of separation from the main body of Germany than were the British, American or French occupations of their zones. The economic and industrial organization of the Russian zone was of course, already in 1945, given a strong Marxist bent, but the political organization of the country remained much as it had been under the Weimar Republic. Hopes for all-German elections were sustained by the East Zone authorities until 1949, and were the basis of the (Communist organized) People's Congress movement in the years 1947–49. Western fears had, however, already been roused by the socialization of the East German economy, and by the fusion of the SPD with the Communists to create the SED party front. Russia's rejection of help from the Marshall aid scheme, and her application of pressure on her eastern satellites to follow suit, suggested that the western and eastern economic systems were not susceptible of harmonization, and that Russia distrusted American intentions.

The differences between the Big Four powers became increasingly sharp, especially after the proclamation of the Truman Doctrine in March 1947 (all peoples should be accorded the right of free elections, to choose their own form of government without pressure from outside) and of the Marshall Aid Plan in June 1947. The Western Powers sought a federal form of government in Germany, the Russians a centralized one in a unitary state (Moscow and London Conferences, of March–April and November–December, 1947). There were differences over reparations policies also, the Russians taking a much tougher line on this issue than the Western Powers.

Both Eastern and Western authorities were by now progressively developing their zones of occupation in accordance with their own political thinking, and the cold war had virtually begun. At the same time, they protested at the steps being taken by the other side to grant greater autonomy to the territories within their care. More fundamentally divisive still were the proposals of the British Foreign Minister, Bevin, for the formation of a Western Union (realized in the Five Power treaty of Brussels, 17th March, 1948), and the subsequent plans for the integration of the three Western Zones of occupied Germany into the Western economic and political system. What was envisaged, in a communiqué of March 6th, 1948, was a federal West German state, with provision for eventual reunification, the inclusion of this unit in the European reconstruction programme, and the close collaboration of the three occupying powers in the administration of their respective zones. The Russian response was to accuse the West of a breach of the Potsdam Agreement and of the occupation statutes, and to call for all-German elections, through the second Peoples' Congress meeting in Berlin. A heated exchange in the Allied Control Commission, in March 1948, led to the withdrawal of the Russian delegation, thus leaving the Commission incapable of action. The Russian blockade of Berlin followed, being announced on 1st April and reaching its peak on 25th June, when the American airlift started. It was to last until May, 1949, and constituted the first real physical test of the West's determination to stand firm in Germany. The embargo by the Russians on the import and export of all goods between West Berlin and other parts of Germany was countered by the airlift, which in itself demonstrated for the West Germans the firm commitment of the Atlantic powers to their defence.

The first overt step towards a separate economic policy for the three Western Zones was the major decision by the Western Powers, reacting to the Berlin blockade, to introduce a currency reform in Western Germany, to the exclusion of the Eastern Zone. Attempts had already been made, in earlier discussion with the Russian authorities, to introduce a general currency reform, but these had failed. On June 20th, 1948, the West German currency reform was effected, to be followed by a separate one carried out by the Russians for their own zone, on June 23rd. The refusal of the West Berlin authorities to accept the new East German Mark instead of the West's new Deutsche Mark led to an intensification of the blockade and the declaration by the Russians that the Western Powers' unilateral action had destroyed the basis of four-power control and consequently deprived the Western Powers of their right to remain in West Berlin. The cold war had indeed begun.

The East Germans, for their part, still pinned their hopes on all-German elections, anticipating the emergence of a left-wing majority. There is some reason to think that the parties of the left would have predominated in a national German election, but a merger of the SPD and the Communist Party (on the lines of the East German SED) would have been most unlikely. Indeed, the leader of the West German SPD, Kurt Schumacher, had specifically rejected such an approach from the East in January 1946. Schumacher did, however, attempt to hold back West German commitment to the Western alliance. Under his leadership, the SPD faction in the *Bundestag* opposed West German membership of the Council of Europe, the Schumann Plan and the European Defence Community. His disapproval of the CDU's policy of integration with the West led him to characterize Dr Adenauer as the

Bundeskanzler der Allierten ("Federal Chancellor for the Allies"). There were, of course, personal motives in these attitudes as well.

On 16th April 1948, eighteen West European states became members of the Organization for European Economic Co-operation (OEEC), and West Germany was associated with it through the signature of the military governors of the three zones of occupation. The London Conference of June 1948 called for a democratic constitution for West Germany and the integration of the three occupation zones. The Russian answer to these measures was the holding of the Warsaw Conference on June 23rd–24th, 1948, which accused the Western Powers of dividing Germany and called for an all-German anti-fascist government, the conclusion of a peace treaty along the lines of the Potsdam Agreement, the demilitarization of Germany and the continuation of reparations payments. In January 1949, East Germany was included in the organization of East European states for economic assistance (COMECON), and mutual support was pledged in their opposition to the OEEC powers.

The West German parliamentary council had meanwhile drafted the terms of the Basic Law, which came into operation in May 1949, and the Federal Republic of West Germany was born on 21st September 1949. An East Zone constitution was drawn up in October 1948, ratified in March 1949 and confirmed by the Third Peoples' Congress of May 1949. The East German constitution came into being on May 30th, 1949, and the Democratic Republic in October of that year.

Events so far had been shaped primarily by the occupying powers; now the Germans themselves were to take over. Dr Adenauer, as the first West German Chancellor, was doubtless only too pleased to align West German policies with those of the West. His fear and distrust of the Communists were deep-seated, and his dedication to the Catholic cause also made the Western Alliance attractive. The eastern half of Germany is predominantly Protestant (roughly 15 million Protestants to 2 million Catholics) and would certainly have voted SPD in preference to CDU, there being a strong radical tradition in industrial Saxony and the Berlin region. Turning his back on his eastern neighbour, Adenauer sought to bind West Germany ever more firmly to Western Europe. In July 1951, the state of war between West Germany and the Western Allies was terminated, and on May 5th 1955, the Federal Republic achieved full sovereignty. The European Community, formed in May 1952, contained a West German contingent, and the Paris Treaties of October 1954 led to West German membership of NATO and Western European Union—the forerunner of EEC.

During Adenauer's period in office, no real attempt was made at a reconciliation with East Germany, though negotiations with Russia were pursued, resulting in the signing of an agreement for the repatriation of German prisoners of war still in Russia (September 1955) and for the exchange of ambassadors between the two countries (January–March 1956). East Germany herself was ignored, and her legality diplomatically denied by West Germany. The Hallstein Doctrine, formulated on December 9th, 1955 by the West German Foreign Minister of that name, threatened the breaking of all diplomatic relations with any state which recognized the East German government. The threat was an effective one, for West German connections were far more important to the majority of the world's trading nations than East German links, and the DDR was consigned to a diplomatic limbo, from which she struggled hard to emerge. Only the Communist states, and certain non-committed countries, accorded her official recognition. The only country to achieve diplomatic relations with both parties was Yugoslavia, whose favours both East and West were attempting to win.

Certain contacts between the two German states could not be entirely avoided. They were, after all, adjacent territories, and there was the particular problem of West Berlin. The physical control which the East Germans exercise over West Berlin's access to the West gives them a most useful lever with which to exert pressure on their neighbour, and it has been exploited with a consistent degree of skill and cunning. Access by road, rail and waterway lying across East German territory has been closed innumerable times on the slimmest of pretexts and with little or no warning. Considerable transport dues have also been charged—and regularly revised in an upward direction. They amounted to the sum of £4½ millions in 1969, and were increased in April 1970 by a further £1¼ millions per annum. The West Germans, in their refusal to treat with the East German authorities and thereby accord them a measure of recognition, always dealt with the Russians on matters affecting Berlin, as the power still fundamentally responsible in the area (together with the three Western Allies, of course). Other negotiations were conducted by the West Berlin government, acting as the local representative of authority, and Bonn was thus able to protect itself from involvement with the other side and the official recognition which would thereby be implied. West Germany's interests have also frequently been represented by the Western Control Powers, who have taken up with Russia threats to the security of West Berlin, arising out of East German actions.

Despite the icy diplomatic temperature, certain trade exchanges did take place between the two German states, though these had no official blessing in the West and the balance of goods received generally worked in East Germany's favour. In 1961, West German exports to East Germany accounted for only 4% of her exports total, and imports from the DDR stood at less than 5% of the overall figure. There was a steady decline up to the year 1963, mainly as a result of the West German government's embargo on strategic goods deliveries, in particular iron and steel, hard coal and engineering and machine products, but the trade exchange began to improve slightly from 1965 onwards.

The nadir of inter-German relations was probably reached on 13th August 1961, with the building of the Berlin Wall, which closed off the last open link between the territory of the two states. The East German authorities were virtually compelled to take this step by the continued exodus of large numbers of their citizens to the West through this loop-hole in the Iron Curtain. Something approaching a quarter of a million East Germans had been leaving the DDR annually, seeking a new life in West Germany. They were mostly young people and many of them were highly qualified workers and intellectuals. Some were fleeing from a politically oppressive regime, some sought to avoid East German conscription, others were attracted by the greater financial lure of the West or by the simple desire to be reunited with relatives living in the Federal Republic. Together, they constituted a serious drain of East German labour, at a time when the DDR's reviving economy was sorely in need of workers to man the new factories and institutes. West Berlin was a thorn in the flesh of East Germany for other reasons too. As a shop window of West German prosperity, it put East Berlin and the whole DDR economy under a shadow, which could only be productive of social discontent. Furthermore, it had proved a useful base for Western intrigues and interventions in the affairs of East Germany, ranging from currency speculation against the East German mark to espionage and subversive infiltrations of various kinds. The building of the Wall removed all these circumstances. It was, all the same, a moral defeat for the East German authorities. One additional negotiating card was, however, placed in the East Germans' hands: West German citizens wishing to visit the East Zone, and vice versa, had to apply to the DDR authorities for permission to cross the border. Once again, the West Berlin government was forced to step in, to negotiate on behalf of Bonn for the granting of free access to her citizens, but the East Germans played their new card skilfully to narrow down the West German government's freedom of manoeuvre.

In the years that followed West Germany's acquisition of full sovereignty in 1955, CDU, SPD and FDP put forward various plans for German reunification which differed in their details, but all subscribed to the basic policy of the Federal Government, which called for free elections throughout Germany to decide the issue of unification, the incorporation of a united Germany in a European security system, and the rejection of the policy of neutralization. The principle of two separate German states was categorically rejected, and the Big Four reminded of their responsibility to restore German unity. The Russians, however, made it clear to Adenauer on his visit to Moscow (September 1955) that they regarded the question of German unity as a matter to be settled between the two German régimes, thus forcing the issue of recognition of East Germany into the foreground once more. West German insistence on the prior holding of free elections merely led back to a situation of deadlock. The Russians regarded the question of Germany's frontiers as having been settled for all time by the Potsdam Agreement; the West Germans insisted that this issue must remain open until the signing of a final peace settlement, to which the Germans must be a party. In a memorandum of 17th February 1961, the Russians warned the West Germans to come to a speedy agreement with East Germany, or else to be prepared for the signing of a separate peace treaty between the Communist states and the East German government. The West Germans, characterizing the East German régime as a Soviet puppet state, ruled against the will of its inhabitants, refused to be moved, and took energetic steps to assert internationally their claim to be the sole legal spokesman for both parts of Germany.

The basic West German (and West European) approach up to 1970 was that of the so-called Herter Plan, outlined by the US Foreign Secretary of that name in May 1959. This re-asserted the responsibility of the four major powers for the solution of the German problem, and reaffirmed the independent status of Berlin, until such time as Germany was reunited. A mixed commission from East and West Germany was called for, which would propose plans for the holding of free all-German elections for a national assembly, which would then evolve a new constitution. This was to lead to the formation of a national government and the final signing of a German peace treaty. (Negotiations on this plan actually broke down as early as August 1959, when the Russians insisted on parity of representation for East and West Germany.)

The idea of an initial confederation, leading to a closer unity only after the solution of major problems, was from this date the basic element of East German proposals on re-unification. They also made the conclusion of a general peace treaty a prerequisite of political unity—the reverse pattern of the West Germans' order of priority.

As we have indicated, the building of the Berlin Wall in August 1961 led to an even more bitter note in exchanges between East and West Germans. At the same time, as the growing affluence of

West Germany brought employment and security for the whole population and successful integration for their displaced millions from the East, so did their attention turn increasingly to the country's manifold links with the West, and the East Germans were largely forgotten by the man in the street. Official circles in West Germany strove hard to keep alive an awareness of the East German problem, and one encountered frequent public posters encouraging the sending of relief parcels *nach drüben* ('over there').

The East German régime, for its part, was concentrating on the thoroughgoing reinforcement of its political and economic system and on its ever closer integration into the Soviet bloc and COMECON planning. It bent its efforts increasingly towards the acquisition of diplomatic recognition as a sovereign state, while its citizens, witnessing the apparent unconcern of the West Germans over their situation, came to feel aggrieved in their sense of isolation.

It was to cut a way through the jungle of misunderstandings and mutual recriminations that the SPD/FDP coalition of 1969 embarked on a new approach to the problem, building up to the exchange of visits between the Prime Ministers of the two states in 1970.[1] The more realistic approach of the Brandt government abandoned the pretence of West Germany's sole right to speak on German affairs and to lay down the terms for national unity. It accepted instead the existence of two German states, which must find ways of growing together, by a gradual process of agreement on specific issues, until such time as political association becomes a realistic prospect. Communications and trade contacts were suggested as fields likely to be least controversial, in initial discussions. Sporting contacts had already been resumed by November 1970, after a 'freeze' of nine years. The recognition of East Germany as a separate sovereign state was evaded in this new policy, by the explanation that although she was a separate entity from West Germany, she was nevertheless a constituent part of Germany as a whole, and is not to be thought of as a separate nation. West Germany thus sought to speak to East Germany not as a foreign power, but as an estranged brother within the German nation-state.

The policy initially met with very limited success, the meetings of 1970 being succeeded by nothing more significant than discussions between officials to explore the possibility of proceeding further. On the broader diplomatic front, however, the Brandt ad-

[1] The West German Chancellor, Willy Brandt, travelled to Erfurt in East Germany, on March 19th 1970, and the East German Prime Minister, Willi Stoph, paid a return visit to Kassel in West Germany on 21st May 1970. The enthusiastic demonstrations in Erfurt were a personal triumph for Willy Brandt, but the discussions themselves remained at the exploratory stage.

ministration made noteworthy progress towards a détente with the East, and this may well prove to have beneficial repercussions on relations with the East Germans. An agreement with the Russians was initialled in August 1970, which in addition to promising friendship between the two states, also provided for certain West German help for the Russian economy, in particular, for the development of her technology.[2] This treaty was followed by one with Poland, in early December 1970, in which the Oder–Neisse Line was accepted as the valid frontier between Germany and Poland. A trade pact with Rumania had been concluded earlier in the year, and Hungary and Czechoslovakia also showed clear signs of wishing for agreements with the West Germans. The treaties with Russia and Poland were only initialled, however, and still required the assent of the *Bundestag*—and a strategic decision by the Bonn government. The stumbling block was Berlin, where the Big Four Powers were engaged in discussions on West German access rights and the sovereignty of West Berlin. The Brandt government hoped to use the proposed Russian and Polish treaties as a lever to gain their point over Berlin: no formal signature before the guaranteeing of West Berlin's independence. The Russians on the other hand demanded the signing of the treaties as a prerequisite for a settlement of the Berlin question. To stress their advantageous position, the East German authorities, in December 1970, had imposed one of their customary freezes on traffic between West Germany and Berlin, and the diplomatic temperature dropped several degrees again. (The CDU had, somewhat provocatively, staged a party conference in West Berlin.)

Much was made by Herr Ulbricht of the absolute loyalty of East Germany to the Communist cause, during the troubled events of 1968–1970 in Czechoslovakia and Poland, despite West German attempts to outflank her by trade treaties with East European states and the proposed treaties with Poland and Russia. The imputation was that Russia was conniving at Western plans to break up the Communist bloc, in her urgent seeking of West German technical advice and economic aid. The point seems to have been taken by the Russians, who suddenly lost their enthusiasm for West German collaboration after Christmas 1970. At the end of February, 1971, however, the Russians stated that they had no intention of going back on their policy of rapprochement with the Brandt government; and the East Germans partially restored the long-severed telephone links between East and West Berlin. The readiness of

---

[2] An important codicil attached to this treaty speaks of the West Germans' ultimate objective that "the German nation *will recover its unity in free self-determination*" (our italics).

the Ulbricht government, announced at the end of February 1971, to discuss the reopening of the Berlin Wall, after almost five years, was a further hint that progress might yet be made; it was, however, conditional on progress being made in the Four Power talks on Berlin's status. These reached a successful conclusion only in December 1971, when the western access rights were guaranteed.

Willy Brandt's approach to the Big Powers, in his seeking of a German settlement, is proof of his political realism. For the basic decisions will be taken, not by East and West Germany in mutual negotiation, but by the power blocs of East and West, having regard to their own long-term interests. That the major powers of the Western and the Communist world hold the strings has been illustrated time and again throughout the post-war years as West German ministers have hurried to Washington, London and Paris to report on negotiations or receive advice, while East German ministers have similarly hurried to Moscow or Warsaw. During the West German negotiations with Poland, in the autumn of 1970, advance consultations were necessary in Western capitals, and the progress of the discussions was regularly reported back.[3] In the treaty which eventually emerged, the Big Powers have reserved for themselves the right to a final say in the settlement of the Oder–Neisse question, in an eventual German peace treaty.

There are, indeed, a number of compelling reasons why the major Western and Eastern powers should oppose the reunification of Germany. With a combined population of 77 millions, she would constitute a major political force in central Europe, and would control vital communication links. What is more, she would represent a major challenge to the leading economies of the world; West Germany in 1970 already stood as the world's third largest trading nation, and East Germany was estimated to occupy eighth position. The Communist world in particular still lives in dread memory of Germany's military might and political ascendancy in Europe. Both Russia and Poland, it must be remembered, hold considerable areas of former German territory, the claim to which has not yet been renounced by powerful factions in West Germany. The West German contribution to NATO is the greatest among her European partners, and East Germany also possesses a considerable military force. Already the dominant economic power in the European Common Market, West Germany could soon assume political dominance also, and there were suggestions in 1970 that Britain's

[3] British Conservative M.P.s, in December 1970, still complained that the West Germans were failing to consult and inform their European partners as fully as they ought, and suspicions were even voiced that the Brandt government was trying to "go it alone" in a private pact with Russia.

application for membership was welcome to France as a prospective counterbalance to German influence in the community. The European balance of power is indeed a delicate one, and will be closely guarded by those who control it.

Russia and America themselves have reasons for delaying the achievement of German unity. The negotiation of a German settlement would be likely to secure Russia's frontiers with the West, leaving her free to deploy her forces elsewhere in the world, and particularly at those points where she is confronting American and Chinese interests in the Middle and Far East (particularly Egypt and Vietnam). Hence one of the reasons for America's lukewarm approach to a German détente. The Russians for their part see the tension in Germany as a potent means of keeping American armies and their equipment tied down in Europe, through their NATO commitment, and are reluctant to release the Americans from this restriction. Only a lessening of tension and growing trust between Russia and America will bring the prospect of a German agreement closer. Hence the extreme degree of caution and tact with which the West Germans are moving.

A complicating factor is that the Russians and other East European states, by proceeding with their rapprochement with Bonn, which is an expression of their desperate need for Western modern technology, are likely to harm the East Germans, who are at present the chief suppliers of such equipment and skills to the Eastern bloc. The East German government would thus lose much of the political and economic influence which it can at present wield, as well as much of its exports; a poor reward for years of dedicated service to the Communist cause, and a likely encouragement to disaffection in other East European states. The Russians here face a personal problem.

Even the restricted negotiations between the West and East German governments are fraught with difficulties. The East Germans, before all else, seek official recognition. By negotiating directly with them, the West Germans imply recognition of their status as legal representatives of the East German population, yet refuse to concede the point. In his theory of two-states-within-one-nation, Willy Brandt walks a diplomatic tightrope where one false step could prove fatal to his case. The East Germans have so far accepted the situation, while exploiting it in other ways. The question of membership of the United Nations Organization has been raised, with the proposal that East and West Germany should separately become members. To deny the right of East Germany to join, while permitting West German membership, would constitute a direct affront. The preferred consequence has been the exclusion from membership of both German states. Here again, Big Power con-

241

Q

siderations have also played a part. To admit Communist East Germany to UNO would also entail the necessity of admitting other Communist régimes similarly unacceptable to the West. Moreover, to admit the East Germans would confer on them a degree of international acceptability which would then make it hard to refuse them diplomatic recognition.

Russian fears are equally great. A re-integrated Germany could in time swing back to a Western-type democratic structure, with a capitalist basis, and a dangerous lure to the smaller East European members of the Communist bloc, who are already finding the blandishments of the West very attractive. Russia would lose a valuable watchdog over Poland and Czechoslovakia, and a buffer-zone in the West. More than this, she might be deprived of the very considerable supplies of machinery and other equipment which the East Germans at present supply for her economy, plus the expert technical skills of the DDR's research scientists. The entire structure of COMECON would then need to be changed. Only a comprehensive European détente, followed by meaningful co-operation between East and West, could avert these dangers. Certainly, West German financiers and industrialists have seen very considerable prospects for expanding trade connections with a friendly Russia.[4]

The mere physical difficulties which stand in the way of German unity are enormous, and even given goodwill on both sides, their solution is by no manner of speaking obvious. The East Germans still, fundamentally, seek full diplomatic recognition as a prerequisite of serious negotiation, and if the West German government is to persuade them to drop this demand it must clearly offer considerable compensations of another sort. Yet any such concessions by the SPD/FDP coalition to the DDR would immediately rouse the hostility of the CDU, particularly its CSU wing under Franz Josef Strauss, and the various extreme right-wing factions of the Federal Republic. On the other hand, to grant the East Germans the recognition which they seek would rouse the opposition at Bonn even more. There is also the suspicion that having won their desired international legitimation, the East Germans would break off negotiations for an association which would, almost certainly, involve greater concessions by them than by the West Germans. Nonrecognition would seem to be Willy Brandt's strongest card; he cannot, however, afford to overplay his hand.

The balance of forces representing the two states in an eventual German confederation would constitute a fundamental issue. The

4 Already, in 1969, the Federal Republic was the principal Western supplier of Eastern Europe. These supplies then represented only 5% of her total exports, but it was estimated that improved relations with the East could raise this proportion to 20% within a few years.

East Germans claim equal representation; the West Germans have in the past called for proportional representation (3 : 1 in favour of the West). A proportional allocation of votes would automatically provide the West Germans with an overwhelming majority in all decisions, and could hardly be acceptable to East Germany.

The West Germans operate from a position of strength, in the sense of their superior economic power and greater population and geographical extent. Yet the East Germans can speak with one voice, their policy decided by the central body which represents the only political reality in the state; whereas the West German government speaks only for its supporters, a bare majority of the West German electorate. The SPD/FDP cabinet must enjoy a convincing vote of confidence for its policies, if it is to operate with any credibility;[5] otherwise there is the possibility of agreed terms even being withdrawn by a future West German government of a different political complexion. Another factor which must be taken into account is the rights of the individual *Länder* to object to *Bund* policies. Any amount of delaying tactics could be indulged in by a reluctant *Land,* through obstructive legislation and appeals to the Federal Constitutional Court.

Yet Willy Brandt, as leader of the SPD, can hardly afford to fail in his attempts. Much of the prestige of his administration has been staked on the achievement of a détente with the East and some measure of progress towards intra-German co-operation. The CDU in the course of twenty years achieved little in this field, and it was the SPD claim that it would end this era of stagnation that helped to bring it to office in 1969. The Brandt administration has certainly achieved much in the field of domestic reform, in education, the social services and legal matters, but for the West Germans its vote-winning propensities depend primarily on its record in the new *Ostpolitik*. But failure to reach agreement with the East would not only be an SPD setback. The likely consequences would be an even tighter identification with the West, the strengthening of the hands of the extremists and a hardening of East-West attitudes, perhaps producing a new 'cold war' mentality.

To argue in favour of maintaining the *status quo* (as the CDU have done) is to overlook two vital factors: West Berlin and the determination of the East German government to achieve general diplomatic recognition. West Germany may well seek to mark time; East Germany will not permit it, and has the means at her disposal to prevent it. Her growing economic power will raise her in political

---

5 Certain CDU and right-wing opposition groups demanded a two-thirds majority vote in support of the Polish treaty in November 1970, on the grounds that it constituted an amendment to the Basic Law.

importance, rendering it less simple to ignore her existence diplomatically. Western states have been engaging increasingly in trade with her in recent years. And when pressure needs to be applied directly to Bonn, it is only necessary to obstruct the access routes to West Berlin. Here, however, the East Germans must act in accordance with the overriding aims of their Russian mentors, and the vital importance of a general East–West détente becomes obvious. A German rapprochement would be an earnest of the major powers' sincerity in seeking peaceful co-existence.

By the end of 1971, both sides seemed to be making concessions. The West Germans were showing a readiness to set aside the question of re-unification and even to accept equal status with East Germany in certain international bodies (special committees associated with the UN, and even the UN itself), while seeking solutions to specific problems of mutual interest. The East Germans for their part were less insistent on diplomatic recognition as a pre-requisite for negotiations. Their claim that the West Germans had moved considerably in the direction of their own mode of approach was probably justified.

The replacement of Ulbricht by Honecker in 1971 will almost certainly have led to some changes in East German policy, and the slow pace of negotiations since that event could be seen as arising from the need to formulate new attitudes. The future alone can prove or disprove the commentators who predicted that Honecker would show himself to be a little less inflexible than his predecessor. For Willy Brandt, the inflexibility of CDU policies seemed in 1971/2 to constitute at least as great an obstacle to progress as the tight-fisted negotiating of the East Germans.

Select Bibliography

A. FEDERAL REPUBLIC OF GERMANY

Heidenheimer, A. J. The Governments of Germany. University Paperbacks, 1965.

Hiscocks, R. Democracy in Western Germany. London, 1957.

Hubatsch, W. Die deutsche Frage. Würzburg, 1961.

Jones, A. G. The Germans. An Englishman's Notebook. Pond Press, 1968.

Kitzinger, U. The European Common Market and Community. London, 1967.

Leonhardt, R. W. This Germany. The Story since the Third Reich. Pelican, 1964.

Meyn, H. Massenmedien in der Bundesrepublik Deutschland. Berlin, 1969.

Montagu, I. Germany's new Nazis. Panther Books, London, 1967.

Pollock, J. K. German Democracy at Work. Ann Arbor, 1955.

Preece, R. J. C. 'Land' Elections in the German Federal Republic. London, 1968.

Strauss, F. J. The Grand Design. London, 1965.

Tilford, R. B., and Preece, R. J. C. Federal Germany. Political and Social Order. London, 1969.

Official Publications

Knoll, J. H. The German Educational System. Inter Nationes, 1967.

Education in Germany. Inter Nationes. A monthly publication.

Deutschland. Published by the West German Trade Union Federation. Düsseldorf, 1954.

Co-determination Rights of the Workers in Germany. Published by the West German Trade Union Federation. June, 1967.

Bundesverband der deutschen Industrie. Jahresbericht 1969/70. Cologne, 1970.

Handelskammer Hamburg. Bericht 1969. Hamburg, 1970.

Die Bundesrepublik Deutschland. Einführung in ihren Aufbau und ihre Entwicklung. Erich Schmidt Verlag, Berlin. Fifth edition, 1968.

Meet Germany. Published by Atlantik-Brücke, Hamburg, 1966 and 1969.

Federal Press and Information Office

Deutschland Heute. Second Edition, 1954.
Germany Reports. Second edition, 1955.
Facts about Germany. Wiesbaden, 1956.
Public Finance. 1961.
Pfizer, A. The German Bundesrat. 1962.
Deutschland in Vergangenheit und Gegenwart. Seventh edition, 1963.
Tatsachen über Deutschland. Sixth completely revised edition, 1963. (Now discontinued.)
Arbeitsmarkt und Arbeitspartner. Wiesbaden, 1966.
Berlin. In brief. 1967.
Soziale Lage, Soziale Sicherung. 1968.
Die Industrie der Bundesrepublik Deutschland. Wiesbaden, 1968.
Wirtschaft und Aussenhandel. Wiesbaden, 1969.
Landwirtschaft, Forsten, Fischerei. Wiesbaden, 1969.
Germany Reports: Cultural Life. Wiesbaden, 1969.

B. GERMAN DEMOCRATIC REPUBLIC

Ersil, W. The two German States and European Security. Dresden, 1967.
Klenner, H. Civil Rights in the German Democratic Republic. Berlin, 1967.
Childs, D. East Germany. Benn, London, 1969.
Hornsby, L. (ed.) Profile of East Germany. Harrap, London, 1966.

Official Publications

300 Questions. 300 Answers. Berlin, 1959 and Dresden, 1967.
The GDR. A modern Industrial State. Verlag Zeit im Bild, Dresden, 1966.
State and Law. Verlag Zeit im Bild. Dresden, 1966.
GDR. A Chronological Table, 1945–1965. Verlag Zeit im Bild. Dresden, 1966.
GDR. Culture Mosaic. Verlag Zeit im Bild. Dresden, 1966.
Youth. Verlag Zeit im Bild. Dresden, 1968.
The Constitution of the German Democratic Republic. Verlag Zeit im Bild. 1968.
Democracy in the GDR. Verlag Zeit im Bild. Dresden, 1968.
Education and Training in the German Democratic Republic. Staatsverlag der DDR. 1966.

Deutsche Demokratische Republik. Statistisches Taschenbuch 1969. Staatsverlag der DDR. Berlin, 1969.

Periodicals

Survey. A Journal of Soviet and East European Studies.   London (quarterly).

Poland and Germany.   London (quarterly).

Der Spiegel.   Hamburg (weekly).

The German Tribune.   Hamburg (quarterly Review of the West German Press).

Appendix

COMPARISON OF DIRECT AND INDIRECT LEVIES ON INCOMES IN THE FEDERAL REPUBLIC AND EAST GERMAN DEMOCRATIC REPUBLIC

Year	Social Insurance Payments*		Income Tax Deductions*		Net Income Remaining	
	BRD	DDR	BRD	DDR	BRD	DDR
1960	9·4%	7·5%	6·3%	6·0%	476 DM	483 marks†
1961	9·1%	7·2%	7·3%	6·2%	522 ,,	503 ,,
1962	9·2%	7·5%	7·6%	6·3%	567 ,,	495 ,,
1963	9·2%	7·2%	8·0%	6·6%	602 ,,	513 ,,
1964	9·2%	7·0%	8·5%	6·7%	652 ,,	531 ,,
1965	9·2%	6·8%	7·8%	6·8%	716 ,,	551 ,,
1966	9·5%	7·0%	8·6%	7·0%	759 ,,	563 ,,
1967	9·7%	6·8%	8·8%	6·9%	788 ,,	578 ,,
1968	10·1%	6·6%	9·4%	7·2%	830 ,,	603 ,,
1969	10·5%	6·3%	10·3%	7·1%	893 ,,	630 ,,

* Expressed as a percentage of gross income.
† The East German unit of currency is the *Mark der deutschen Notenbank* (MDN), but statistics are usually quoted simply in marks.

THE LARGEST WEST GERMAN INDUSTRIAL AND TRADING COMPANIES, 1970

Company Name	Turnover in Mill. DM		Persons Employed (in 1000s)	
	1970	1969	1970	1969
1. Volkswagenwerk	15 791	13 934	190,3	168,5
2. Siemens	11 763	9 685	301	272
3. Farbwerke Hoechst	11 591	9 747	139,5	98,1
4. Farben Bayer	11 129	10 225	135,8	126,2
5. Daimler-Benz	11 054	9 091	144,4	136,4
6. Thyssen-Hütte	10 881	9 099	97,5	106,3
7. Badische Anilin u. Soda-Fabrik	10 520	8 892	106,8	94,7
8. AEG-Telefunken	8 543	7 040	178,0	164,3
9. Klöckner-Gruppe	8 300	7 100	•	•
10. Veba	8 060	6 942	53,7	50,8
11. Ruhrkohle AG	7 600	6 500	186	183
12. Mannesmann	7 363	5 059	88,2	63,6
13. Gutehoffnungshütte	6 344	5 655	95,8	95
14. Krupp	5 812	5 248	80,3	79,5
15. Metallgesellschaft	5 600	4 600	•	•
16. Bosch	5 500	4 700	117	110
17. Rheinisch-Westfälisches Elektrizitätswerk	5 442	5 084	54,6	53,6

Company Name	Turnover in Mill. DM		Persons Employed (in 1000s)	
	1970	1969	1970	1969
18. Flick-Gruppe	5 425	4 657	75,3	73,9
19. Esso AG	5 274	4 515	5,2	5,1
20. Adam Opel AG	5 126	4 854	56,9	54,3
21. Rheinstahl	4 766	4 201	71,1	71,9
22. Ford-Werke AG	4 643	3 884	53,4	45,4
23. Deutsche Shell AG	4 586	3 970	5,8	5,6
24. Hoesch	4 547	3 893	53	52,4
25. Unilever	4 526	4 057	45,1	43

Note: Not all West German companies publish a statement of their annual accounts, but legislation of 1970 will necessitate the publication of the accounts of all firms with an annual turnover in excess of 250 million DM, or a balance of 125 million DM or which employ over 5,000 workers. The "league table" printed above is expected to show some interesting changes as a consequence.

COMPARISONS OF AGRICULTURAL PRODUCTION IN THE BRD AND DDR

Category	BRD		DDR		DDR in % BRD	
	1957/61	1968	1957/61	1968	1957/61	1968
Agricultural area (million hectares)	14,26	13,87	6,44	6,30	45,2	45,4
Head of cattle (millions)	11,89	12,44	5,06	4,96	42,6	39,9
Engaged in agriculture or forestry (1000s)	3,794	2,630	1,416	1,068	37,3	40,6
Tractors (million horse power)	15,15	30,98	2,30	6,25	15,2	20,2
Gross production (million tons)	48,05	58,01	19,17	23,35	39,9	40,3
Net food production (million tons)	40,82	49,50	13,95	17,86	34,2	36,1

AGRICULTURAL PRODUCTIVITY IN THE BRD AND DDR (DDR EXPRESSED AS A PERCENTAGE OF BRD)

Year	Gross Production per hectare unit	Animal Production per unit weight	Labour Productivity	Net food production per unit.
1957/61	88%	81%	—	76%
1960	91%	79%	—	73%
1961	78%	76%	—	73%
1962	84%	68%	—	62%
1963	80%	73%	—	69%
1964	86%	74%	58%	70%
1965	98%	84%	64%	85%
1966	92%	84%	63%	81%
1967	91%	82%	60%	78%
1968	88%	84%	61%	79%

(From *Bericht der Bundesregierung zur Lage der Nation*, 1971).

Index

Note: For collective treatment of topics, see headings under Table of Contents on pp. 5–6.

GERMAN FEDERAL REPUBLIC (WEST GERMANY)

Adenauer, Konrad 10, 21, 25–7, 32, 33–6, 44, 75, 117, 142, 233–4, 237
APO (*außerparlamentarische Opposition*) 40
Armed forces 18

Basic Law 11–13, 17, 18, 22, 33, 38, 47–8, 49–50, 55, 86, 118, 186, 234, 243
Berlin (West) 9, 12, 14, 51–2, 117, 125, 144, 187–9, 191, 200, 233, 235–6, 239–40, 243–4
Bavaria 11, 44, 127, 144, 192
Berufsschule see Vocational training
Bezirk 51
BHE (*Bund der Heimatlosen und Entrechteten*) 31, 34
Brandt, Willy 9, 27, 36, 39, 41, 238–244
Broadcasting 192, 200–1, 227
Bundeskanzler see Chancellor
Bundesrat 13–18, 35, 44, 51
Bundestag 13–24, 41–3, 46–7, 51, 239
Bundesverfassungsgericht see Constitutional Court

CDU (*Christlich-Demokratische Union*) 24–7, 33–42, 45, 80, 122, 130, 185, 191, 202, 236, 239, 242–4
Chancellor (Federal) 13–14, 23–4
Civil servants 47, 76
Communists 32–3
Constitutional Court 12, 18, 19, 30, 32, 35, 243
Cost of living 115–9, 121–6, 133–4, 144, 165, 173, 177–8, 182–3, 196, 210, 214–5
CSU (*Christlich-Soziale Union*) 25, 30, 33, 34, 36, 37, 40, 41, 45, 202, 242

d'Hondt system (PR) 20–21, 24
DFU (*Deutsche Friedens-Union*) 33, 36, 37
DKP (*Deutsche Kommunistische Partei*) (1968) 32–3
DP (*Deutsche Partei*) 31, 33, 34, 35

Educational reform 190–4, 197–8
EEC (European Economic Community) 34, 78, 139–44, 240
Einheitsschule 191
Equalization of burdens *see Lastenausgleich*
Erhard, Ludwig 25, 36–7, 38, 77, 117, 121
Exports *see* Trade balance

Family allowances 172–4
FDP (*Freie Demokratische Partei*) 28–30, 31, 33–41, 45–6, 55, 125, 236, 238, 242–3
Foreign labour 123, 135–6, 181

Gastarbeiter see Foreign labour
GDP (*Gesamtdeutsche Partei*); also GB (*Gesamtdeutscher Block*) 31, 34, 36
Gemeinde 12, 49–50, 121–2, 123, 186, 194, 200, 203
Gesamtschule 191
Grundgesetz see Basic Law
Gymnasium 188–190, 191

Hallstein doctrine 235
Health statistics 175, 180–2
Heinemann, Gustav 32
Holidays 80, 88–9, 175, 184
Housing 78, 117, 119, 125, 165, 176–9, 210, 215

Imports *see* Trade balance
Inflation 121–5, 177, 183
Insurance 171–6; accident 172, 174;

GERMAN DEMOCRATIC REPUBLIC (EAST GERMANY)